THE
RIGHT
THING

THE RIGHT THING

"I know this fine American patriot feels terrible about what took place.
It was a terrible accident. And like any good commander, he's taken the heat,
he's taken the hit. I read in the newspaper that the man is actually going
to go over to meet with some of the parents, which I think is an act
of great compassion. This is an officer who bears all the responsibility,
and to me, that says something about the man's character."

—President George W. Bush
NBC *Today Show* interview

CMDR. SCOTT WADDLE (RET.)
WITH KEN ABRAHAM

INTEGRITY
PUBLISHERS®

Nashville

THE RIGHT THING

Published by Integrity Publishers, a division of Integrity Media, Inc.,
5250 Virginia Way, Suite 110, Brentwood, TN 37027.

HELPING PEOPLE WORLDWIDE EXPERIENCE *the* MANIFEST PRESENCE *of* GOD.

Scripture quotations used in this book are from the New American Standard
Bible (NASB), copyright © 1960, 1977 by the Lockman Foundation. Used by
permission.

Cover Design: The Office of Bill Chiaravalle, www.officeofbc.com
Interior Design/Page Composition: PerfecType, Nashville, TN

Library of Congress Cataloging-in-Publication Data
Waddle, Scott.
   The right thing / by Scott Waddle ; with Ken Abraham.
      p. cm.
   ISBN 1-59145-036-5
   1. Waddle, Scott. 2. United States. Navy—Officers—Biography. 3. Greene-
ville (Submarine) 4. Ehime Maru (Training ship) 5. Collisions at sea—
Hawaii. 6. Submarine disasters—Hawaii. I. Abraham, Ken. II. Title.

V63.W23 A3 2002
910'.9164'9—dc21
[B]
                                                        2002038835

Printed in the United States of America
03 04 05 06 07 RRD 9 8 7 6 5 4 3 2 1

DEDICATION

This book is dedicated to the two most important people in my life—my wife, Jill, and daughter, Ashley. Thank you for loving me so unconditionally and for standing by me! I am truly a blessed man to have you both in my life.

I also dedicate this book to the members of the armed forces, along with their families, for their personal sacrifice in defending our freedom and protecting our way of life.

Special recognition goes to the men who served with me on board the USS *Greeneville* during my two years in command. I will never forget you shipmates and am proud to have served with you as your captain.

ACKNOWLEDGMENTS

Just as driving a nuclear-powered submarine is an adventure that requires the assistance and expertise of numerous talented and dedicated individuals working together to accomplish a common goal, I've discovered that writing and publishing a book is a collaboration between many highly skilled and deeply committed individuals.

I extend my heartfelt appreciation to Ken Abraham for helping me put thoughts and words into coherent text, and to Byron Williamson and his staff at Integrity Publishing for believing in me and for making this book possible. May you continue to be blessed, and may you always live up to your name.

CONTENTS

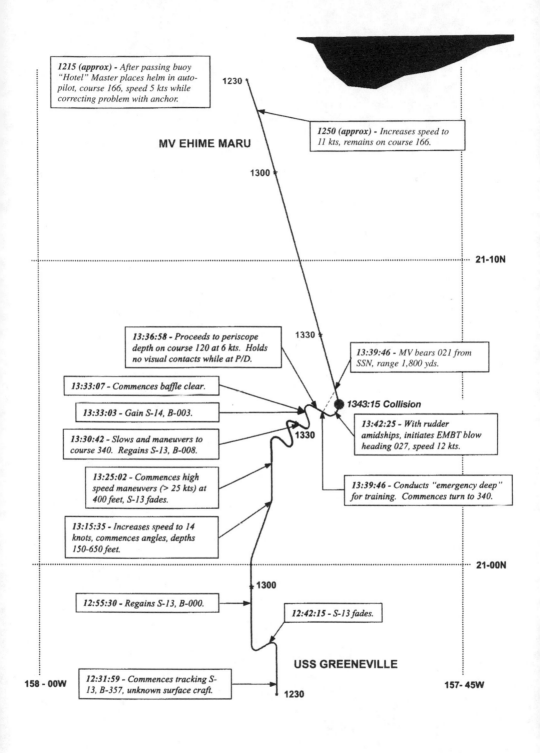

1215 (approx) - After passing buoy "Hotel" Master places helm in auto-pilot, course 166, speed 5 kts while correcting problem with anchor.

1230

1250 (approx) - Increases speed to 11 kts, remains on course 166.

MV EHIME MARU

1300

21-10N

13:36:58 - Proceeds to periscope depth on course 120 at 6 kts. Holds no visual contacts while at P/D.

1330

13:39:46 - MV bears 021 from SSN, range 1,800 yds.

13:33:07 - Commences baffle clear.

13:33:03 - Gain S-14, B-003.

1343:15 Collision

13:30:42 - Slows and maneuvers to course 340. Regains S-13, B-008.

1330

13:42:25 - With rudder amidships, initiates EMBT blow heading 027, speed 12 kts.

13:25:02 - Commences high speed maneuvers (> 25 kts) at 400 feet, S-13 fades.

13:15:35 - Increases speed to 14 knots, commences angles, depths 150-650 feet.

13:39:46 - Conducts "emergency deep" for training. Commences turn to 340.

21-00N

1300

12:55:30 - Regains S-13, B-000.

12:42:15 - S-13 fades.

USS GREENEVILLE

158 - 00W

12:31:59 - Commences tracking S-13, B-357, unknown surface craft.

1230

157- 45W

CHAPTER 1

A TIME TO SPEAK

"Over my dead body! You are not going to take that witness stand, Scott. Not without immunity! I'll kill you before I allow you to take the stand to testify without immunity," my lawyer, Charlie Gittins, railed. "On second thought, I won't have to—you'd be killing yourself!"

I smiled slightly at my defense counsel's impassioned plea; he had said something similar to me the first time I'd met him, and his attitude hadn't changed over the weeks he had been defending me. I knew Charlie wanted to protect me, but I felt compelled to take the stand. I honestly believed that the truth was not the worst thing that could be known about the sorrowful events in which I had played a part.

"I have to, Charlie. I did it. Nine people are dead because of me."

"It was an accident, Scott. A horrible, freak accident, something that should never have happened, and it was not your fault!"

"No, Charlie. There's a time to be silent and a time to speak up for what is right. I'm the only guy who really knows what happened aboard that ship that day. I'm the only one who knows what I saw through that periscope. I have to tell the truth; I have to take responsibility and let the chips fall where they may. It's the right thing to do."

Charlie Gittins, one of the world's foremost attorneys handling military cases, shrugged his shoulders in exasperation. Charlie knew how to build a strong defense, as well as how to mount a strong offense. He had gained national recognition during the Navy's Tailhook scandal, and he was not afraid to take a risk in court or go for the jugular when necessary. But from the beginning of the trial, Charlie had adamantly opposed my testifying without immunity before the naval court of inquiry, and he had informed the court of that decision early on. When Admiral Thomas Fargo, commander in chief of the Pacific Fleet, refused to grant me immunity, Charlie stuck to his guns. He would not allow me to testify during the inquiry without immunity. The risks were too high. These were serious charges: I was suspected of dereliction of duty, improper hazarding of a vessel, and negligent homicide. If I said the wrong thing or answered the three-officer panel in any way that incriminated me, I could be subjected to court-martial, tried, convicted, and imprisoned. This was no trifling matter. Nine Japanese civilians—four of them teenagers—were dead as a result of my choices.

I had ordered the emergency main ballast tank blow that had brought the USS *Greeneville*, the nuclear attack submarine I had commanded, ripping up through the water and smashing into a Japanese fishing boat, the *Ehime Maru*, off the coast of Pearl Harbor on February 9, 2001. The *Greeneville*'s steel rudder, specially reinforced to tear through ice, tore diagonally through the underbelly of the Japanese ship, causing it to sink within minutes. Worse yet—to the Japanese public, at least—I had been entertaining civilian guests, two of whom were at the sub's controls at the time of the impact. On a broader scale, it was the first major foreign-policy challenge for the newly inaugurated president, George W. Bush.

Devastated as I was at the deaths of the nine innocent people and the negative publicity for our country, I was nonetheless confident that the Navy, the nation, and the world would see the tragedy for what it was—a horrible accident. Although I knew I wouldn't walk away unscathed, I did hope to walk away with my life and my dignity.

But things had not gone well during the inquiry. Several of my officers and crewmembers had testified with immunity, and they had answered truthfully. But through their pointed questions, the admirals had painted a picture of the *Greeneville*'s captain—me—rushing through procedures, running a loose and informal ship environment, and showing off for the distinguished visitors who had been aboard the *Greeneville* for a demonstration cruise that fateful day.

For eleven days, I had sat silently in the courtroom, with the family members of the Japanese victims sitting behind me and drilling holes in my head with their glaring eyes. A Japanese submarine admiral sat facing me on the court of inquiry as a nonvoting adviser, an unprecedented move in American military justice. Every time some detail of the *Ehime Maru*'s plight was discussed, the Japanese officer winced, sending the victims' families into loud wails and sobs resounding throughout the inquiry room.

Despite the perilous odds and awkward circumstances, Charlie Gittins had outdone himself, challenging evidence, pointing out contradictions in the testimony of witnesses, and subtly cautioning the court against looking for a scapegoat. Still, as the inquiry dragged on for days, it became increasingly clear that the court was doing precisely that. This accident was a huge embarrassment for the Navy and for our nation at a time when everyone in the military, me included, hoped that with the change of political guard in Washington would come a change in attitude toward the nuclear submarine force that had played such a vital role in winning the Cold War. Now those hopes had been dashed. Somebody had to take a fall for it, and, as the court of inquiry progressed, it became more and more obvious that the court had already decided that the sacrificial lamb would be me.

I recognized that, and in some ways I even accepted that as part of the responsibility for my role in what had happened nine miles off the coast of Oahu. But if I was going down, I wanted the truth to be known. Beyond that, my crew was my family; I didn't want anyone else to go down with me. I had to testify, with immunity or not.

To admit my mistakes publicly did not come easily to me. While I had always appeared bold and self-confident in public, I'd spent my entire life craving the approval of my parents, my peers, and my superior officers in the military. Inwardly, I was crying out for attention and acceptance, and I'd do almost anything to prove that I deserved it. Throughout my career I had driven myself not just to succeed, but to excel. As captain of the *Greeneville*, I'd pushed my crew hard, and together we'd become the envy of the Pacific Fleet.

To admit my wrong decisions was to acknowledge failure on a colossal level. No longer would I be touted as the Navy's golden boy, on a fast track to higher command positions within the submarine community, with hopes of possibly rising even higher in Navy echelons. No longer would I be respected and praised as I had been for most of my naval career. To admit my mistakes would be to admit defeat, something I had been well trained never to do. By taking the witness stand, I would willingly subject myself to further public disgrace, derision, and condemnation. But in my heart and mind, I knew I had no choice. I had to tell the truth.

"Okay, Scott," Charlie acquiesced. "If you're going to do this, let's at least try to prepare. Let's meet after dinner to go over some of the questions the court will likely ask you."

"Okay, fine," I replied. "Better yet, why don't we have our legal team—you, Mark Patton, Kimberlie Young, and Jennifer Herrold—come to our home for dinner, and we'll get an earlier start? I'll even cook."

Charlie gave me his best "you've-got-to-be-kidding" look, but he agreed.

That evening, I made dinner for my wife, daughter, and legal team. We ate quickly, and then it was time to get to work. "You better sit down," Charlie nodded to me. "This is going to take awhile."

My wife, Jill, brought in some refreshments from the kitchen of our comfortable home on Hospital Point, in the heart of the U.S. naval base at Pearl Harbor. Since the Navy owned the property, it was a foregone conclusion that if we lost our case, we'd also lose our lovely home, my salary, and the pension I had earned by serving nearly twenty years in the military. The stakes were high, not just for me, but also for Jill and our thirteen-year-old daughter, Ashley.

I could see the tension in Jill's face as she set some drinks on the coffee table. I knew this ordeal had been extremely draining for her, but she had valiantly stood with me, going to the courtroom every day, dealing with the media frenzy surrounding our every move, and enduring the public humiliation of having her husband's every thought, word, and action analyzed for hidden defects. She sat stoically as the court of inquiry castigated everything from my brash personality to my less-than-perfect eyesight.

All the while, Jill continually encouraged me and lovingly cared for me. While I could not—dared not—speak to the press, for fear that my comments could be used against me, Jill did. She attempted to protect me as much as possible.

Jill possessed the rare combination a military man looks for in a wife—the ability to be soft and sweet, yet firm and tough. She understood the pressures of Navy life, including the inherent tensions that accompany leadership positions. She was vocal when it came to expressing her opinions, but as an officer's wife, she recognized that discretion is often the better part of valor. Jill knew how to keep me happy when I was home, and she could be happy even when I was away. She was extremely competent to run our household while I was on a six-month-long deployment at sea.

Nevertheless, the prolonged absences took a toll on our marriage. Together for more than fourteen years, our relationship had been rocky at times, and on more than a few occasions we both wondered if our family could survive. But in recent years we had developed an almost spiritual bond that had deepened with time, and our love and commitment to each other were stronger than ever. Indeed, the *Ehime Maru* accident had galvanized our hearts together. If for no other reason, I owed it to Jill to fight for the truth.

I took a sip of coffee. "Okay, guys. Let's get going."

The defense team—comprised of Charlie; my friend and Naval Academy classmate Commander Mark Patton, serving as our technical expert; Kimberlie Young, a lawyer who worked in the legal services office at Pearl Harbor; and Jennifer Herrold, a defense lawyer who had been assigned to me early on—both members of the Navy judge advocate general's corps

(JAGC)—went to work grilling me in preparation for what was sure to be the most probing, nerve-racking day of my life. Throughout the night we worked. Again and again, Charlie and the others asked tough questions, going through the accident from every angle. Over and over again, I asked myself a more searing set of questions: *How could this have happened? Why did God allow this set of circumstances to occur? What's going to happen tomorrow?* I had spent my entire adult life preparing to go to war. How could I be forty-one years of age, at the pinnacle of my career, and suddenly, in a matter of minutes, see my whole world blown apart? Nothing in my earlier experiences could possibly have prepared me for this.

CHAPTER 2

AIR FORCE BRAT

It's interesting to look back on one's childhood and wonder, *How much of my early life has influenced me in later years?* I'm convinced that God doesn't waste any of our experiences. He uses them to refine us, to equip us to help others, and to prepare us for what lies ahead. In my life, it's easy to spot His hand shaping me long before I really believed in Him.

My grandfather, James Stuteville, lived and breathed Texas oil, working his entire adult life as an account manager in Mobil Oil's administrative office. A quiet sort of man, Jim didn't require a lot to be content. He simply went to work, did his job, and came home. He was the kind of guy to be found in every big company—a man who went to work every day for twenty or thirty years, and when he retired with a gold watch, most people hardly noticed that he was gone.

Jim married Molly Wright, from White Wright, a small Texas town about sixty miles northeast of Dallas. The common joke in our family was that Grandma came from the "right" family and lived on the "right" side of town. Molly was a strong-willed woman who had grown up on a farm, and she definitely wore the pants in the family. She was a schoolteacher who later taught at Southern Methodist University. Papa Jim usually demurred to her wishes, and he was perfectly content to let "Nonnie," as we called her, run the family. My mom, Barbara Lou Stuteville, was their only child. Papa Jim contracted diabetes in his fifties, and, making matters worse, he often neglected to take his insulin on time. He died before I ever got a chance to know him.

My dad, Dan Waddle, was born in Dallas, the youngest of two in his family. His father, Daniel Thad Waddle, was a hardworking house painter. Dan and his sister, Ava, attended Sunday school at the Methodist church and went to Sunset High School in Dallas, where he was a popular, charismatic, athletic guy. It made sense that he soon took notice of Barbara Lou Stuteville, the new girl at school. Barbara was an outgoing, talented young entertainer with a great singing voice. They fell in love, and, to my grandparents' chagrin, my parents eloped while Mom was still in high school and Dad was a student at Southern Methodist University.

When his mom got sick, Dan Waddle started college at Texas A&M, but when his father became sick as well, Dan dropped out of college for a while to help with the family business. His mom died of a heart attack at the age of forty-nine, when Dan was only eighteen. Following his mom's death, Dan went back to school at Southern Methodist University, where he earned his degree. Meanwhile, Dad's sister, Ava, became an accomplished clothing designer in New York.

Dad's family didn't have enough money to send him to college, so he went to school under the Air Force Reserve Officers Training Corps (ROTC) program. The Air Force paid for Dad's college education in return for Dad's commitment to becoming an Air Force officer for a minimum of five years after college. When he graduated, he stepped straight out of college into Air Force training at College Station, Texas. He was commissioned as an officer in 1953. His first assignment was in Bryan, Texas, not far from Texas A&M.

Dad was stationed in Japan at Misawa Air Force Base when I was born on May 20, 1959. I was rushing right from the start, taking Mom and Dad by surprise—I was more than two months premature. Eighteen months later, my sister, Michelle, was also born in Japan, on December 6, the eve of Pearl Harbor Day. We lived in Japan until I was a toddler, and we had a Japanese maid named Tama who cared for me and carried me around with her as she worked at the house, helping my mom. My first spoken words, I'm told, were in Japanese.

Dad loved to fly Air Force jets, and from all I've heard, he was a mighty good pilot. But even a good pilot can sometimes encounter problems. One morning, just three months after I was born, Dad was streaking across the skies of northern Japan, flying his F-101 Voodoo jet, when it started to come apart on him. Fragments of the jet literally began disintegrating as Dad flew. Thinking quickly of what he could possibly do to save his own life and avoid killing other people, Dad decided to point the jet toward the Pacific Ocean and eject. There was only one problem: He knew that if he parachuted in that area, he couldn't possibly survive for long in the frigid North Pacific waters. He had only one choice. He'd eject just as the jet crossed over the beach area heading toward the sea. He hoped the winds would carry him close to land as the plane continued on into the Pacific.

The plan seemed to make perfectly good sense under the circumstances. Dad timed his moves carefully, pulling the ejection handle just as the plane approached the beach, flying at several hundred miles per hour. The ejection seat catapulted him out of the cockpit, and Dad's chute opened cleanly.

Unfortunately, the now pilotless plane didn't stay on course once the cockpit was exposed. The jet suddenly turned 180 degrees in the sky and streaked straight back toward the land. Worse yet, the plane roared right at an elementary school!

At the last second, the jet jerked downward, hit a telephone pole adjacent to the school, and exploded. The jet crashed onto the schoolyard, the fireball just missing the school building. Fortunately, the children and the teachers escaped with little more than a frightening experience to share over their next batch of orange juice and cookies.

Dad never mentioned his near miss with death. Not for forty-one years, that is . . .

Interestingly, I didn't grow up with a love for sailing; I wanted to fly like my dad. Although I wanted to be an Air Force pilot, maybe a love for the sea was born in me and I didn't realize it. The sea was Japan's life. Everybody on the crowded islands lived within one hundred miles of it. Maybe being a sailor was in my blood.

I was always a good kid. Honestly, I was! Even when I tried to do something wrong, I couldn't make it work. Shortly after our family moved to England, when I was in third grade, some boys goaded me into stealing some comic books from the military bookstore. I tried to stash the comic books under my white T-shirt, and I got caught. No wonder. The clerk could see the bright-colored comics right through my cotton T-shirt.

"Sorry, pal, you're not walking out of here without paying for those comic books," he said. "Stay right here; I'm gonna call your mom and dad."

Mom came to the store and picked me up. She gave me a lecture hot enough to burn my ears off. I'd have rather been spanked, but Mom knew the lecture hurt me more.

I was never any good at being dishonest.

Because Dad was in the military, we moved a lot during my sister's and my childhood. We lived in Japan; Valdosta, Georgia; Alconbury, England; Huntingdon, England; Sherman, Texas; and Austin, Texas—all before I was in eighth grade.

My father was sent to Vietnam when I was in the fourth grade. Maybe that had something to do with the demise of my parents' marriage. Regardless, Michelle and I noticed that Mom and Dad seemed to argue a lot prior to Dad's going to Vietnam. Still, they sincerely loved each other, and they tried desperately to keep the marriage together. I vividly recall Mom and us kids filling reel-to-reel tapes with conversation and sending them to Dad in the mail. He then would send a tape back to us, filled with great stories about his flying exploits. I'd been raised around Air Force bases, and I was fascinated. As a little boy, I had watched my dad taking off in his jet and wondered what it would be like to ride with him. As I listened to him recounting his flights over places I could barely pronounce, I could imagine being in the cockpit with him. *One of these days, I'm going to fly too,* I'd dream.

Mom, Michelle, and I lived in Sherman, Texas, at the time. I enjoyed being the man of the house while Dad was gone. And Dad was gone a lot. His life revolved around his work.

When my father returned from Vietnam, he and Mom separated and later divorced. I was in the sixth grade when my father left, and I was devastated. I didn't really know what divorce meant. Since Dad was gone much of the time anyhow, our lives were not thrown into any major turmoil; but even as a youngster, something told me that divorce was not a happy experience.

I desperately missed my father and was disappointed at his not being around more during my growing-up years. We played catch in the backyard once in a while and did a few other father-son activities, but for the most part, Dad was absent. He was always busy working. Although my father and I have forged a solid relationship today, I have almost no memories of us spending time together—just the two of us—during my childhood.

Despite the instability in our home, I was a good student in school, excelling especially in math and science, two areas that many of my friends didn't really care for. I yearned to do well and craved the praise of other people, including coaches, teachers, and especially my mom. Maybe unconsciously I was missing the father figure in my life. Although I exuded confidence, I always felt insecure. I had an element of doubt, not knowing whether I'd be big enough, fast enough, strong enough, or smart enough to compete with the other kids. When I did something that brought any success or approval, I lapped it up like an eager puppy getting a treat for doing a trick. I relished any recognition that came my way.

We moved to Austin, Texas, where I played on the Pop Warner football team Richard's Raiders, sponsored by Richard's Sporting Goods Store. I probably wouldn't have played football, but Mom made me. She thought it would be good for me, and it was, I suppose. I wasn't so convinced, however, when I came home from the first two days of practice crying my eyes out. I'd been beaten all over the field. I begged Mom not to make me go back. But if I thought that I was going to get any sympathy from Mom, I was wrong! "Toughen up, boy," she said. "You're going back in there."

After Dad left, we lived in a tiny house on Chatham Street, near T. G. Harris Elementary School. Mrs. DeLang was my favorite teacher at Harris. She noticed that I'd get bored easily and aggravated if I wasn't active. She recognized that I had more energy than a lot of the other kids. In those days, nobody diagnosed my excess energy as attention deficit disorder, but maybe it was. Regardless, Mrs. DeLang had the perfect cure. When I'd get fidgety, she'd make me run to the fence and back, again and again, until I was nearly exhausted. Then when I was all wrung out, I could sit in my chair, focus on schoolwork, and do well.

Mrs. DeLang also realized that I'd do almost anything for a little praise and recognition. "Oh, Scott. That is so good!" she'd exclaim over one of my pages of schoolwork. I would beam with pleasure. And I'd work even harder to make her happy. I wanted to be liked by everybody, especially by people in authority.

Mom went to work for Snelling and Snelling, a well-known job placement firm, and did a bit of modeling on the side. Mom had an uncanny knack for matching the right person with the right job. I derived much of my work ethic, as well as many of my personal character traits, from my mom.

Our finances were tight most of my early life, so Mom worked hard all the time. She was so tired, sometimes my sister and I had to literally drag her out of bed in the morning to go to work. But Mom always found time to attend my sister's and my school activities. A compassionate, sensitive, and emotional woman, she also found time to teach us about God. We prayed before meals and went to church every Sunday. Most of all, she modeled genuine faith in God—not the kind of faith that believes when everything is going well, but the kind of faith that believes even when everything is falling apart, when you are hanging on for sheer survival. That's the kind of faith Mom had.

In 1971, Mom married John Coe, a strong, quiet man from Vero Beach, Florida, who was also an Air Force pilot. I got along well with John, and he was extremely supportive of me throughout my teen years. He never denigrated my father or tried to undermine or usurp his role in any way. John understood that my father was halfway around the world, serving his country and trying to do all that he could for me. But John Coe was there for me at a time when I desperately needed a strong male role model in my life, and I'll always be grateful to the man who loved me enough to raise me as his own son.

We moved to Laredo, Texas, where I enrolled in seventh grade at United Intermediate School. I was placed in an advanced math program for children who could do mathematics problems in their head, without the aid of pencil and paper. I went to the state finals in math competition.

On the other hand, I was terrible in English. I was placed in a remedial program because of reading comprehension problems. Throughout my seventh-grade year, I had a tutor to help me, and I attended special classes outside of school to enhance my reading comprehension skills. It was kind of embarrassing. While the rest of the class was having regular English classes, I had to get on a van and travel to an off-campus site to work with flash cards.

While at United, I played football and was the captain of the team. I tried out for basketball, too, but I got cut because I couldn't dribble very well. I had never really played basketball, but it looked easy enough. Wrong! I was a lousy basketball player. I was content to play football and run on the track team while at United.

About that time, I also joined the Boy Scouts in Laredo. I had been in Cub Scouts before that in Sherman and in Austin. Scouting was a natural for me. Raised in the southwestern part of the country, "Yes, sir; no, sir" and "Thank you, ma'am" came easily to me. The emphasis on manners, morality, and respect for God, country, and family fit well with the military principles I lived with every day. I was a "Boy Scout" even before I joined the organization.

I wasn't an outdoorsman, but I found the scouting program to be extremely challenging and rewarding. I especially liked the idea of wearing a uniform and earning various merit badges for my accomplishments. Give me a badge that I could wear on my chest, and I'd climb the highest tree, help an elderly lady across the street, learn how to tie a knot, stay out for a weekend campout, or do whatever was necessary. I was a good Scout, too, advancing all the way to Eagle Scout by the time I was sixteen.

It wasn't part of our scouting program, but for entertainment, my friends and I would sometimes go out and catch tarantulas. We'd get a big jar, put it over the tarantula nest, and then pour water down the other side of the hole, forcing the tarantula out of the hole into the jar. We'd take the tarantula to school and scare all the girls or put it on our favorite teacher's desk. Needless to say, there wasn't a lot for teenagers to do in Laredo at that time.

It wouldn't have mattered to me if there had been plenty of things to keep an active teenager busy. Just about the time I started feeling at home there, we got word that John was being transferred to Naples, Italy.

CHAPTER 3
A NEW START

Naples, Italy, is one of the most fascinating cities on earth. Lying at the foot of Mount Vesuvius and stretching lazily at the edge of the Mediterranean Sea, Naples is a seaport rife with beauty and history. The city is the center of commerce for southern Italy, and it boasts a population of more than 1.2 million people. It's often compared to San Diego because of its picturesque location and its combination of the "old Italy" with a new, bustling business community. It is also a strategic military outpost for American air and sea presence in Europe.

My family and I lived outside the city, about a half-hour's drive in the country. I attended Forrest Sherman High School in Naples, a school run by the U.S. Department of Defense school system and attended mainly by U.S. "military brats." It certainly wasn't your everyday, typical school. It was an American school located right in the heart of downtown Naples.

Even though I was surrounded by other Americans, I gradually became conversationally fluent in Italian. I loved the sound of the Italian words rolling across my tongue. And the food was delicious!

As a military kid, I sometimes felt awkward being the new kid in school all the time, but in Naples, almost everyone in the school came from somewhere else. I learned how to interact with kids from different cultures who had grown up in various parts of the U.S. and around the world. Adaptability was the name of the game. It was great training for life as a naval officer. Actually, it was great training for anything!

My eighth-grade year, I was taking a ninth-grade English class and I misspelled the word *angelfish* as *anglefish* on a writing exam. The teacher placed my paper on an overhead transparency and put it up on the screen for all the other kids to see. He then proceeded to criticize my work in front of the entire class. I hated him for doing that. It was bad enough that I'd made a mistake. He didn't have to humiliate me in front of my classmates. But he did. And I never forgot that awful feeling.

In high school, as I had in Texas, I went out for the football team at Forrest Sherman. I played offensive guard and middle linebacker on defense and soon became a leader on the team. I was team captain during my senior year.

I didn't date a lot in high school, but the one blossoming relationship I had during my senior year was with a young lady named Donna Zimmerman. Donna was the captain of the cheerleaders, a spunky young woman with the look of a gymnast and a vivacious, outgoing personality. We became great friends. Donna's brother, David, eventually became a squadron commander of F/A-18 fighter jets. Ironically, it was David's plane that dropped three bombs during a training mission in Kuwait, killing five U.S. servicemen and a New Zealand soldier in mid-March 2001, barely a month after the *Greeneville–Ehime Maru* tragedy in Hawaii.

Forrest Sherman was a wonderful educational environment. In the middle of the winter, if my friends and I wanted to go skiing for the day, all we had to do was clear it with our teachers and get our assignments in advance. Then we were off to the Italian Alps. Incredible! We rode the train past Rome and did our homework on the way. We'd get back late that same night and would be back in school the next day.

Throughout high school, I worked as an assistant to Marvin Perry, our chemistry teacher. Besides chemistry, I was also in Mr. Perry's classes for algebra, physics, and other math and science courses. I liked Mr. Perry, and his positive influence on me academically was one of the reasons I pursued chemistry at the Naval Academy.

Another teacher who greatly influenced my life was Eleanor Holstein. Teaching Latin, Greek mythology, and English, Mrs. Holstein didn't believe in simply learning correct answers from books. The world was her classroom. She took her students on field trips almost every week, taking full advantage of the caves, catacombs, and ancient ruins around Naples. Mrs. Holstein brought literature to life, taking the class out to the Mediterranean Sea to visualize the Greek mythological characters going off to war. She was an incredible teacher, and she inspired within me a love of learning and a desire to explore the world.

Sometime around my sophomore and junior years in high school, I really began to wonder about some of the basic tenets of the Christian faith my mom had taught Michelle and me since childhood. We attended an Episcopal church, and the formal, high-church atmosphere left something to be desired for a teenage boy looking for spiritual reality. Although I was an acolyte in the church, I thought it seemed extremely cold and impersonal.

I always believed in the existence of God. My analytical way of looking at things demanded a Creator. I could see God's handiwork in the world around me, and I knew this world simply could not have happened by accident. Nature is much too orderly, too predictable. Some people talked about taking a leap of faith. I really wanted to do that. I sometimes even prayed, "God, please show me how to take that leap of faith. I really want to know You."

It wasn't that I disbelieved; I was just having trouble putting my faith together with my intellectual, analytical, mathematical approach to life. I'd heard that the great mathematician Blaise Pascal was a sincere Christian, and that was an encouragement to me. *Maybe I'm just not seeing how it all works yet,* I thought. *Maybe there's another piece to the puzzle that I haven't found, another part of the equation that I haven't discovered.*

How did God come to earth in the form of Jesus? I couldn't figure it out. How could faith in Christ affect my life?

During my junior year of high school, I was intrigued by what I saw in the life of Bob Wolfkill, a friend of mine on our football team. Bob was a senior, a bright guy, the son of an Air Force sergeant, yet he seemed to have a simple faith in Jesus that permeated his entire life. He didn't try to figure it all out; he accepted that some parts of his relationship with God required faith, and he was willing to trust his life to that faith.

We were riding on a bus in the middle of the night, on the way to a game in Vicenza, Italy. I looked over and noticed Bob reading a small booklet.

"Hey, whatcha reading?" I asked.

"I'm reading the Bible," he said, "and this little book is helping me to understand it."

"Really?"

"Yeah, do you want to see?"

"Sure." I started reading some of the scriptures in the Bible that Bob showed me, and for the first time in my life, the formula started coming together. It made sense. Mankind was lost because of our sin. God sent His Son, Jesus Christ, to pay the price for our sin by giving His life for us. I was especially impressed that Jesus would lay down His life for people He didn't even know, and who didn't care a bit about Him. To me, that was the ultimate sacrifice. But it didn't stop there. He rose from the dead—that part was tough for me to believe—and now He intercedes for us, making a way for us, sort of as a bridge, the one true way by which we can have a relationship with God. By believing in Jesus Christ, I could be forgiven of my sins and be guaranteed a spot in heaven.

"What a deal! No wonder they call it good news!" I said. "This stuff is amazing."

I didn't understand everything, but enough of the dots connected that I could see the picture for the first time. In the dim blue lights of the bus, in the middle of the night, riding up the Italian autostrada, Bob introduced me to Jesus Christ. Bob prayed and led the way. I prayed, too, and invited Christ to come into my life, acknowledging my willingness to trust Him from then on.

There were no lightning bolts, no thunderclaps, and no voices out of heaven. But I knew that a transaction had taken place between God and me.

I recognized that He had made a total commitment to me by dying for me on the cross; now I made a serious, irrevocable commitment to Him by being willing to live for Him in the world. I didn't have all the answers; in fact, I still had many questions and doubts, but I knew that I had done the right thing.

I didn't try to force my faith on anyone else, nor did I initiate conversations about spiritual matters. I was just a learner myself; I didn't feel that I knew enough to help anyone else. I was very private about my faith, yet when people asked me, I was quick to share openly what I knew. To me, when it came to telling other people about the Lord, I was just one beggar telling another beggar where to find food.

Trusting in Jesus gave me an incredible sense of peace and a refreshing outlook on life. I felt almost like a new baby, seeing the world from an entirely new perspective. Obviously, the world hadn't changed, but something had changed within me. One of the most tangible changes took place in my attitude. I was still ambitious, focused, and intense, but I was also able to mellow out a bit.

In my senior year, Mr. Vogle, the music teacher, was having trouble getting enough students to sign up for choir. "Scott, I need your help," he said one day. "Would you be willing to sing in the choir? If we don't get some people to join, we'll have to cancel the class."

"Sure, I'll join," I said. I talked a few of my football buddies into joining too. Before long, we had most of the football team singing in the choir! It became the "cool" thing to do. We weren't half bad either. We went on a choir tour and sang all over Italy, including a concert in Florence, and we even sang at the Vatican in Rome.

Becoming a Christian, however, did not turn me into a wimp or a nerd. Nor did it mean that I was less aggressive or less competitive. I still played hard and fought to win. During the championship football game in my senior year, playing once again against Vicenza, I wanted the team to play well, and I wanted to win so badly I could taste it. Unfortunately, I had a lot of zeal, but not a great deal of wisdom.

About ten minutes into the game, I was playing so tenaciously that I kept going after the opposing player on a downfield block, long after the referee had blown the play dead. I hadn't heard the whistle, so I kept blocking. Apparently, the referee thought I was trying to instigate a fight, so he called a penalty for unsportsmanlike conduct. When I protested too vehemently, the official ejected me from the game.

It was bad enough that I had been tossed off the field in the most important game of the season, but my mom and stepdad had driven twelve hours, all the way from Naples to Vicenza, to see me play in the championship game. I felt like an idiot. Our team eventually won the game and the championship, but my contribution was mainly as an encourager on the sidelines.

That night, while the team and cheerleaders celebrated our victory with pizza and Cokes, I noticed that the base theater had enough letters on the marquee to spell out a derogatory epithet about Vicenza. I climbed up on the roof to rearrange the letters and had just gotten them into position when the military police pulled up and caught me. They hauled me down to the station, and my coach had to come down and verbally bail me out of the brig.

Despite my mischievous tendencies, I had a strong sense of right and wrong even before becoming a Christian. My newfound faith bolstered my determination to do the right thing all the more. That's not to say I wasn't tempted. Drugs were available in our school, as they are in most schools nowadays. If you wanted them, you could usually find what you were looking for. More than the high they provided, drugs were a doorway to acceptance. To me, that was a far greater temptation, because if I wanted anything in the world, it was to be accepted, approved of, and appreciated. But I knew drugs were harmful to my body, as well as illegal, so I avoided that trap.

Sexual immorality was a far greater temptation for me, as it was for most of my friends. Although our school was extremely conservative in many ways, it was well known that many of the students in the upper grades were sexually active. I decided I wanted to be different. I chose to follow the path of sexual abstinence throughout high school and college. Again, my

Christian faith helped strengthen me to avoid or overcome temptations, but my decision to abstain from sex outside of marriage was based as much on common sense as it was the Bible. Potential premarital pregnancy, the possibility of venereal diseases, and guilt all loomed large as valid reasons to refrain from having sex in high school. Besides, I saw many of my friends who used other friends simply for their own gratification, and I didn't want to be a user.

I caught some flak for my stand on celibacy. One girl went so far as to write aspersions about me on the wall of the girls' restroom in school. That was embarrassing in some ways, but oddly enough, it actually caused many of my classmates to respect me more.

Increasingly, I was becoming known for my leadership abilities. Besides being the captain of the football team my senior year, I also had served as junior class president. It sounds more significant than it really was, since our class had only 110 students. I was also president of the National Honor Society.

That's not to say I was perfect, not by a long shot. One of my most embarrassing moments in high school came when I got caught trying to cheat on my Scholastic Aptitude Test. I had done poorly on the English section of the preliminary SATs the year before, scoring in the bottom percentile of everyone who took the test. I did little better the first time I took the real test, scoring in the twentieth percentile of students who took the test across America. I was frustrated. I was ranked in the upper 10 percent of my high school class, but I could not do well on the standardized tests. I struggled to read and comprehend the questions, and I simply couldn't grasp them.

Knowing how important it is to score well on college entrance exams, I was desperate; I brought in a crib sheet for the test when I took it as a senior. Of course, it's almost impossible to cheat on the SAT, but I didn't realize that. I figured anything was worth a try when it came to raising my English scores. I was found out, though, by my guidance counselor and forced to resign as president of the National Honor Society. It was horribly humiliating.

When I took the ACT college entrance exam, a test formatted in a manner more conducive to my comprehension abilities, I scored among the top

5 percent in the nation. On the basis of these test scores, I was able to get into college.

I knew that I wanted to go to college, but since I had spent my high school years in Italy, I felt no close affinity to American colleges. One of the last places on my list was the Naval Academy in Annapolis, Maryland.

I had a bitter taste toward the Navy from watching the sailors coming into port in Naples. When the carriers arrived, that was always our cue to have a class fund-raiser. We quickly discovered that the Navy guys would pay exorbitant amounts of money for cookies or brownies from a pretty young girl, hoping that his purchase might lead to other delights. Unfortunately, all too often the young sailors coming off the aircraft carriers were simply look-ing for a good time at the expense of one of my female high school class-mates. It was not unusual for one of the young women in our school to turn up pregnant after the carriers had headed back to sea.

Since my father was an Air Force colonel and my stepfather was a lieutenant colonel in the Air Force, I felt sure that I'd be a shoo-in to be accepted at the Air Force Academy, where I could study to become a pilot. Not so.

I had my tonsils out when I was sixteen years of age to alleviate severe sinus problems. When the Air Force reviewed my medical records, they found a long history of sinusitus. Unfortunately, sinus problems and flying a fighter jet don't mix. I was turned down for health reasons. I could have still attended the Air Force Academy, but I'd never be able to get in the cockpit and fly. That would be like taking a kid to an ice cream store and saying, "You can look, but you can't have any." Moreover, the sinus problems pre-cluded me from receiving an Air Force ROTC scholarship.

I could, however, get into Annapolis or West Point. I received appoint-ments from both military schools, and I also qualified for ROTC scholar-ships that could be used to pay for my education at any accredited college to which I was accepted. That made my choice rather simple.

CHAPTER 4
THE ACADEMY

I really had my heart set on going to the Air Force Academy to be a pilot like my dad. When I discovered my sinus problems would keep me out of the Air Force, I looked around to see where else I could fly.

Hey, the Navy has planes too, I thought.

Growing up in the home of an Air Force officer, I wasn't content to join the Navy and work my way up through the enlisted ranks. Like my dad, I wanted to be an officer. The fastest route to a Navy jet looked to be through Annapolis, where I could graduate as an ensign and then head for flight training.

Unlike many seamen who grew up on the water and couldn't leave it if they wanted to, my boyhood was spent in dry, dusty towns like Sherman and Laredo, Texas, a long way from the ocean. We barely had big mud puddles in those parts of Texas, let alone the sea. Nor had living along the Mediterranean seacoast during my teenage years inspired any passion within me for the seafaring life. But I knew the military lifestyle and felt the subtle (and sometimes not-so-subtle) pressure from friends and family to carry on the military tradition.

It was an exciting day when my stepdad brought in the mail, and there was a personal letter to me from the superintendent of the Naval Academy and signed by the president of the United States, congratulating me on my appointment to the Naval Academy. I was thrilled to receive the signed letter from the commander in chief, until I received a similar letter from West Point as well, with the exact same signature printed on the letter. Silly me, thinking that the president of the United States would know my name!

Nevertheless, I was honored that two great military schools were offering me scholarships. I chose Annapolis for one main reason—I wanted to fly.

I majored in chemistry at the Naval Academy, and I was an above-average student, but "book-learning" was never my forte. I enjoyed a more hands-on approach. If I could see how something worked, I could figure it out much easier than merely studying it for hours in a book.

I played "lightweight" football during my first two years at Annapolis, sort of an intramural league for guys weighing between 150 and 200 pounds, hoping for a shot at Navy's varsity team. I played hard, but I never made varsity, so I went out for cheerleader. The Naval Academy cheerleaders were not a bunch of effeminate twerps. Quite the contrary, the Naval Academy cheerleaders were as vigorous as gymnasts. Nevertheless, questions of virility came up frequently, and they were often settled with vicious verbal sparring matches since fistfights between midshipmen were taboo and could lead to expulsion.

I actually enjoyed cheering on the other players. I was always a "rah-rah" sort of guy, and the cheerleading gave me a legitimate way to express that part of my personality. Besides, somebody had to do it, and as a perk, I got to travel for free to all the away games and visit a number of interesting parts of the country. Years later, as captain of the *Greeneville*, I'd often find that my cheerleading skills came in handy, especially when it came to motivating my men, speaking to civic groups and colleges on behalf of the Navy, or conducting public relations cruises for the Navy.

I loved championing someone else's cause other than my own. If someone was bullying a weaker person, I was quick to step in and say, "Hey, knock it off. If you want to pick on someone, come on; your fight is now with me."

I had a sincere desire to help people maximize their potential. As a plebe in the Naval Academy, one of the things we had to do as a test of upper-body strength was climb a rope hanging from the ceiling of the gymnasium. One of the guys in our group did okay climbing up, but then when he got to the top, he froze. There he was, hanging at the top of the rope, thirty-five feet above the floor, paralyzed with fear, and he couldn't climb down. I saw that his face was flushed and his arms had started to shake, and it was plain to me that at any second he was going to come down, one way or the other.

The female instructor, a lieutenant, was yelling at him. "Come on. Get down! Make it happen. Let's go!"

That wasn't helping him a bit.

Without even thinking about it, I grabbed hold of the rope next to the stranded classmate. I climbed up the rope and hung there at the gymnasium ceiling along with my classmate.

"How ya doin'?" I asked.

"I'm scared!" the guy wailed.

"Hey, you can do this," I said. "Come on, let's go back down. Because if you don't, gravity is going to help you."

He smiled weakly, and I said, "Here, let me help you down." I swung over and wrapped my legs around his waist. "I'm here to help you, to let you know that we can do this. We can get down."

We started down, inch by inch. It took us awhile, and we both ended up with a few rope burns, but we got down safely.

The instructor wrote up a glowing evaluation for me because I went up the rope, at risk to myself, to help a classmate in need.

On the other hand, I wasn't above cutting a corner if I thought I could get the same results. During my plebe summer, I went into the boxing ring with Gary Chambers, a friend from Houston, Texas. Gary was a good boxer, and I had never really boxed before. Gary cleaned my clock, giving me a bloody nose!

The next fall, during boxing class, another friend of mine, Stanley Bashaw, and I conspired to choreograph our fight. We had it all worked out so we could both get in a few good licks, knock each other down, and make it look good for both of us. We figured that we'd both get an A in the course, without either of us getting killed.

But that boxing instructor hadn't started teaching yesterday.

After a few minutes of watching Stanley and me flail away at each other harmlessly, he roared in a gruff voice that sounded like a chain-smoking Popeye the Sailorman, "All right, you clowns! Get out of the ring. You," he pointed to me. "Stay in there."

He then went to a midshipman classmate who looked about as big as an oak tree. "You," Popeye growled. "Get in there and fight."

The Tree climbed into the ring with me. He was at least three or four inches taller than me, outweighed me by twenty-five pounds, and had at least a five- to six-inch reach on me. The bell rang, and the Tree came out swinging. I'm sure we looked like a cartoon for a while as he just stood there and pummeled me. I knew that if I didn't do something soon, the Tree was going to kill me!

Somehow I crossed my legs, and the Tree came across with a powerful right hook that lifted me right off my feet and landed me on the canvas. Any sane person would have said, "Okay, that's it. I've had enough." But not me. The guy had embarrassed me, and that made me mad!

I stumbled to my feet and began swinging wildly for all I was worth. I had arms and legs going every direction, and I beat the daylights out of the Tree. When Popeye finally called the fight, both the Tree and I had earned an A in boxing class!

During the fall of my senior year, I went to have my eyes tested in a routine exam to qualify as a Navy pilot. Following the exam, the Navy eye doctor looked perplexed.

"What's wrong?" I asked.

"I'm sorry, Scott. We have a bit of a problem," he said.

"Problem? What kind of problem?"

"Your eyesight is 20-25, and the Navy requires 20-20 vision of its pilots. On a good day, you might pass, but on a typical day, probably not."

"What do you mean? I can see just fine. I don't even wear glasses."

"I know, Scott. But that's not good enough."

"Do you mean that after four years here at the Academy . . ."

"I'm sorry, Scott."

For four years I'd looked forward to my graduation day so I could start flight school. I was disappointed, but I was learning to roll with the punches. Now I had to reevaluate my career options. It wouldn't be the last time. Consequently, I found myself looking into the submariners program.

Actually, my first brushes with the submarine community came during my freshman year at the Academy. The first submariner I had anything to do with was my company officer, a lieutenant in his midtwenties who did everything by the book. He seemed incapable of using common sense and couldn't make a decision about anything that wasn't specifically spelled out in the *Midshipman's Held* publication. I was less than impressed with his leadership skills.

The second submariner I met was my sponsor. All plebes have sponsors, usually a civilian family or friend who lives off the Academy grounds. The sponsors offer an opportunity for the midshipmen to get away from the Academy on Saturday afternoons for a brief break from the military regime. My sponsor was Captain Dan Branch, a battalion officer at the Academy and a former submarine commander who lived on the Academy grounds. Not only was I still immersed in the Academy during my Saturdays, I had to stay in uniform and go to Captain Branch's home to baby-sit his kids!

Nevertheless, I was fascinated listening to Captain Branch's submarine stories, and his enthusiasm piqued my interest. Captain Branch convinced me that going out on a submarine for a few weeks during a summer training program would be an exciting adventure.

He spoke so passionately about the submarine program, I was intrigued. Submarines harbored a unique aura and a lot of mystique to me. Since the submarine force had a reputation as the "silent service," the public didn't know or understand much of what the U.S. submarines did during peacetime. And the Navy liked it that way, since many of the sub force's activities were classified or covert.

Although I had no great love for the ocean, I was fascinated with the high-tech wizardry that could take 140 men hundreds of feet below the surface, perform difficult maneuvers, and keep them alive to tell about it. When the opportunity came up to take a ride on a submarine, I couldn't pass it by, if for no other reason than just to say that I had done it.

The midshipmen originated their trips from Submarine Base New London in Groton, Connecticut, where we were housed in the rat- and roach-infested, condemned portion of the bachelor officers' quarters, one of the oldest buildings in the complex. During the late 1970s, the American economy was in the pits, interest rates were approaching 20 percent, and the Navy had its pick of top-notch men. It didn't have to cater to the cream of the crop; they just came. The deplorable conditions for the midshipmen and young officers sent a subtle message: "Don't think you're so special. We can get guys like you a dime a dozen." Of course, within a decade, that would change dramatically.

My first trip out on a sub was in 1978, aboard the USS *Skipjack* (SSN 585), the first of six boats built in that class. Nuclear-powered submarine series (designated SSN) are named for the first ship built in that class, for example, the *Skipjack* class, the *Thresher/Permit* class, the *Sturgeon* class, the *Los Angeles* class, the *George Washington* class, and the *Ohio* class, which are armed with ballistic nuclear weapons (designated SSBN), America's primary remaining strategic nuclear deterrent now that our number of silo-based and bomber-carried missiles has been dramatically reduced.

At the time I took my first ride, the *Skipjack* was the first submarine to use the new *Albacore* teardrop-shaped hull, enabling the ship to dive deep and fast. The basic hull of the ship cost more than forty million dollars, an astronomical figure at that time. Of course, the price tag on nuclear subs has risen exponentially through the years. As I climbed down the hatch of the long, black cylinder, the first thing to strike me was the unusual smell. Submarines, then and now, have a unique odor due to the amine, a chemical used to cleanse the air of carbon dioxide. Added to that were the pungent odors of diesel oil, hydraulic fluid, coffee, cigarette smoke, and 140 men in a very confined space. Once I got aboard and grew accustomed to the smell, I was okay.

I was riding the fastest, most expensive submarine in the world, and I was hooked! I was doing fine until, suddenly, I heard a series of alarms over the general communications system: We've had a collision! There's flooding in the battery well! Toxic gas! Toxic gas! All hands in the forward compartment don breathing equipment!

Someone tossed me a gas mask. I put it on my head, but I didn't know where to plug it in for air. I wasn't getting air! I couldn't breathe, but I didn't want to take it off because I didn't want to die. Finally, a crewmember saw my predicament, grabbed my mask, and plugged me into the low-pressure, emergency air manifold just seconds before I was ready to pass out.

While I was still gulping huge breaths of air, I heard the words, "Secure from the drill," an announcement that meant the shipwide emergency drill was completed. My mentors were standing around laughing hilariously—I had thought the entire emergency was the real thing!

It wasn't just the amazing machine that impressed me. It was the amazing crewmen. I was assigned to "A" gang, the auxiliary division, and the crew took me under their wing and made me one of the guys. I studied hard and actually excelled as a messenger of the watch. I stood watch as a helmsman, a planesman, and as a lookout, and I worked in every position I could learn. By the end of the three-week deployment, I concluded, *This life is cramped, and it's not very comfortable, but the men sure are intellectually sharp.*

I was most impressed when I was standing up on the bridge with Commander McGhan, and the submarine was ripping though the slot between Race Rock and Long Island at about eighteen knots. The water is cold and rough in that area, and it's extremely windy. McGhan wanted to light a cigar, but the wind kept blowing out his lighter.

Finally, Commander McGhan ordered the officer of the deck, "Ring up all stop!" The OOD obeyed instantly. "Now all back full!" The OOD echoed the commander's words. The submarine heaved to a dead stop.

Commander McGhan nonchalantly pulled out his lighter and lit his cigar. "Okay, all ahead full!"

The submarine lurched forward in the water.

I looked at Commander McGhan and thought, *Now that's power! I want that guy's job.*

Submarines have played an important role in American naval history, as far back, believe it or not, as the American Revolution. In the Civil War, both the Union and the Confederacy employed submarines, and both sides scored significant "kills." The submarine played an important role throughout World War I and World War II, employed effectively by both the Germans and Japanese in their quests for world domination. When the Japanese decimated our surface ship fleet at Pearl Harbor on December 7, 1941, the American submarine force was called upon to mount meaningful counterattacks in the Pacific. What the American submarine force lacked in numbers they made up for by sheer daring, skill, and courage. By the end of World War II, the U.S. submariners had earned a nickname that has stayed with them to this day—the "silent service."

After the war, the Soviet Union closed its grip on the nations it occupied, creating the Iron Curtain, which prohibited people from coming in or leaving the Soviet-controlled territories without the communists' permission. Moreover, as other countries were backing down their military production, the Soviets continued to build a large fleet of diesel-powered submarines. Eventually more than three hundred heavily armed Soviet submarines lurked in waters around the world. Compared to the American subs, they were noisy and easily tracked, but they posed a formidable force nonetheless. Relations between the U.S. and the Soviets soon frosted, and we entered a period that came to be known as the Cold War. During this time, the two countries were not engaged in active battle, but tensions between the U.S. and the Soviets ran high. Both countries lived with the constant potential threat to a very fragile peace.

In the midst of this extremely tense environment, the nuclear submarine was born, spearheaded by a cagey U.S. Navy captain, Hyman G. Rickover. An engineer, Rickover was one of the first to recognize not only the potential of nuclear-powered submarines, but also the possibility, and the necessity, of building them before the Soviets did. Besides the fact that a nuclear-powered submarine could travel thousands of miles without refueling, it also meant that the sub could stay below the surface for very long periods of time, something diesel-powered subs could not do.

Rickover received the U.S. Congress's blessing to begin work on a nuclear-powered submarine in the early 1950s, contracting with the Electric Boat Division of General Dynamics, in Groton, Connecticut. The first nuclear-powered submarine, *Nautilus*, took nearly three years to build and was commissioned on January 21, 1954. The sub soon proved its worth, breaking all existing speed and endurance records; and in 1958, the sub became the first to reach the North Pole, traveling 1,830 miles under the ice—an important and muscle-flexing accomplishment for the U.S., considering the tense relations between the U.S. and the Soviet Union. *Nautilus* remained in service for twenty-five years and was one of the subs involved in the Cuban Missile Crisis blockade in 1962.

As the Cold War intensified and espionage increased between the Soviets and the U.S., the Navy's priorities for our submarines changed from speed to quietness and diving depth. Submarines traveling at high speeds are easier to hear, but with technological advances, the U.S. subs could literally sneak up right behind the Soviet subs, tailing them at a distance close enough that if the Soviet subs ever threatened our nation's interests, our boats would be in a position to intervene. Fictionalized accounts of tension-packed encounters between U.S. and Soviet submarines, such as Tom Clancy's lauded *The Hunt for Red October*, and ostensibly factual accounts of U.S.–Soviet intrigues, such as Sherry Sontag's *Blind Man's Bluff*, are not completely accurate, but they aren't far-fetched either.

Nowadays, most people are aware of the existence of stealth aircraft, planes that can avoid detection by radar or normal surveillance methods. I've always looked at submarines as the original stealth platform and modern nuclear subs, which have the ability to go out to sea for as long as six months at a time, as the "ultrastealth" platform. The nuclear submarine is not limited by the amount of fuel it can carry; it produces its own power as it goes. It is limited only by how much food and coffee a crew can carry!

CHAPTER 5
SUBS ARE US

Enlisting in the Navy is relatively easy; getting assigned to a submarine is a bit more involved. Following basic training, a new recruit moves on to "C" school, where he is specially trained in sonar, mechanics, electronics, navigation, or some other area in which he demonstrates an aptitude. If he hopes to serve aboard a nuclear submarine as an engineer, a reactor operator, an electrician, or a machinist mate, he will probably go to nuclear power school, which was in Orlando, Florida, at the time I attended and is now located in Charleston, South Carolina. He will study at nuclear power school for six months, followed by six more months of training on a nuclear reactor prototype. Then he's off to Groton, Connecticut, to attend submarine school, where he'll learn the basics of sub life, followed by his first tour of duty, which usually lasts four to six years.

Once the sailor is actually on board his first sub, his next goal will be to earn his "dolphins," the warfare pin signifying that he is certified as a true submariner. From there, the sailor continues studying and earning promotions. If he chooses to reenlist, he can continue his career and advance in rank. If an enlisted man demonstrates team leadership and aptitude, he can apply for a program to become an officer. Or he may choose to go to college and enter the officers' ranks through that door. The highest enlisted men's rank is master chief petty officer; the most senior position for an enlisted man on the boat is chief of the boat, the noncommissioned officer responsible for the other enlisted men on the ship. He is the principal enlisted adviser to the ship's captain.

Becoming a naval officer is a somewhat more stringent process. Many officers are graduates of the U.S. Naval Academy in Annapolis, Maryland, but nowadays, other commissioning sources are growing in number. Some choose to attend nonmilitary colleges and enroll in the Reserve Officers Training Corps, a four-year program that offers financial aid to a student in exchange for a five-year commitment to the Navy. Upon graduation, the young man or woman is commissioned as an ensign or a second lieutenant. College graduates who have not gone through ROTC may become officers by enrolling in Officers Candidate School. In this program, they are put through an intensive, rigorous ninety-day training, coming out as commissioned ensigns or second lieutenants, and affectionately known ever after in the Navy as "ninety-day wonders."

To become a submarine officer, a young man must be selected by the Director, Naval Reactors and pass a series of interviews with the director, a four-star admiral, to confirm the candidate's technical knowledge and ability to handle stress. When I was at the Academy, this interview was conducted by Admiral Hyman G. Rickover himself! Talk about intimidating. And Admiral Rickover didn't make it easy on candidates. His interviews were legendary around the Navy. His questions tended to be extremely personal, outlandish, and sometimes downright bizarre. But his decisions were final, and an interview with the director set many careers sailing and many others tumbling backward.

Following his selection for the submarine program, the prospective submarine officer heads off to Nuclear Power School for six months in Charleston, followed by six months at a land-based prototype reactor plant at either Saratoga Springs, New York, or in Ballston Spa, New York. Then he goes to three months of sub school, after which he will be assigned to his first ship. Like the enlisted man, the officer will probably spend twelve to eighteen months qualifying for his dolphins and usually about three years at his first assignment. Just because he is an officer does not mean he automatically receives his dolphins. Quite the contrary, the dolphins must be earned.

After two and a half years, during his first tour aboard a submarine, the young officer will take the engineer's exam. This comprehensive examination on all aspects of the nuclear reactor design, operation, the sub's propulsion plant, and the complex electrical systems, is proctored by someone from the office of the Director, Naval Reactors. The four- to six-hour test is followed by a two-hour period of oral interviews. This is a pivotal point for an officer. If he passes, he can remain in the submarine program, and he can be assigned as chief engineer of a boat or work in some other engineering capacity. But if he fails the test twice, he is released from the submarine program and shuffled off to some other part of the Navy.

After a tour of duty onshore, the officer returns to the submarine school at Groton for the Submarine Officers Advanced Course, which is six more months of training. This course is intended to prepare the officer as a department head or specialist in some area on the boat, whether navigation, engineering, weapons, or other specialty. During this time, he learns submarine tactics, ship operation, maintenance planning, leadership training, warfare tactics, weapons employment, sensors, and threat recognition. It is a detailed, challenging curriculum that focuses on knowing your adversary and how to beat him. Next, the officer puts in approximately three years as a department head.

Following another shore tour, he is ready for the next big thing in his naval career: becoming an executive officer (XO). A senior lieutenant by this time, he must first screen for the position, and then he has two more months of training in the Prospective Executive Officers Course, which prepares him for his position as the XO on board a nuclear submarine. Following his XO tour, he will most likely do a shore tour, and from there he screens for his first command and then heads to Prospective Commanding Officers (PCO) training, perhaps the most important training course in the officer's career.

The PCO course is comparable to the Navy's Top Gun program in that only the best make it through the selection process. During the nine-month course, ten to twelve specially qualified and highly skilled officers are immersed in the tactical and operational intricacies of commanding a nuclear submarine. Besides learning detailed information about running a nuclear reactor, the officer must know every system on the ship, including the handling and firing of torpedoes and missiles, the placing of mines, and the delicate matters of intelligence gathering. Any mistake can be grounds for disqualification from the course. If and when the instructor decides the PCO is ready, the officer is assigned as commander of his own submarine. The admirals in Hawaii, the commander of the Submarine Force, U.S. Pacific Fleet (COMSUBPAC), and the commander of the Submarine Force, U.S. Atlantic Fleet (COMSUBLANT) decide which commanders go to which submarines.

This path has some flexibility—but not much—and a few variables, so every commanding officer won't follow exactly the same curriculum, but every commander will be qualified in each of the areas I've mentioned. Regardless, it is a long, challenging, and at times frustrating journey to become a commanding officer of a nuclear-powered submarine in the U.S. Navy. But once an officer has achieved that position, he is confident he can do just about anything.

The Navy is rather picky about who gets to drive a nuclear submarine loaded with torpedoes, Tomahawk missiles, and some with nuclear ballistic missiles powerful enough to wipe out a city fifteen hundred miles away. The Navy may permit a high school graduate who demonstrates great skills to drive the admiral from place to place in a car, or a physical education major may get to fly an F-18 Hornet, but the person at the helm of a nuclear sub must be a college graduate with knowledge in some engineering discipline. Beyond that, the Navy prefers its sub drivers to have master's degrees. All this emphasis on education in the submarine community is not wasted. One look around the control room of an attack submarine, and it's easy to understand why the man at the controls better be able to think clearly, accurately, and quickly.

In the fall of my senior year, during November 1980, I interviewed with Admiral Hyman Rickover for possible placement in the submarine program. I was nervous going in to see the admiral, and he did absolutely nothing to relieve the tension I felt.

Rickover was an odd blend of nuclear engineer, political insider, and Navy bureaucrat. In his heyday, he personally interviewed and selected every individual who served in the nuclear power program. Rickover prided himself in being a quick study; he could tell who was going to make it in the nuclear sub program and who wouldn't after a brief conversation. And his track record was extremely accurate. Rickover liked two types of officers: "Boy Scouts" or "rebels." The Boy Scouts would carry out his orders without questioning. The rebels would stand up to him and challenge him whenever they thought he was wrong, out of line, or simply over the top in his methods. I was a rare breed to him, part Boy Scout and part rebel, and I think Rickover liked that.

When I walked in his office, the admiral was dressed in a business suit—he rarely wore a uniform—and perched behind a big desk. Maybe the desk just seemed large, since the admiral himself was a rather diminutive person. It struck me as strange that a man of such tiny stature wielded so much power.

Rickover motioned to a wooden chair where he wanted me to sit. It looked like an ordinary chair at first glance, but the front legs were actually cut an inch or two shorter than the back legs. This forced the interview candidates into an uncomfortable position to keep from sliding off the smooth wooden seat. The man spent billions of dollars building nuclear submarines! Could he not afford a decent chair in his office? Of course he could. Admiral Rickover could have had a gold chair had he requisitioned one. This was, after all, the era of six-hundred-dollar toilet seats in the military. And Rickover's name was golden in Congress.

But Rickover's office chair was not a manufacturing defect or a discount-store special. It was a classic Rickover tactic, intended to put the candidates he interviewed at a disadvantage.

I walked over to the chair, sat down, and carefully slid my ankles around the outside of the front legs of the chair, which allowed me to sort of lock onto the chair, sit up straight, and be relatively comfortable. I sat silently, waiting for the admiral to speak.

Rickover ignored me. He sat at his desk holding a piece of paper in his hands, studying it as though it was his income tax return.

Finally, he looked up at me and said, "So, you're a @/x!#?&!% *cheerleader.*" He spat the term out with such derision it hit me like a punch in the gut. "So Mr. Cheerleader, give me a cheer."

Despite my nervousness, Rickover's abrasive demeanor made me angry. I thought, *All right, buddy, you asked for it.*

I unclasped from the chair, stood to my feet, and bellowed the U.S. Naval Academy cheer. I channeled every ounce of energy and anger into that cheer, and I yelled so loud I thought the lights were going to shatter.

Rickover leaned back with a satisfied look on his face. "Okay, sit down, Mr. Cheerleader."

My rear end had barely hit the chair when Rickover was all over me again. "Your grades have been up and down like a @/x!#?&!% roller coaster. What are you going to do about it?"

"I'm going to study more, sir."

"How much more?"

"Ten hours a week, sir."

"Not enough!"

"Twenty hours, sir."

"Not enough," Rickover snapped. "You will study an additional thirty hours a week and write me a report every Friday to show me what you have done."

"Yes, sir."

That's what I said. In my mind, I was thinking, *How in the world am I going to be able to do that on top of what I'm already doing?* But of course, I didn't dare broach that question to the admiral.

Rickover held the paper in front of him again. "So you're a Boy Scout, are you? What are you going to do, generate a submarine merit badge?"

It was clear to me that Admiral Rickover was attempting to rattle me any way he could, so I simply replied, "No, sir."

"Oh, and you've been to Fort Benning jump school and were honor graduate in your class, huh? What are you going to do, parachute onto one of my submarines, Mr. Airborne?"

"No, sir."

"Why do you want in my program?" Rickover roared. "What have you ever done to deserve being in this program?"

It was obviously a rhetorical question, so I remained silent. My heart was pounding and my brain was screaming, *You little man, I could snap you over my knee like a twig right now if I wanted to! How dare you talk to me that way!*

But Hyman Rickover was a four-star admiral, dressed in civilian clothes. So I sat silently.

Finally, Admiral Rickover leaned forward and yelled, "Get the h___ out of here!"

"Yes, sir," I stood and started for the door.

"Not so fast, Mr. Cheerleader. Give me another cheer."

I glowered back at this man—he was, after all, just a man—and the only cheer that came to mind was the old standard. "Give me an N!" I yelled as loud as my lungs could scream.

From somewhere out in the waiting rooms, where my classmates were fretting about their own interviews with Rickover, came the response, "N!"

"Give me an A!" I roared.

The response in the outer offices was louder, "A!"

"Give me a V!" I yelled at the top of my lungs, glaring at Rickover while I awaited the response from the outer offices.

"V!" the cheer was louder yet outside Rickover's door.

"Give me a Y!" I gave it all I had.

"Y!"

"What do you have?"

"NAVY!" came the shout from outside.

"What do you *have?*"

"*NAVY!*" The sound nearly shook the building.

Admiral Rickover went over to the door and poked his head out to his four secretaries in the outer office. "What do you think, ladies?" he asked them.

The four women stood to their feet and applauded.

Rickover waved an arm at me. "Get the h___ out of here!"

Gladly, I thought.

I left Rickover's office that day never wanting to see him or his submarines ever again. "The guy's loony tunes," I said aloud to myself. "He may be the father of the modern nuclear submarine age, but the guy is certifiably nuts!"

I actually held an advantage over Admiral Rickover during my initial interview with him. Rickover thought he was God, and I knew he wasn't!

A short time later, I received a letter from Admiral Rickover, welcoming me into the Naval Reactors Program when I graduated from the Academy. The reactors program was the doorway to the nuclear submarine program. *Oh, God*, I said silently when I saw Rickover's letter. *What have I gotten myself into?*

During my four years at the Academy, the highest grade point I attained was a 3.5 in the spring of my senior year, thanks to Rickover's study demands. Rickover taught me a lesson: With a little extra effort, I could excel. Right before graduation, however, I dropped to 2.97 and felt as though I had failed miserably. I decided I'd work harder to prove myself as an officer. The "if onlys" haunted me: "If only I'd have studied harder for that test," or "If only I hadn't spent so much time goofing off." But it was too late for could haves and should haves.

I graduated from the Naval Academy in the top third of my class, which was okay, but certainly not great. I was commissioned as an ensign on May 27, 1981. Getting my education at the Naval Academy was a challenge for me, but I will always be grateful for the training I received there. I made a lot of lifelong friends at the Academy, enjoyed many opportunities to develop as a leader, learned how to motivate people, and perhaps most important of all, realized that the military was not just in my blood, it was in my future.

Patriotism came naturally for me. Some people serve in the U.S. military because it is a tremendous career opportunity. Others serve as a desire to be a part of a bigger cause. For me, every time I say the Pledge of Allegiance or look at the American flag or hear the "Star-Spangled Banner," I feel something special, something that far surpasses any satisfaction I could receive from a career or a cause.

Nevertheless, I never confused my commitment to my country with a blind faith in naval infallibility. From the very beginning of my naval career, I always bucked the system. I challenged authority when I believed it was wrong. I didn't just go with the flow, and I wasn't a yes-man.

A few years later, my friend Tim Anderson saw the sharp dichotomy between my career choice and my personality. He said to me one day, "Scott, you're either going to be an admiral or you're going to get kicked out of the Navy!"

I knew Tim's mom wrote books about angels, but I never dreamed he was a prophet.

CHAPTER 6
BUILDING THE BOAT BUILDER

My first assignment after graduation from Annapolis was to Submarine Group Eight, located in Naples, Italy. I was thrilled! Not only did I get to go back to the same city where I had attended high school, but my father and his wife were now living there. I was excited to see them and stayed with them for several months before finding my own place. My first tour of duty lasted from July 1981 to December of that same year. Then it was off to my next assignment.

In January 1982, I began a six-month training course at the Navy Nuclear Power School in Orlando, Florida. I hated the rigorous academic requirements. It was similar to getting a master's degree in nuclear power within an extremely short period of time. I simply couldn't grasp the complex information about the nuclear reactors aboard modern submarines by reading concepts in science books. I've always been a hands-on learner. I needed to see it, to feel it, to touch the parts to truly understand how the system worked. But if I was ever going to get a chance to see a working nuclear reactor, I had to pass the comprehensive exam based on the books.

A few weeks before the final exam, I was called in to the Nuclear Power School's equivalent of the dean's office to see Captain Greenman.

"Waddle, your average is 2.79, and typically most students score .2 below their average on the final exam. That leaves you with a 2.59 estimated performance on the final exam. That means you'll have .09 gravy, and that's not much."

I looked back at Greenman with frustration. "If this information is meant to be motivating, it's not," I said. "Nor encouraging, sir."

At that point, Captain Greenman invited me to leave his office.

I was in class with some of the most brilliant "nukes" in America; every one of those guys could have been the top of his class somewhere. I was frustrated and almost ready to quit when my roommate, Jim Murphy, came to my rescue. Jim was a Notre Dame graduate who was ranked number one in our class of seventy-one guys; I was ranked seventieth. "Come on, Scott. We'll study together. I'll help you," Jim offered. We studied for hours the night before the comprehensive final exam. This was the one test that we had to pass . . . or else. Jim worked with me and helped me figure out what I needed to know, translating the book material into practical information that made sense to me. The following day, we took the eight-hour exam. I scored the tenth highest in the class!

I was thrilled to have done so well and couldn't wait to see Captain Greenman. As it turned out, he couldn't wait to see me, too, but for different reasons. He called me to his office once again.

"Waddle, you've been jerking us around the entire time you've been here," Greenman carped. "You really weren't in academic trouble at all. Here you scored the tenth highest score in the class. You were just pulling our chain."

So much for a pat on the back.

While I was studying at the Nuclear Power School in Orlando, an event took place in South America that convinced the world of what can happen when the real threat of a submarine attack is added to the mystique of a vessel that can strike an enemy and then slip silently away into the deep. In April 1982, Argentina and Great Britain became embroiled in a dispute over who controlled the Falkland Islands, a group of islands relatively unknown to most of the world prior to that time. The Argentinean troops landed on the Falklands and took over several cities. The British responded by moving ships into the Falklands to blockade the islands. The Argentines' aircraft dropped some bombs and destroyed some warships, and the battle continued to heighten until a Royal Navy nuclear attack submarine sunk the Argentinean cruiser *General Belgrano* as it attempted to leave the islands. More than fifteen hundred sailors perished, causing Argentina to reevaluate its position in the war.

The mere threat that the British may have one or more nuclear subs lurking out there in the sea, just waiting to pick off the Argentinean vessels, kept the Argentinean Navy in port. The British controlled the seas around the islands, and before long, the Brits once again controlled the islands as well.

While the Falkland Islands War went down in history as a relatively minor skirmish as far as military conflicts, it was the first major example of the potential for war or peace held by the nuclear submarine. As an ensign fresh out of Annapolis, the impression was not lost on me.

Because of some highly publicized scandals, many people think the military is populated by a plethora of promiscuous people. They're not far wrong . . . but they are wrong. Granted, any job that takes a person away from home in a foreign environment carries with it the potential for sexual temptations. Whether it is a businesswoman who spends five nights a week on the road, a professional athlete, or a traveling sales representative, it is all too easy to compromise sexually nowadays without strong moral values. The military is no different.

While I was stationed in Orlando as a single, young ensign, one Navy nurse took me on as her personal project. She was convinced that I was a homosexual because I refused to sleep with her. "I can help you change," she said sincerely.

"I don't want to change," I replied.

"Well, it's my goal to convince you that you need to be heterosexual."

"I'm *very* heterosexual," I told her. "I respect you, and I respect myself. I don't consider sexual intimacy to be just a roll in the hay."

It wasn't easy to maintain that sort of standard, but I soon discovered that the right kind of person respects someone who chooses to do what is right.

In December 1982, following my stint in Orlando at the Nuclear Power School, I went to Ballston Spa, New York, where I studied at the Nuclear Power Training Unit for another six months. There I got to work in a prototype, with a land-based nuclear reactor identical to the one in the submarines at sea. This time the work came easily to me, since it was hands-on training. I could actually see the reactor and the systems, rather than merely reading about them and memorizing a bunch of statistics. I scored at the top of my class. Clearly, my aptitude was in seeing and doing. I didn't simply want to know information; I wanted to put it to use.

Because I had done so well in school, I was given a choice as to where I'd like to go for my first stint aboard a submarine. I chose a "new construction" ship, one that was still being built. I wasn't too keen on going to sea yet. As far as I was concerned, I was going to do the five years that I owed the Navy in return for paying for my education, and then get out. At this point in my life, I had no intention of being a career naval officer.

In September 1983, I transferred back to Groton, Connecticut, for my first tour of duty aboard a nuclear submarine. I was assigned to be part of the Pre-Commissioning Unit helping to build a new submarine, the USS *Alabama*, a Trident outfitted with ballistic missiles.

Well, not so fast. Building a boat is a long, slow process. For instance, it took nearly seven years from the time the Navy designed the *Los Angeles*–class subs to the time they started showing up in the U.S. fleet. The two main companies employed to manufacture American submarines are the Electric Boat division of General Dynamics, in Groton, Connecticut; and Newport News Shipbuilding, in Norfolk, Virginia. Of course, computer parts, electronics, and nuclear reactor components are produced in various places around the country.

Once the funding for the boat is submitted in the president's defense budget and approved by Congress, the shipbuilder must parcel out the various components that require long amounts of time to produce, items such as the nuclear reactor, the heavy turbines, and gears for the ship. It usually takes a year or more before these components of the submarine begin showing up at the construction site. Meanwhile, Electric Boat or Newport News Shipbuilding gets busy manufacturing the steel-barrel, cylindrical hull sections of the sub. The hull of the ship, most of which remains underwater even when the vessel is surfaced, is enormous. More than six hundred feet long, in dry dock the Trident submarine stands about the height of a six- to ten-story building. Imagine the Washington Monument lying on its side, and you have a general idea how enormous these boats are! The hull is formed from huge, barrel-like pieces of steel. The sections are welded together into one long cylinder to form the pressure hull. These welds are checked and rechecked by civilian inspectors. One weak weld can lead to a leak, which can lead to the loss of the submarine and her crew.

The largest items on the sub, such as the nuclear reactor, sonar, weapons launch systems, and other intricate systems, have to be installed early in the construction process. They would be much too large to maneuver inside the sub once the hull is complete.

Next, it's time for the most important component to be brought in—the crew. The technological wonder of a nuclear submarine is simply a mass of metal without good men, qualified and trained to operate it. During the time a U.S. submarine is being built, the Navy brings in a number of seasoned officers and some of the chief petty officers who will actually be taking the ship to sea for the first time. Obviously, these people have a vested interest in seeing that the work on the sub is done correctly. This group is known as the Pre-Commissioning Unit (PCU), until the time that the ship is actually commissioned as a USS, a United States Ship. This was the group to which I was first assigned to work while building the *Alabama*. The PCU works with the shipbuilders to install and test all the interior equipment. This can take up to twenty-four months for a Trident if things are going well, and much longer if they are not. The *Los Angeles*–class submarine PCUs usually run about twelve months.

By the time the PCU crew arrives, the reconnaisance tower, or sail, has been placed and the bow and the stern end caps have been sealed on the boat, so all the interior equipment has to be taken down the hatches of the sub to be installed. As huge as the modern submarines are, the working conditions are still cramped, with little space allotted for "crew comforts." The ship is tightly crammed with high-tech observation and detection equipment. Although there are no windows on *Los Angeles*–class or Trident submarines, technology helps the crew to "see" what is outside the boat in the water. The modern submariner's detection equipment is so good, if a dolphin swims by in the water, someone on the sub probably knows about it. The difficulty, of course, is discerning the myriad sounds and "contacts" that are picked up by all the high-tech equipment once the ship is submerged.

Things really get interesting when the nuclear reactor is powered up, or "achieves criticality," for the first time. Like any land-based nuclear facility, this must be done with precision and care. There is no room for error when working with a nuclear reactor. All the same inherent dangers of a nuclear reactor meltdown such as that experienced at Chernobyl, or nearly experienced at Three Mile Island, are real possibilities aboard a nuclear submarine if people don't perform their jobs. The long-term effects of such a disaster could be devastating. Fortunately, there has never been a nuclear accident aboard a U.S. sub. This is a credit to the methodical testing that takes place on the sub prior to commissioning and the rigid adherence to established procedures. The director actually embarks on the initial test runs with every new nuclear submarine the U.S. puts in the water. It's a tremendous statement of confidence in the building program that the director goes to sea with the sub the first time the submarine is put through its paces during the shipbuilders' initial sea trials.

When the shipbuilder and the PCU crew have finished their work, the remainder of the crew is brought aboard for training. These are the guys who will actually "fight" the submarine, turning themselves and the long, black cylinder into an incredible war machine. When the Navy decides that the ship and crew are ready in every way, a commissioning ceremony is arranged either at Groton or Norfolk. Political leaders and high-ranking Navy officials are usually asked to say a few words in honor of the occasion. Most say far too many words, but that's okay. Everyone is patient. The commissioning has been a long time in coming; nearly six years have passed since the ship's inception. A few more minutes won't hurt.

Finally the new ship's captain gets to speak, and then the ship's pennant is presented, the name becomes official, and the crew stands topside for the first official moments of the ship's career. "Set the watch on the below decks!" comes the order, and the sailors burst into motion, heading for their positions. All in all, it is a powerfully moving ceremony when the bottle of champagne is broken over the bow and the submarine enters service. The Navy has invested enormous amounts of time, energy, and money into the ship and her captain and crew. It would be a shame to waste any of that investment.

This was the process I went through during the building and testing of the *Alabama*. My first captain oozed obsessive-compulsive traits, especially when it came to dirt on his submarine—a characteristic that eventually I came to better appreciate—but at the time, I just thought the guy was nitpicking. More importantly, the captain was extremely slow to praise and quick to criticize. Everything was done "by the book," and anyone having any fun on his boat seemed to be suspect.

For instance, prior to pulling the *Alabama* into port at the ship's namesake, Mobile Bay, Alabama, the captain painstakingly warned the crew about revealing too much information about the new SSBN sub. He especially stressed that we should be noncommittal in answering any questions about the weapons carried aboard the boat.

When the new submarine pulled into the pier, we created quite a stir. Reporters and politicians all lined the shore, looking over and commenting about the new sub. A number of national dignitaries, including Admiral James Watkins, the chief of naval operations who eventually became the secretary of energy, and Jeremiah Denton, a congressman and former prisoner of war, were also in attendance.

The people of Alabama were rightfully proud of "their new boat." Everything was going along well, until a local reporter scratched his chin and asked, "How many torpedoes do you carry on this baby?"

The captain's stock answer was, "I can neither confirm nor deny the presence of torpedoes on board the *Alabama.*"

"How 'bout nukes?" another man asked. "I read in the paper that you boys got some nukes in there."

"I can neither confirm nor deny the presence of nuclear weapons aboard the *Alabama,*" the captain spouted. Of course, the media had already informed the public about the potent destructive capabilities of the SSBN. The only questions were, How much damage could we do? And how far away? It was ludicrous to pretend such weapons weren't aboard.

It got to be such a joke that when reporters asked any question to one of our crewmembers, Lance Milion, he rattled off the captain's response.

A camera crew was interviewing crewmembers when Lance got on a roll. "How's the food on board the sub?" a television reporter asked.

"I can neither confirm nor deny the presence of good food on board the *Alabama,*" Lance deadpanned.

"What about entertainment? Do you have good movies on board?"

"I can neither confirm nor deny the presence of good movies on board the *Alabama.*"

"What do you do with all the waste products when you're out at sea for long periods of time?"

"I can neither confirm nor deny . . ."

The reporter didn't even bother to ask about nuclear weapons.

Two weeks prior to the *Alabama*'s mooring in Mobile Bay, my friend and fellow shipmate Rich Volkert and I had completed qualifications for our dolphins, so we had a great idea. "Let's see if we can get Admiral Watkins to pin our dolphins on us," Rich said. With all the special emphasis on the *Alabama*, and with the admiral in town along with numerous other luminaries, it seemed like a winning idea to us. When we suggested the notion to the captain, however, he wouldn't hear of it. Instead, he insisted on handling the dolphins ceremony himself, back in Bremerton, Washington, a few weeks later.

The encounter was typical of the way he ran his boat, and I started long-ing for the day I could get off his ship. I vowed to myself that if I ever got the opportunity to create a different sort of work environment aboard a sub-marine, I'd do it.

Fortunately, near the end of 1986, several significant changes took place that probably kept me in the Navy. First, a new captain, Garnet C. "Skip" Beard, took charge of the *Alabama,* and the morale aboard the *Alabama* changed almost overnight. Captain Beard didn't do things all that differently than the previous captain had done. He was, however, quick to praise his crew and slower to criticize. Even when he corrected or disciplined a crew-man, he tried to find something good to say about the man's work or his character. For the first time since joining the Navy, I enjoyed going to work each day. I flourished so well, Captain Beard recommended me as a junior officer to take my engineer's exam at Naval Reactors.

More importantly, I had discovered a person who kept my mind better occupied than worrying about the peccadilloes of my captain. Her name was Jill Elise Huntington.

CHAPTER 7

SCOTT AND JILL

When Rich and I finally received our dolphins, the prestigious warfare pin worn over the chest pocket and so highly valued by every submariner, we were back in Bremerton, Washington, in late 1986. The dolphins are awarded when a submariner learns the boat's systems—including in-depth knowledge of all the sub's systems and detailed knowledge of all emergency systems—and passes the necessary tests proving that he knows what he's doing aboard the sub. More importantly, the dolphins are the sign that a sailor has "arrived" in the submarine community. Prior to earning his dolphins, he is simply another "non-qual"; once he has earned his dolphins, he's *family*.

The Navy does a good job of honoring the achievements of its sailors with various promotion ceremonies, change of command ceremonies, and recognition ceremonies. None of these is more highly regarded than the bestowing of the dolphins. I invited my fiancée, Jill, to attend the ceremony.

Prior to the occasion, the captain had asked me, "Who do you want to pin on your dolphins?"

"In all respect, sir," I replied, "I don't want you to pin on my dolphins. I'd like to have my fiancée pin on my dolphins."

If the captain was offended, he didn't show it. When the time came, he stood aside as Jill stepped to the front, took the dolphins, and pinned them on my uniform. She's been an integral part of my Navy career ever since.

I first met Jill when I was relocated to Bremerton, Washington, the home port for the *Alabama*. Lieutenants get precious little room to store extra clothes, personal belongings, and toiletries aboard a submarine, so I rented a small condominium in town. While the *Alabama*'s gold crew was back at General Dynamics for the boat's additional sea trials, I was part of the blue crew, the "off" crew stationed on the West Coast. One afternoon I decided to go to the Silverdale shopping mall to pick up some necessities. I was walking through a Bon Marché department store, passing by the cosmetics section, when a stunning blonde salesclerk working behind the counter caught my eye. I nonchalantly ambled over in the direction of the men's cologne section nearby, watching the young woman out of the corner of my eye. I pretended to be interested in the men's cologne, which I really was, since the colognes were positioned perfectly to give me the best view of the pretty young woman.

After getting a better look, I thought, *Oh, man! She is cute!* The blonde was tall and shapely with sparkling hazel eyes and distinctly Norwegian facial features. She wasn't just good-looking; she was drop-dead gorgeous! I thought, *I want to meet this woman.*

I walked closer to the men's fragrances counter, thinking that she'd come over to wait on me. Instead, another saleswoman, wearing a nametag bearing the name *Betty*, came over to wait on me. Betty was an attractive woman as well, but I was mesmerized by the blonde.

"Can I help you?" Betty asked.

"I'm sure you can," I said, "but I'd really rather that other girl over there help me." I nodded toward the Norwegian-looking woman.

Betty looked back at me coolly, running her eyes up and down my frame. I was wearing khaki pants and a long-sleeved, button-down shirt with a sweater-vest. I must have passed Betty's inspection because, without batting an eye, she rattled off, "Well, listen pal, to get to her, you've got to go through me, and that will cost you forty bucks; so you better pick out what you want." Betty gestured toward the cologne showcase.

I didn't need any cologne, but I bought forty dollars' worth of Aramis products, keeping an eye on the blonde woman while I pulled the cash from my wallet.

"Plus tax," said Betty.

I hauled out a few more dollars.

Meanwhile, the blonde was motioning behind my back to Betty to get my name and address.

Betty called to the blonde, "Jill, come on over. Here's another guy who wants to meet you."

Jill sashayed over to where I was standing, and she didn't even have to open her mouth. I was smitten!

"Hi, my name is Jill Huntington," she said with a beautiful smile as she reached out her hand to shake mine in a very businesslike manner.

I introduced myself and told her that I was a lieutenant in the Navy. We talked briefly and I asked her out for a drink after she was done working. "No, I don't date Navy guys," she answered curtly.

"What? Why not?"

"I just don't," she replied in a manner that said, "And don't ask again." So I didn't.

"Well, in that case, I guess I'd better return this merchandise."

"You can't do that," she said sweetly.

"Why not?"

"Because then Betty won't get her commission."

"Hey, I don't care about Betty! I don't even know Betty!" I said.

"No, but I do, and Betty's my friend. It's been nice talking to you," Jill said.

Another customer called for Jill's attention, so she waved good-bye and went back to her station behind the cosmetics counter. I left the store, frustrated but determined. I wanted another chance.

A week or so later I came back again, and Jill and I talked some more. I asked her out again, and she turned me down again.

We went through the same routine the following week.

"What's it going to take for you to go out with me? Come on! Give me a chance."

"Well, you are rather persistent," Jill said.

"Come on," I begged, "we'll just go out for coffee or something. Some place where there are lots of people."

"Well, okay . . ." Jill softened. "But Betty will have to come with us."

"*Betty!* What's Betty got to do with anythi . . . well, okay. Yeah, sure, we'll take Betty with us."

For our first date, I dressed in my typical preppy look—slacks, button-down shirt, and a sweater—because the late-summer, early-fall temperatures in Washington had already begun to cool. I picked up Jill at work and was delighted to discover that Betty couldn't make it! Jill and I went to the Sandpiper Inn, a restaurant close to where I worked. She was a classy dresser, and I was proud to be seen with her. We talked for hours, and I was more intrigued than before, so I asked her out again the following week. Her dad worked as a communications officer at Fort Lewis, the Army post, and he was a captain in the National Guard, so Jill was familiar with the pressures of the military experience and lifestyle. That may have been one of the reasons that she had been reluctant to date Navy guys. Her mom worked in the local school cafeteria, and several of her close relatives were professors and teachers nearby. Jill herself had a great gift for teaching, and it was easy for me to imagine her one day being a schoolteacher.

On our second date we went to the Boatshed, a popular restaurant on the waterfront. During the conversation, I said, "This is a great dinner, but it's not as good as I make."

Now it was Jill's turn to be intrigued. "A sailor who cooks?"

"Yeah, I love to cook!"

The following week I invited Jill to my place, where I cooked a sensational meal of steak, potatoes, and green beans, complete with Oreo ice cream for dessert. Jill was living with a friend, Judy Manley, and together the two of them were struggling to make ends meet. To have a home-cooked meal was a real treat for her.

I knew I'd won her heart! We dated for several months and fell head over heels in love.

In late November I took my engineer's exam, a crucial, pivotal point in my career. The engineer's exam is the turning point at which most men either continue in their training toward a command position in the Navy or stall in their careers.

I took the engineer's exam at Naval Reactors, in the same building where Admiral Rickover had interviewed me. Afterward, I waited around until I received word that I had passed—and I'd done so with flying colors! What a relief!

That afternoon, feeling pumped up, I decided to stop by Annapolis and visit some friends at the Naval Academy before heading back to the *Alabama*. It was my first visit to the Academy since my graduation. While I was in the rotunda of Bancroft Hall, then deputy commandant of midshipmen, Captain Albert Konetzni, came out of an office and saw me in my Navy whites. He came up to me and introduced himself.

"What's your name, shipmate?" he asked me.

I told Captain Konetzni my name and that I had just passed my engineer's exam and had stopped by to visit some friends at the Academy.

"That's great!" He slapped me on the back and said, "Come in to my office. Let's talk." He held the rank of captain at that time, but nobody who knew him doubted that Captain Konetzni would soon be Admiral Konetzni. I'd never seen the man before, but I recognized him instantly the moment I laid eyes on him. Everyone in the Navy, it seemed, knew "Big Al, the sailor's pal." A gregarious, big, teddy bear of a man, Captain Konetzni was a highly regarded submariner, but more importantly, he was a motivator of men.

He sat down with me and we talked for more than an hour! It was the first time in my career that a captain, a submariner I didn't even know, took such an interest in me. Captain Konetzni and I hit it off immediately. He said that he saw a lot of himself in me, and I took that as a high compliment. Neither of us could ever have dreamed how intertwined our lives would become over the years to follow.

Jill's and my relationship was progressing rapidly when suddenly, right before Christmas, I received bad news: I was being shipped out to Naples, Italy. I was scheduled to report to Italy on January 5.

When I told Jill that the Navy had transferred me to Naples, probably for the next two years of my life, she was devastated. Our love had grown deep, fast. Although we both had always known the possibility—more accurately, the certainty—that I'd be reassigned sooner or later, we had hoped it would be later rather than sooner. Now the thought of a two-year separation seemed untenable. I had been considering asking her to marry me, but the fact that within weeks I'd be halfway around the world from her caused me to make up my mind quickly.

We were at the Boatshed restaurant when I got down on one knee and blurted, "Jill, I know it's crazy; I don't even have a ring to give you, and we don't have much time, but would you marry me? I love you."

She smiled lovingly, put her hand in mine, and said, "Yes, let's get married."

The Christmas holidays were a blur. Besides all the usual festivities, we were planning a New Year's Eve wedding. On top of that, we had lots of details to deal with, everything from buying wedding rings, to getting military identification cards and a passport for Jill, to finding a place to live in Naples before we arrived.

During a quick visit to Texas, we went to a jewelry store looking for rings and found a spectacular one-and-a-half-carat, pear-shaped loose diamond at the Galleria mall in Austin. Jill went nuts over it. When we asked the price, I went bonkers myself. The stone alone sold for more than fifteen thousand dollars. On my lieutenant's salary, that was more than half my income for a year!

I told Jill, "I love you, but I just can't afford that ring."

Jill agreed, but I saw that it was too late. She'd already fallen in love with that diamond.

When I told my mom how disappointed I was that I couldn't afford the stone for Jill's ring, she said, "Let's try something else." She called some friends in the diamond business, described the stone, and asked if they could help. "Give me a little time, and I'll see what I can find. Come on over in a couple of days," Mom's friend said.

A few days later we went to the diamond broker's home, and there, for a fraction of the price, was the exact same stone that we had just seen in the mall. We bought it and had it mounted, and Jill is wearing it to this day.

Through all the wedding plans and preparations, Jill's attitude was incredible. Every woman has dreams she's carried from childhood about the kind of wedding and honeymoon she'd like to have. Jill's dreams of a big, fancy wedding were suddenly altered. We planned a small, intimate ceremony at Puget Sound Naval Shipyard Chapel, conducted by the Episcopal priest of St. Bede's, the church where Jill and I had been attending. The tiny, cedar-paneled chapel was decked out in Christmas décor, with pine branches and poinsettias, and it was beautiful in its quaintness and charm. Because of the haste of our plans, only a few of our closest friends could attend. Nonplussed, Jill sloughed off any sacrifices of her dreams as merely minor nuisances. My stepdad, John Coe, was my best man. Jill's friend Judy Manley was the maid of honor. Jill looked radiant in her hastily purchased wedding dress. We were in love, and we were committed to each other; that's all that mattered.

We married on New Year's Eve, celebrated Jill's birthday on January 2, and picked up her passport and identification cards on January 3. On January 4 we flew on a commercial jet from Seattle to Philadelphia, and then we boarded a military transport plane for the flight to Rota, Spain, on our way to Naples.

We arrived in Naples and set up housekeeping in Quarto, a gorgeous location on the edge of a dormant volcanic crater, high above the Mediterranean

Sea. We had a great view of the sea, looking out our front windows. It was fabulous, and Jill loved it!

Jill had never before driven an automobile with a stick shift, let alone driven in the frenetic Italian traffic patterns—or lack of patterns. But she took on that challenge as well. Before long, she was driving chaotically, yelling, and gesturing out the windows at motorists who got in her way, just like the locals!

Getting married is a shock to a person's system under the best of circumstances, even after the most meticulous preparation. Jill and I married after a whirlwind courtship and a brief period of pastoral counseling in our church. Then, not only was she thrust into a military lifestyle, she was whisked from the security of her friends, family, familiar sights, sounds, foods, and shopping malls to begin marriage in an entirely new country! Worse still, she didn't know anyone outside of the military base, and she couldn't speak a word of Italian!

Even for a strong woman such as Jill, that's an enormous amount of change in an incredibly short period of time. Not surprisingly, we experienced stress in our relationship right from the start. But our love was strong, and our commitment to each other was unconditional. We were in this thing for the long haul, come what may.

We lived in Italy from January 1987 to January 1989. It was a fabulous experience for Jill and me. One of the best things that happened during our tour in Naples was the birth of our daughter, Ashley Nichole.

We were excited when we learned that Jill was pregnant, though somewhat concerned. We hardly had had a chance to get settled, and now we were taking on the responsibility of bringing another human being into the world. *How are we going to handle it all?* I wondered.

Complicating matters further, late in Jill's pregnancy the doctors discovered that our baby was breech, had crossed legs, and was facing forward. A week past our due date, the doctor said that a Caesarian section was required. We set a date and reported to the hospital for the birth of our baby. It was a strange feeling, driving to the hospital, knowing that we'd be coming home with a baby.

I was permitted to be in the operating room with Jill. As I scrubbed and put on the outfit and booties the hospital provided, I was excited but nervous. Once inside the operating room, my nervousness changed to stark terror. There was Jill on the operating table, with both of her arms strapped down. One arm had an intravenous needle, and the other arm had a blood pressure monitor. She was anesthetized, so she couldn't feel anything from the waist down, but she was awake.

I'm a strong man, but it challenged my intestinal fortitude like nothing else ever had to stand there and peer over the drape as the doctors sliced my wife's belly and opened her up like a book. Several times I came close to fainting, not so much from the blood, but from the knowledge that my wife was going through this to bring our baby into this world. I never loved her more than at that moment, when she looked at me pleadingly, as if to say, "Why are you allowing these people to do this to me? Can't you do something to help?"

All of those feelings disappeared a few moments later when the doctor removed the baby from Jill's stomach and held up the child. "Congratulations," said the nurse standing next to me. "It's a boy, I think."

I started doing a little jig right there in the operating room. "Yeah!"

"Wait a minute, no. It's a girl."

"Hey, get out of the way, and let me check," I crowed.

I looked down at the baby. Jill groaned, "Honey, what is it?"

"Aw, it's a girl," I sighed in mock disappointment.

Just then the little girl let loose her first cry, "Whaaaahh!" My heart melted instantly. *That's my baby!* I thought. And that little girl has held my heart ever since.

The nurse washed the baby and handed her to me as the doctors sewed Jill back together. I leaned over Jill's head and said, "She's our little girl!"

We named her Ashley Nichole because she was a beautiful baby, and she deserved a beautiful name. The nurses pressed Ashley's foot against an inkpad and then placed her tiny foot on some paper, creating an image of her footprint. I carried that little footprint with me all around the world, and I still carry it in my wallet today.

When we took Ashley home, often after Jill and I had put her in her bassinet, we'd stand together looking over her, and we'd just stare. "Isn't she beautiful?" Jill would ask as we'd cling to each other and thank God for the incredible blessing of our baby. No other feeling I'd ever known compared to the joy of having a child of our own to hold, to hug, and to kiss good-night.

I went back to work for Submarine Group Eight, located in Naples, which was great since I spent much of my time onshore and had to go out on infrequent deployments for only a few weeks at a time. It was during this second tour of duty in Naples that I ran into a major conflict with a senior officer in the Navy. It wouldn't be my last. Throughout my naval career my mouth occasionally got me in trouble when I told a boss what I sincerely thought.

I worked hard to do the right thing, but for some reason I got across the breakers with one particular captain. We had hit it off well at the beginning of our relationship, especially when he heard that I had played football for Navy. When he found out that I'd never made the varsity team and had instead joined the male cheerleading squad, he was less than impressed.

For my part, I was less than impressed with him when I learned that he had "hit on" Jill at a party at the Officers' Club.

"What's a good-looking and smart woman like you doing with a loser of a man like your husband?" he had blatantly asked Jill.

This was the man who was my boss in Naples, where I served as the submarine scheduler. As a staff watch officer, I stood twelve-hour watches keeping track of all the submarines operating in the Mediterranean, both U.S. and allied boats. My job was to know what ships were out there and where they were going, and a secondary part of my job involved scheduling the various logistical needs of our subs, including the advance arrangement of diplomatic permissions and other matters.

One day, just before Jill and I were going to take our baby girl, Ashley, and go on leave for a week, I submitted a schedule change for one of our subs to our radio group. For some reason, the change never got through, but I didn't know that. I went on leave, thinking that everything was taken care of. We didn't have cell phones in those days, so I was completely out of touch with the office.

When I returned, I walked into a hornets' nest in the office. Apparently, while I'd been away, an admiral had been aboard a submarine going from Gibraltar to La Spezia, Italy, and the diplomatic clearance had not been obtained to allow the submarine to pull into port. The admiral was forced to transfer to a small boat more than twelve miles out at sea. That's a long way to ride on a small landing-craft type of boat, and, putting it nicely, the admiral was not a happy sailor.

Neither was my boss.

Since the diplomatic arrangements were my responsibilities, my name was worse than mud around the office. As a result, I was removed as ship scheduler. Worse yet, my fitness report—the file used to determine future promotions—showed a black mark against my name.

I was reassigned to work for Lieutenant Commander Bob Nestlerode in the office. One night I was working late and walked by Nestlerode's office when I noticed some notes, written on his calendar. I read some of the notations such as: "Left to go get a haircut without telling me" and "Went to the operation control center without telling me." The operation control center was one floor below us. Another note said, "Didn't route a message to me."

As I looked at the mundane list of minor offenses, I realized what it was. Lieutenant Commander Nestlerode was keeping tabs on me!

I picked up the phone and called him at home. "Commander Nestlerode, this is Scott Waddle," I said when the commander came on the line.

"What do you need, Scott?" he asked.

"I just want you to know that it's late . . . and I'm here at the office working on this project. I could be home like other guys, home with my wife and new baby, but I'm here. I certainly hope you are keeping a list of the good things I'm doing, as well as this other list on your desk."

"Well, er, ah . . . Scott, this isn't the time to talk about this."

"No, it's not. But I'll see you first thing tomorrow morning, and we'll discuss it then."

The following morning I confronted our chief of staff about the commander's list. "I know what this list is," I said, "and I don't like it. If you have a problem with me, come to me about it. Don't keep a scorecard behind my back."

"Well, Scott, we were gathering information to issue a nonpunitive letter of caution to you, to address your performance."

I was irate, and I didn't hold in my anger. "If you want to address my performance, let's talk about what I do around here, spending 65 percent of my time covering my rear end and 35 percent doing my job."

The chief of staff told me the contents of the letter they had planned to give me. The letter was never issued, but I received an adverse fitness report anyhow. I was given a C in judgment and response to stressful situations, which was a kiss of death in the Navy. Any mark less than a 4.0 is enough to destroy an officer's future.

I was furious, but there was nothing I could do about it. After two years, I left Naples with less-than-glowing marks on my record. I did not receive an end-of-tour award, the Navy's medal given at the close of a successful tour of duty. The missing medal would be conspicuously absent to any review board evaluating me for potential future service. Two years later, the black marks against my name were removed from my record by Admiral Hank Chiles, but they nearly destroyed my career before it got started.

CHAPTER 8

ALOHA, INSPECTOR WADDLE

In January 1989, we moved from Naples to Naval Submarine School in New London, Connecticut, located just across the Thames River from Groton, "the submarine capital of the world." A short drive along the seacoast from New York City, the quiet town of Groton is the quintessential New England seaport, the kind of place you imagine when you look at paintings of New England seascapes. But this is no ordinary community along the seacoast. Here in Groton are the Navy's core submarine schools and training facilities that will at one time or another host every U.S. submariner serving aboard ship. While the classroom buildings on the hillside look like those of most any small college, inside these nondescript exteriors reside some of the most complex and sophisticated training machines and simulators ever devised by man. These classrooms are where both new officers and enlisted men learn how to operate the various systems aboard a sub. This is also one of the places submariners return to periodically for refresher courses. In these simulators a seaman can practice everything from driving a submarine to fighting a fire aboard a submarine to simulating an emergency blow, a rapid surfacing maneuver.

Downriver a few miles from the sub base, close to the banks of Long Island Sound, is General Dynamics' Electric Boat shipyard, where the majority of today's active submarines have been built. Here, the dock is lined with new ships under construction. It's an amazing sight, one that every submariner carries near to his heart.

I studied and worked at Groton from February 1989 to July 1989. From there, I was assigned to the exciting task of working as an engineer, helping to build a new submarine, the USS *Kentucky*, "a boomer," an *Ohio*-class SSBN designed to carry as many as twenty-four Trident missiles—enough thermonuclear explosives to destroy most of the major cities of the world.

It took more than two years to build the *Kentucky* and then test it on sea trials. I was part of that process from August 1989 to October 1992, and during that time I worked like a maniac, trying to prove to my superiors that the negative comments on my fitness report from Naples were wrong. By now I was thirty-three, and I held the rank of lieutenant commander, serving under Michael Regal and Captain Joseph Henry. Captain Henry had been on the *Key West*, serving under Admiral Hank Chiles, who had by now moved up the ladder to be the commander of the Submarine Force, U.S. Atlantic Fleet.

Building the *Kentucky* was a complicated affair. The first two years were spent in construction, testing, and then sea trials before the ship was commissioned. The contractors do an incredible job of getting the boat seaworthy, but there is always a measure of risk during the test periods. One nuclear sub actually sank off the coast of New England during tests, and all of the crewmembers perished.

Apparently, my work aboard the *Kentucky* impressed Captain Joseph Henry immensely, because he went to bat for me with Admiral Chiles. It was through Captain Henry's efforts that the black marks against my name were removed. In a real sense, I owe my Navy career to him. Without the change in my fitness report, I'd have never been allowed to screen for executive officer, one of the last big steppingstones to commanding my own ship.

Although the years working on the *Kentucky* were hard years, they were extremely productive. That's where I found my niche. I discovered that what I really enjoyed was motivating men, bringing out the best in them, training them, instilling in them standards of excellence, and then turning out an exceptional product for the Navy.

After the *Kentucky* was commissioned, I moved to Kings Bay, Georgia, for about six months, while Jill and Ashley remained behind to sell our house in Groton. The house had barely sold, and Jill and Ashley had joined me for only about a month and a half in Kings Bay, when we received word that the Navy was moving us again!

This move, however, was every submariner's dream come true. We were being assigned to Pearl Harbor, Hawaii. We drove across the country from Georgia, stopping to spend some time in Austin and Houston with my family members, and then going on to Olympia, Washington, to visit Jill's mom before it was time for me to report to duty in Hawaii. A widow now, Jill's mom was thrilled to have the company, especially that of her granddaughter, who was almost five years old.

We moved to Hawaii in November 1992 and lived there until January 1995. There I worked for the commander of the Pacific Fleet, serving as part of the U.S. Pacific Fleet Nuclear Propulsion Examining Board. Mine was an engineering job, but it felt more as though I was a member of the Navy's version of the Internal Revenue Service. My job was inspecting nuclear-powered submarines, surface ships, and shore-based facilities having to do with servicing ships' propulsion plant operations. I had been selected for this duty because of the success of my department and my engineering team aboard the *Kentucky*, where we had worked through two arduous years in the shipyard with a flawless safety record.

I was one of five junior members of the board, along with two captains. I was honored to be a part of the team, because I knew the Navy didn't send just anyone to inspect their nuclear submarines. They sent the best of the best. I was also quite aware that the men who move up to command positions are mostly engineers.

My responsibility was to issue and audit the operational reactor safeguards exam given to the crew of all nuclear submarines. I interacted with a lot of sailors, conducting fifty-four inspections over a twenty-four-month period.

Usually, our team flew to a location and spent two to three days aboard a submarine. We did administrative and material inspections, and then we had the crew perform six to eight hours of engineering casualty drills to see how they responded to emergency situations. We wrote our evaluations that same night. After a few hours of sleep, we interviewed the crew and then graded them. We'd leave the ship for a while, caucus in an office somewhere, and then return to the ship and give the crew the results of our inspections.

The inspections were taken very seriously, not simply for safety reasons, but for the rating of the submarine and its crew. They were the benchmarks against which they measured themselves and the method of comparison against other submarines in the fleet.

I spent two years as an inspector and earned a reputation as being tough but fair. I always tried to consider how I'd feel if someone were examining every nook and cranny of my ship and analyzing every move of every person on board. Nobody likes to have someone come in from the outside and be a critic, nitpicking about every little thing. While I never let a crew get away with anything, I didn't always make an official entry in the final report when I found something not quite right.

For instance, on one ship I was inspecting at Puget Sound Naval Shipyard, I saw a warning light come on around the nuclear reactor while the engineers were performing a test of the equipment. A young sailor hit the reset button, assuming that I hadn't seen his action. That in itself was not an infraction. Obviously, the warning light alerted the crew to a problem that needed to be fixed, but that was not insurmountable. Unfortunately, sometimes crewmembers became so driven to be perfect, they'd overlook something rather than admit something was wrong or being done incorrectly.

When I approached the division chief later and asked if there had been any problems in performing the evolution, he said, "No, sir, none at all."

I knew better. I'd seen the warning light with my own eyes! Now it was an integrity issue. I told my boss what I'd seen, and he said, "Let's find out what's going on."

We went to the ship's engineer and reported what we found. He was mortified to think that one of his guys might endanger the ship by trying to hide a problem with the reactor equipment. I asked the chief about the warning light incident. "Did this happen? Was there a problem?"

"No, sir. The equipment is working fine."

"Okay, let's run the test again," I said. We ran the test again, and the equipment failed.

The sheepish looks on the faces of the reactor controls chief and the engineer told the story. They were dead meat and they knew it. I could have failed them right there. One comment in my report pertaining to a breech of integrity could have sunk their careers. But rather than hammering the guys, I chose to take a different tack. I wrote up the problem without penalizing the crew or failing them in the inspection, but they learned from the experience that they dare not fudge on the facts, and that's what mattered most to me.

On another occasion, I was inspecting an attack boat returning from a six-month deployment and came across a sailor who was supposed to be standing watch, but he had fallen asleep! I woke up the sailor, and I told the engineering watch officer and the engineer to get him out of there. "Put somebody on the watch who's awake ," I said.

Later the captain pulled me aside in his stateroom and said, "I just want you to know that I've had that guy written up. I'm going to take him to captain's mast, and I'm going to bust him. I'm going to fine him, and this crew will learn the importance of standing an alert watch!"

"Captain, how about *not* writing him up," I said. The captain's eyebrows furled at the thought. "And how about determining the cause of why he was so fatigued. Find out what his schedule has been for the past forty-eight hours. Let's find out if your scheduling set up this sailor for failure."

The captain cringed. I could imagine the wheels turning in his head. *Wait a minute! If it turns out to be my fault or my staff's, that's going to reflect poorly on me!* He didn't want that responsibility, but he dared not balk, for fear of failing the inspection. "Chances are, sir, it's your fault," I continued, "or your subordinates' fault that this man fell asleep on watch. Certainly, he has responsibility here, but you have contributed to it, and you're not getting to the root cause simply by putting this man on report."

"Well, I thought that if I put him on my report, you wouldn't have to put him in your report."

"Just the opposite," I said. "If you put that sailor on your report, I'll put the incident in my inspection report."

I wasn't covering for the sailor's mistake, but when we investigated the circumstances, we found that the sailor had been awake for more than thirty-six hours. No wonder he fell asleep on the watch! Incidents such as those earned me the reputation that I was more concerned about solving the problem than about giving someone a poor grade that could impair his progress. That earned me enormous respect with the men on the waterfront.

CHAPTER 9
SHOWTIME

In February 1995, I became the executive officer on the USS *San Francisco*, a *Los Angeles*–class nuclear fast-attack submarine. The *Los Angeles*–class subs came on line in the late 1970s. Although the *Los Angeles*–class submarines were not designed to carry nuclear ballistic weapons similar to the Trident submarines, they were known as the fleet's "hunter-killer" subs and were the quietest fast-attack submarines built at the time. The story of how the *Los Angeles* almost *didn't* get built is an interesting part of Admiral Rickover's legacy.

In the late 1960s, during a particularly tense time in the Cold War, the U.S. was planning to build a new breed of nuclear attack submarines. Admiral Rickover wanted a fast sub able to protect the U.S. carrier battle groups against possible attack by other submarines, and he was willing to give up some diving depth to get the speed and maneuverability he wanted.

The Naval Sea Systems Command favored a ship design known as "Conform," which wasn't as fast as Rickover's, but provided enhanced habitability for the crew. Rickover wasn't interested in creature comforts. He wanted speed and agility. The two camps remained at loggerheads until the infamous *Enterprise* affair.

In 1969, as U.S. soldiers were sloshing through the humid jungles of Vietnam, the aircraft carrier USS *Enterprise* and the ships escorting her left their base in California, heading toward Vietnam. Shortly after the carrier group embarked, U.S. intelligence intercepted a message indicating that the Soviets were dispatching one of their new nuclear attack subs to intervene.

Navy brass didn't really expect the Soviets to attack the carrier group, but nobody could be sure what the Russians were up to. Regardless, the sub design groups saw the chase as something of an experiment. "Let's see how good these Russkies really are" was their attitude. The *Enterprise* carrier group was provided with antisubmarine warfare aircraft surveillance and ordered to outrun the Russians. The Naval Sea Systems Command "Conformists" assumed the Russian subs could travel at maximum speeds of around twenty knots, and the U.S. ships would leave the Soviets in their wake, thus proving that the faster speeds Rickover was demanding were unnecessary.

It didn't happen. The Russians stayed right with the *Enterprise* group at fifteen knots . . . twenty knots . . . twenty-five knots, and the Soviet nuclear attack submarine was still right on the carrier's tail! The *Enterprise* pegged thirty knots, and the Russian sub was still closing in on them! The U.S. carrier group backed down to normal speed and continued on to Southeast Asia, tailed the entire way by a Russian sub.

Back in Washington, Rickover went wild. Making full use of his acerbic tongue and personality, as well as his formidable clout with Congress, he pressured the Navy to drop the Conform class and to go with his fast-attack ships. Ironically, it was later discovered that the reason the Soviet nuclear sub had been able to keep up with the *Enterprise* group was due to extremely poor radiation shielding. Notoriously indifferent to the health and well-being of its seamen, the Russian Navy had stripped its nuclear submarine of everything that weighed it down—including a large measure of the lead shielding around the nuclear reactor so necessary to prevent radiation exposure to the men on the sub.

Whether Rickover knew about the lack of shielding or not is a part of the lore surrounding the admiral. Rickover's initial order was for twelve boats, so legend has it that to help secure the votes needed in Congress to provide the megabucks funding, Rickover decided to name the boats after the home cities of the twelve congressmen who voted in his favor. Instead of the longstanding Navy tradition of naming submarines after sea creatures, such as the *Sturgeon, Haddock, Halibut, Snook,* and others, Rickover named his first boats the *Los Angeles, Baton Rouge, Philadelphia,* and *Memphis.* When asked why the change in naming practice, Rickover supposedly cracked, "Fish don't vote."

Regardless of Admiral Rickover's eccentricities and his penchant for publicity, he was passionate about the nuclear submarine program. "The Kindly Old Gentleman," as he uniquely thought of himself, conceived of the first nuclear-powered submarine; he went on to develop an entire fleet of the ships, ranging from the *Skipjack* class to the Trident missile-carrying subs, to the mininuclear subs, to the *Virginia* class, the Navy's latest and greatest sub yet (at this writing). Rickover's lore and legends notwithstanding, his legacy includes the building of the *Los Angeles*–class submarine. A total of sixty-two *Los Angeles*–class subs were eventually designed and built, at a whopping base price of more than nine hundred million dollars each! One of the last ships built in the class was a submarine named USS *Greeneville,* commissioned on February 16, 1996.

For the most part, I enjoyed my time working as executive officer aboard the *San Francisco,* serving under Captain Mike Cregge. After nine months on the job, I was rated as the top XO in the entire squadron. More importantly, I was able to bring our engineering department's performance rating up from marginal to excellent. When I first went on board, the crew of the *San Francisco* could not adhere to the "Plan of the Day," the posted, written plan designed to keep the ship's crew on schedule. They referred to the POD as the "Possibility of the Day." Rather than sticking to the POD, a fifteen-minute meeting on the *San Francisco* often stretched to an hour and a half to two hours. The sub was never where it was supposed to be at any given time in the day. I had to be tough and demanding at first, but once we got the ship squared away, we stayed that way.

Once I had things under control, I was able to relax a bit, and the crew and I often engaged in good-natured bantering and pranks. For instance, one day while we were at sea, the crew stole the door to my stateroom and hid it under a mattress of some guy's bunk. Rather than making a big deal about it, I decided I'd do just the opposite. I'd pretend like everything was normal.

I had a drop-down sink in my stateroom, and when I came out of the shower, I'd normally stand there in front of a mirror to shave. So I did, sans door. I stood there wearing my flip-flops and a smile. Guys walking by my doorway could look right in. "Oh, man, XO, put some clothes on, please! Don't subject us to such a sight!"

"Well, give me back my door!" The door was back on that afternoon.

At other times, the guys would steal my pillow and freeze it. It was all in good-natured fun, and the guys were always ecstatic when they knew they'd pulled something on me. Surprisingly, for as much fun as we had on that ship, the captain was a stickler for the rules and regulations. I didn't mind that, but sometimes, real life demands some flexibility.

On May 4, 1996, Mom called me in Hawaii where the *San Francisco* was in port. She told me that the doctors had found cancer in her lungs, and they were going to remove her left lung. She had surgery the next day. I was on my way out to sea for three weeks, but I was able to talk with her by phone before I left. She was in the intensive care recovery unit and doing okay.

When I spoke with the doctor who had performed the operation, he said, "Don't worry. We got it all. She's going to be fine."

I said, "Thank God. She's going to be okay."

By the time I returned from sea three weeks later, the doctors had changed their prognosis. "We have found some problems in her blood work," the doctor told me, "and we've discovered that the cancer has already spread to the bone."

"What! You've got to be kidding!" I practically shouted at him.

"I'm sorry, Scott. Frankly, had we known the cancer was also in her bone, we probably wouldn't have operated."

The cancer spread quickly throughout my mom's body. She had tumors in her remaining lung, and breathing became increasingly difficult for her.

I was able to visit with her on May 23, three days after my thirty-seventh birthday. That was the last time I saw my mom alive. I deployed in June to Japan, Guam, and other special operations that prohibited me from coming home.

In the meantime, Mom's condition continued to deteriorate. I asked my commander if I could possibly get a leave to go see her, but he denied the request. "You're mom is going to be okay. You already had a chance to see her before we left."

My commander was mistaken.

On October 18, 1996, while I was at sea serving as the XO on board the *San Francisco*, my mom died. I was not able to talk to her before she passed away, but my sister was at her bedside, as was my stepdad. By now tumors riddled her body. Fluid was filling her lungs, and she was taking megadoses of morphine to dull the pain. Her throat and mouth were ulcerated. Mom knew that she was dying, but she had a calm, peaceful faith in the Lord.

Michelle held one hand and John held the other while Mom told them about a dream she had just had. "I saw Jesus," Mom told them, "and He said that He was ready for me."

Shortly after that, Mom's face suddenly brightened and she said, "They're beautiful!"

"What are you talking about, Mom?" Michelle asked.

"Can't you see them?" Mom said excitedly. "The angels. They look like my friends. They're beautiful. They're here! They're waiting for me."

"Then go ahead, Mom," Michelle said softly. "Go to Jesus."

My mom exhaled calmly and passed away.

Next to my wife and my daughter, my mother was the most important person in my life. I was extremely distraught that I was not able to attend her funeral. Eventually, I joined my sister and stepdad for a private interment ceremony in a little cemetery in White Wright, Texas, where Mom's other family members were buried.

A few years later, when I was a commanding officer, a fellow named Glasner was serving aboard the *Greeneville*. While we were out at sea, we learned that his mom was dying of cancer. I knew how heart-wrenching it must have been for him to know that his mom was near death while he was so far away. I insisted that he go to be with his mom, and I made sure that we got him off the ship and back home to see her before she passed away.

Mike Cregge, the commander of the *San Francisco*, was a good man, but he was not very creative, nor did he want to do anything that might seem as though he was pushing the envelope.

Once we were on a port visit in Yokosuka, Japan, at the same time as Admiral Gene Fluckey, a World War II submarine hero and former commander of the diesel sub *Barb*. Admiral Fluckey was a Medal of Honor winner who had earned two Navy Crosses and was one of the most decorated submariners in history. He was there for the commissioning of the new communications building on the naval base.

Admiral Al Konetzni, now the commander of Submarine Group Seven, headquartered in Yokosuka, Japan, was also in attendance that day. I hadn't seen the admiral since we had talked in Washington, D.C., after my engineer's exam, and it was exciting to catch up with him.

A lieutenant named Ross Orvik had qualified for his dolphins, so I suggested to Captain Cregge that it would be a great idea to have Admiral Fluckey pin on Orvik's fish.

"Oh, no. I don't want to bother the admiral," Cregge said.

I kept the matter in the back of my mind, though. If there was an opportunity to make Orvik's dolphin presentation special, I wanted to find it. I saw my chance in a conversation with Admiral Konetzni. "Admiral, we have a guy who's ready to have his dolphins pinned on, and Captain Cregge thinks it would be a great idea if we had Admiral Fluckey do the honors. What do you think?"

"Hey, that's a great idea!" Admiral Konetzni agreed. "Yeah, let's do that!"

He walked over to Captain Cregge, slapped him on the back, and said, "Hey, Cregge. Good idea. I love it! Way to take care of your troops! What a great skipper. Way to take care of your men!"

"Er, ah . . . well, thank you, Admiral," Cregge said. He glared at me.

I just raised my eyebrows, shrugged my shoulders slightly, and smiled.

The following day, we had a private ceremony in Admiral Konetzni's office in which Admiral Fluckey presented Ross Orvik his dolphins. It was one of the most moving dolphin presentations I've ever seen. As was customary at such presentations, we read aloud excerpts from a book describing the exploits of World War II diesel submarines. Today's readings, however, were about Admiral Fluckey's exploits on the USS *Barb*. We read about Fluckey's nighttime submarine attack on Japanese ships within Chinese coastal waters. Not only did Fluckey earn a Medal of Honor for this daring and dangerous attack, but the *Barb* also earned the nickname "The Galloping Ghost of the China Coast."

At the end of the reading, as I customarily did in dolphin ceremonies, I said to Orvik and the group, "Such is the stuff that submariners are made of, and today we welcome another into our midst." I've seen strong men nearly overwhelmed as submarine history collides with their present honor and their future service, all wrapped up in that one sentence . . . and like a line from a favorite love song or a poignant passage of poetry, it still moves me to this day.

On this day, however, after Admiral Fluckey presented Ross Orvik's dolphins, the admiral gave us all a rare and special honor. He picked up the book from which we were reading, looked at it, nodded slightly, and said, "Now, let me tell you how it really happened."

We sat down, and for the next thirty-five minutes, Admiral Fluckey took us back to the China coast and gave us a play-by-play account of the inside story. He told us what it was like to slip into the busy harbor at night, dodging destroyer escorts that guarded the coast. He painted an incredible picture showing us how the *Barb* attacked the harbor, blowing up large portions of it, as well as several anchored ships, and then taking out one of the destroyers as he maneuvered the *Barb* safely back out to sea. I felt as though

I was watching a movie of one of the boldest American submarine attacks in history.

As the admiral concluded his story, I noticed that Ross Orvik looked as though his chest was about to burst with pride; he was ready to defend America to his dying breath. I wouldn't have missed that opportunity to encourage a young sailor for the world.

Admiral Fluckey's story was so inspiring, even Captain Cregge eventually got over the fact that I had trapped him into the ceremony. I was especially glad that the Orvik dolphins affair had turned out so well, since I'd almost gotten fired for presuming upon Captain Cregge previously, in a similar incident.

Only three weeks into the job, Jill and I attended the 1996 Submarine Birthday Ball and sat at dinner with Captain Cregge and his wife, Sandy. Each year at the ball, it was traditionally a challenge between Squadron One and Squadron Seven to see who could have the most recently qualified submariner. That man got to cut the cake with the oldest submariner at the end of the ball. Over the years, the competition between squadrons became so intense, some captains would wait until five minutes before the dinner to sign the card acknowledging the completion of a man's dolphins qualifications.

In 1996, one of our guys, Lieutenant Steve Guaerky, had completed his submarine qualifications, but Captain Cregge had not yet presented him with his dolphins. I had purchased a dolphins pin and carried it with me to the ball, hoping for an opportunity in which we could present them to Lieutenant Guaerky. Admiral Barr was in attendance at the ball, so I saw an opportunity to honor Guaerky.

During the meal I leaned over to Captain Cregge's wife and quietly asked, "Sandy, do you think your husband would mind if we asked Admiral Barr to pin on Steve Guaerky's dolphins?"

Sandy said, "Oh, that would be great. Mike wouldn't mind at all."

When I mentioned my idea to Captain Cregge, he waved it off, saying, "Oh, I don't know."

He didn't really say no, so to me, that was a potential yes.

Shortly after dinner, Captain and Mrs. Cregge excused themselves and left the ball early. It was then that I did something that any military officer hoping to ascend in rank would never do. After the Cregges were gone, I said to Guaerky, "Let's go find the admiral."

I wasn't afraid to approach Admiral Barr since he knew me. We lived near each other on Ford Island at the time. Guaerky and I walked over to the admiral, and I said, "Admiral, I'd like to introduce you to Submarine Squadron One's newest qualified submarine officer, Lieutenant Steve Guaerky."

"Glad to meet you, Lieutenant!" Admiral Barr said as he shook Steve's hand. Keenly observant, Admiral Barr noticed immediately that Steve was not wearing his dolphins. "Where are your fish?" he asked, referring to Steve's dolphins.

"Well, sir, they haven't been pinned on yet," Steve answered.

I jumped in, pulled the dolphins pin out of my pocket, and asked, "Admiral, would you do us the honor of pinning on these dolphins?"

"Where is your skipper?" he asked, graciously not wishing to rob Captain Cregge of an opportunity to bestow the dolphins.

I answered, "Captain Cregge and his wife have already gone home. He called it a night."

Being a gentleman, Admiral Barr made a noble presentation of Guaerky's dolphins. Somebody took pictures, and Steve Guaerky went home beaming.

Everyone was happy . . . except Captain Cregge. First thing Monday morning, he called me into his office and he presented me with a non-punitive letter of caution, tantamount to saying, "Strike two; one more and you're out of here."

Cregge's letter said, "Your actions embarrassed Admiral Barr, Captain Cregge, and Lieutenant Guaerky. You need to harness your energy, and apply it in areas that would be more productive."

When I left San Francisco a few years later, Guaerky presented me with a blown-up photograph of Admiral Barr pinning on his dolphins, and me standing next to him with an impish grin on my face.

Captain Cregge was a tough man to please. Nothing I did ever seemed quite good enough for him. A key to good leadership is finding out what motivates your people. For some guys, the "that's-not-good-enough" approach was an effective motivational tactic, but not for me. For somebody like me, who had sought approval all my life, a few pats on the back were much more motivating than all the negative remarks, rebukes, and challenges I received. Laying a hand on the shoulder of someone and saying, "I believe in you," was often more powerful than saying, "That's good. But it's not good enough. You can do better."

Captain Cregge never once allowed any report I'd written to go without editing. He'd make changes, even on my most meticulous work.

When Glenn Niederhauser first came on board as the new captain, I wrote a report recommending two of our men for a Navy League Award. The captain signed it and gave it back to me.

I looked at him in amazement. "What? No changes?" I asked.

"Well, should there be?" Captain Niederhauser asked.

"No. No, sir!" I exclaimed. It was the beginning of a new atmosphere on the *San Francisco*. Beyond that, the two men I had recommended won the Navy League Award, based on the report exactly as I had written it. I stayed on board the *San Francisco* for another six months, finishing my tour of duty in July 1997.

Interestingly, Glenn Niederhauser enjoyed a very successful command aboard the *San Francisco* and eventually became the Pacific Submarine Force's prospective officers instructor. A few years later, when my career came under fire, Glenn Niederhauser was a good friend to me. In the midst of the *Greeneville* inquiry, he was concerned about me and as a neighbor visited our home on Hospital Point at Pearl Harbor. During our conversation he asked me, "Scott, how do you hope to come out of this?"

"Well, I don't want to go to prison, I want to keep my rank, and I don't want to lose my retirement." I have no doubt in my mind that Glenn Niederhauser took those words to heart. I knew when he left our home, he would do all within his power to help safeguard my future.

From August 1997 through June 1998, I attended the National Defense University in Washington, D.C., where I earned my master's degree in national resource strategy, which was basically the science of determining how a nation's resources or lack of them could be used in military negotiations. The idea was that military confrontations might be avoided if we know which chips to deal in the high-stakes poker games between nations. For instance, the U.S. could have said to the Soviet Union during the Cold War, "We'll provide you with grain so you can feed your people, if you will talk more seriously about backing off the production of more intercontinental ballistic missiles." Or more recently, we could say to a Third World country, "Look, we'll gladly trade with you, if you will refuse to harbor terrorists." Certainly, that's an oversimplification of the process, but my master's degree gave me a much broader view of the world than that which I could know looking through the lens of a submarine periscope.

With my master's work completed, I was on my way to being the commander of my own ship. To qualify for command, however, I had to take a nine-month refresher course on submarine tactics and the specific engineering design of the submarine to which I was assigned, the *Greeneville*. Three of those months were at Naval Reactors, at the Department of Energy in Washington, D.C., for an intensive exam period again. Overall, my PCO instructors rated me in the top third of my class. By February 1999, finally, after eighteen years in the Navy, I was ready.

CHAPTER 10

LIFE ABOARD A SUBMARINE

It's not natural for a human being to go underwater for long periods of time, to live in a windowless steel environment with artificial light and manufactured air. It takes a special sort of person to be able to handle the lifestyle of a submariner. By the time the food, water, weapons, and personal items are stowed, there's not much living space available for 140 guys. Imagine putting one hundred strangers into the space of a small, three-bedroom house and saying, "Now live together, work together, and everybody get along."

Prolonged trips below the surface are similar to living on a motor home with no windows or doors for a long period of time. Claustrophobia can be a real problem. Some extremely talented surface ship sailors can't handle being cooped up like that; it goes against all their images of sailing the open, wide blue seas, and they wouldn't dare set foot aboard a sub. Others are spooked by the many stories they've heard about the possibility of the submarine going below "crush depth" and never returning. It has only occurred twice in the history of U.S. nuclear-powered submarines, but it could happen.

Despite all the drawbacks, a lot of guys love going into that long, black cylinder. They love the excitement, the danger, the thrill, the technical expertise wrapped all around them, but most of all, they love the camaraderie. Submariners are unlike any other group in the military. They have their own language, their own rituals, and their own culture. Ironically, a U.S. submariner may feel more akin to a submariner from a foreign country than he does to the other sailors in our own Navy. There's just something different about the guys who live on a boat.

Maybe that's why the Navy doesn't just pull one commander off a boat and plop another man in that position. Instead, prior to actually taking command, the new commander, known as the prospective commanding officer, spends about thirty days on board the vessel, getting to know the boat, the crew, the culture, and how things are done on that submarine.

I first boarded the *Greeneville* as a PCO in February 1999. Commander Robert Guy had been the boss on the *Greeneville* since shortly after its commissioning in June 1996. He seemed almost paternalistic about his boat, and rightly so, since in a sense, he had helped bring the *Greeneville* to life. Basically, my job for one month was to watch, learn, and listen, and—the toughest part for me—to keep my mouth shut.

The first time I watched from the bridge as the ship got underway, I was appalled at how loud and nasty everyone was. Commander Guy was yelling at the men, lacing his language with a full repertoire of expletives for all to hear. The officer of the deck was flustered, and he was yelling down at line handlers on the pier. It was a very tense environment.

I'm convinced that people don't perform as well when they are getting yelled at. Usually, quite the contrary, when they get nervous or angry, they don't think clearly and are more prone to make mistakes.

Amazingly, we got out of the Pearl Harbor channel without a mishap, and as we were pulling out toward the open sea, I recalled that the small outboard motor on the underside of the sub was still extended. This motor is used to help push the sub when it is first starting out, and then it is to be retracted. It is not meant to be used at speeds above ten knots, or the shaft could be damaged and the ship cannot get up to speed. A submarine sailing with an extended outboard motor would be similar to an airplane flying with the landing gear and wheels still down.

As we pulled out, the officer of the deck ordered a standard bell, which would put us at a speed of fourteen to fifteen knots. I was standing in the background, trying my best to remain quiet. But I worried, *Oh, goodness. Let's see who is going to pick up on the fact that the outboard motor is still extended.*

I waited quietly, trying to hold my tongue, waiting to see if anyone would notice the problem. The helm acknowledged the order to go to standard bell. The ship's navigator, Keith Sloan, had recently joined the *Greeneville* crew, and this was his first underway. He acknowledged the order and concurred with the speed. Meanwhile the captain was simply sitting on the bridge, and nobody was concerned about the potential problem! Finally, I knew I had to speak up.

I leaned forward and said to the officer of the deck, "Excuse me, but isn't the outboard motor extended?"

The OOD immediately recognized the error and called out to the helm, "All stop!" in an effort to slow the boat in a hurry.

Commander Guy turned around and glared at me. "The next time you have a safety of the ship issue, I'd rather you'd go through me, and not my officer of the deck."

I thought, *Okaayy! Things are going to change when I relieve you.*

One of the greatest days of my life was the day my daughter, Ashley, was born. Certainly, Jill's and my wedding day was also extremely special to us. But the greatest day of my career came on March 19, 1999, the day I took over as commander of the USS *Greeneville* (SSN 772), an improved *Los Angeles*–class, nuclear attack submarine, with vertical Tomahawk missile launching capabilities. The ship was named after the county in Tennessee in which Davy Crockett had been born and was christened in 1996 by Tipper Gore, the wife of then Vice President Al Gore.

The change of command ceremony took place on board the boat as it was moored at the pier in Pearl Harbor, Hawaii. My entire family turned out to see me take command of the *Greeneville*. My father, Dan Waddle, came all the way from Austin, and my mother-in-law, Loretta, came from Olympia, Washington. My stepdad, John Coe, also came, as did my wife's brother, Kent, and his wife, Kathy, along with their boys, Isaac and Jacob. I knew my mom would have wanted to attend, and I felt that maybe God was allowing her to watch from heaven.

Admiral Albert Konetzni, the commander of the Submarine Force, U.S. Pacific Fleet was the keynote speaker, as he often was at change of command ceremonies in Pearl Harbor. Most of the sailors who worked out of Pearl Harbor knew his three-point speech by heart: *people, engagement,* and *efficiency.* Admiral Konetzni always reminded us that *people* were the most important aspect of the sub force. *Engagement* was also imperative, by which Admiral Konetzni meant to reach out in friendship to everyone you could, especially nations such as Japan, with whom we had become allies. The admiral was convinced that our submarine force was the best in the world, but we needed the help of our allies to make it work effectively.

"*Efficiency,* you gotta be efficient," Big Al continued. "They're not building enough submarines these days. So we have to be more efficient." Actually, due to cutbacks in the military budget implemented by the Clinton administration, the U.S. wasn't building *any* submarines at the time, other than the new Seawolf program, which had called for two or three subs that had been previously designed.

Admiral Konetzni always reminded his charges, "The tribe is important; take care of the tribe. You gotta take care of your men." That became a cornerstone in my methods of command.

"Throughout my career, I have urged those I work with to keep a clear vision of where they are and where they need to be headed," concluded Admiral Konetzni. Little could I have known that almost two years later to the day, I'd be reminded of those words over and over again.

It was a rousing speech, and I enjoyed hearing it, especially this time, since it was directed at me. No speech was needed, however, to inspire me. When I looked at the *Greeneville*, that was all the inspiration I needed! When asked to say a few words, I spoke succinctly. "I'm really looking forward to this duty. The crew is superb. Everyone works together, and that's why they're one of the best boats on the waterfront."

They weren't idle words; I truly believed that.

Following the ceremony, the ship prepared for our first underway with me as the new commander. It was my first trip out, and I was extremely nervous. I had worked nearly twenty years to get to this point. Fortunately, the crew of the *Greeneville* was good enough, they could have exited the Pearl Harbor channel, navigating without me.

My father watched from the pier as the *Greeneville* prepared for departure. I was trying to take in all the sights and sounds from the top of the bridge, but it really hadn't sunk in yet that I was the man in charge of the nearly billion-dollar machine on which I was standing. Finally, I heard the officer of the deck ask, "Permission to cast off all lines and get underway, Captain?" I looked over my shoulder to see who he was talking to. It was only then that I realized, *He's talking to me!*

The *Greeneville* crew was good—so good in fact, that before our first underway, I expressed my absolute confidence in their abilities. The officer of the deck, the junior officer of the deck, and I talked through the procedures in my stateroom. I told them that I wanted them to have complete freedom to do their jobs. "My job," I said, "is to stand on the bridge, and I'm not going to open my mouth unless it is necessary for the safety of the boat. I want you guys to take control."

From the time I gave permission to cast off all lines until it was time to submerge, I didn't have to say a word of instruction to the *Greeneville* crew. I acknowledged all reports, but the officer of the deck did such an incredible job of driving the ship, I didn't have to say anything else.

"Well, done, OOD," I said at the end of the transit. He was beaming with pride. It was the beginning of a new era aboard the *Greeneville*.

With 140 men at sea in a small living area, even if you like each other, it's relatively easy to get on one another's nerves. Consequently, I was determined to develop a different ship environment than some of the ships I had served on. I wanted an atmosphere of mutual respect and trust. If I said something, my crew could count on its being true. On the other hand, I wasn't intimidated or offended when one of my crewmembers wanted to challenge me about something.

From the very beginning, I had three tenets that I tried to instill in my crew, three words that summed up our working conditions aboard the *Greeneville*: *safety, efficiency,* and *backup*. Be safe in all that you do. Be efficient; don't waste time. And if you see something wrong, potentially damaging, or something that could compromise the ship's safety, speak up! We're working together, and we need to back each other up.

Like a good baseball team, when a ground ball is hit down the first base line, the first baseman goes for the ball, the second baseman backs him up in case the ball squirts through, and behind the second baseman, the right fielder and center fielder are moving in the direction of the ball. The pitcher runs over and covers first base. Meanwhile, the catcher races down the first base line to back up the pitcher. The entire backup plan is to make sure that if the ball gets by one man, another man is there to catch it. The whole scenario happens almost unnoticeably under normal conditions. The only time fans notice the backup process at all is when it is not done and an error occurs.

Similarly, on the *Greeneville*, we emphasized how important our backup systems were. Nobody is perfect; we all make mistakes; a man staring at the red print on a screen in a darkened submarine for hours on end can get fatigued. We all need backup. If one person misses something, another man is there to catch it.

I repeated these tenets again and again, until they became second nature to every man aboard the boat. For most of my Navy career, and especially during my time on the *Greeneville*, they worked effectively. For eight minutes on February 9, 2001, they did not.

I also sought to provide a more relaxed atmosphere on the *Greeneville*. I knew it was risky to violate Admiral Rickover's tried-and-true methods of using fear and intimidation to make sure the crew performs. "Don't trust anyone; don't even trust yourself," was another "Rickoverism" I hoped to change. In removing the fear factor, I knew I was relegated to trusting that my men would do their duty, and do it right, with a motivation to be the best. I rarely raised my voice aboard ship and, in most cases, spoke in a normal, conversational tone, even when giving orders. I wasn't afraid to laugh with the guys and cut up with them, yet I was still careful to maintain a level of mutual respect that was necessary for a military unit to function. The guys responded well to these new "freedoms." They were professionals, and they knew how to do their jobs. They didn't need someone screaming at them to get it right.

Family issues were important to me as well. When we were working at home onshore, I tried to get the guys off the ship earlier so they could spend more quality time at home with their families. I protected their weekends when I could, so long as it didn't compromise our training. I attempted to accommodate a man's family responsibilities as much as possible, believing that a happy wife made for a happy husband.

Overall, I tried to make life aboard ship as pleasant as possible for my men. I ordered enhanced audiovisual equipment on board, including challenging hand-eye coordination video games. The games provided hours of entertainment and also challenged the guys in their strategic thinking. The truth is, I enjoyed playing the video games as much as the crew! I especially made sure that we had great food on the *Greeneville*. The guys readily acknowledged that the *Greeneville* had the best food in the Navy.

Still, three weeks out without a break was usually the point at which we all had to get some real air and some space between us. After a few weeks, we usually came in to port in some friendly location, even during a long deployment of three to six months.

Quiet is the watchword aboard any submarine, but especially aboard a nuclear fast-attack submarine such as the *Greeneville*. Rare is the loud outburst aboard a submerged boat. After a while, guys get used to speaking more calmly and quietly. Part of this, of course, is due to the many surveillance assignments the "silent service" conducts. The *Greeneville* received numerous glowing accolades for some of our secretive, special operations. Although for national security reasons, I am not permitted by law to discuss most of those operations, I can say that the *Greeneville*'s crew was extremely good at what we did.

I wanted my crew to be the best, the envy of the Navy. My goal was for every other sailor in the Navy to dream, *Maybe someday I'll be good enough to make it on the* Greeneville.

One of the adages I constantly kept before my crew regarded drills and practice maneuvers. I told my crew, "We train like we're going to fight, because we'll fight like we have been trained." The time to learn how to fight is not when you are engaging the enemy.

In October 1999, we set out to fight a mock battle against the John C. Stennis aircraft carrier battle group, off the San Diego coast. The exercises were part of the Stennis group's preparation prior to deployment to the Arabian Sea area, so the *Greeneville* carried a special "noise augmentation unit" to simulate the noises typically created by enemy diesel submarines plying the Arabian Gulf. The maneuvers were monitored by a three-star admiral, and Captain Pete Daly, a destroyer squadron commander in Pearl Harbor at the time, served as an umpire on board the carrier. This was my first major sortie since taking command of the *Greeneville*. I had worked with this crew for more than six months, and we trusted one another implicitly.

We headed out to sea from San Diego, and we were designated as the bad guys, the enemy hoping to engage the carrier group and attack if possible. Obviously, we weren't going to fire real weapons, but we were to plot the targets as though we were shooting the real stuff.

The carrier group included two Arleigh Burke–class destroyers, two Aegis cruisers, a *Knox*-class frigate, and multiple antisubmarine warfare–equipped helicopters. And, of course, the enormous floating airport, the John C. Stennis carrier. More than six ships to one. They had the numbers and the size—the carrier alone is the size of a small town—but we had the stealth. We could hide in the deep water and dart in and out and all around the carrier group waiting for an opening to take our best shot. We had to watch out for dipping sonar from the constantly hovering helicopters, mock bombs from the carrier group, and of course, the very real possibility of getting rammed.

We maneuvered right in the middle of the carrier group, got out in front of them, turned around 180 degrees, and headed right back at them! The carrier group was about two miles away, coming at us at eighteen knots, and we went up to periscope depth. I knew I was taking my guys into the middle of a very dangerous situation. Any one of our own ships could have ripped us apart if they'd have hit us.

I told the men, "We are going to engage those guys. Remember, we train like we're going to fight, because we'll fight like we have been trained. So let's do it."

I could see the looks of nervous excitement on some of the guys' faces. Others weren't sure whether to laugh or cry. War games or no war games, what we were doing was dangerous and the guys knew it.

I told them, "Look, if we go to war, you want to go to war with me, because I will put the enemy on the bottom and we'll come home alive."

I wasn't trying to build them up with bombast and bravado; I was absolutely serious.

The closer we got to the carrier group, the more nervous some of the guys became. I thought one fellow in particular was going to have a heart attack!

At one point, as the helicopters hovered overhead, we broached the *Greeneville*, let them see us, then dove under a merchant ship in the vicinity of the group. We hid directly below the merchant ship, at a depth of about 150 feet, and the carrier group couldn't find us! The merchant ship was so noisy, we could have had a party on the *Greeneville* and they'd have never heard us. The merchant ship sounded like an unbalanced old washing machine on spin cycle, and we slowly rode away to safety. We popped up about a mile away, as if to say, "Ha! Fooled you!"

We did a series of difficult maneuvers and outwitted the helicopters. They couldn't spot us from the air, and the carrier group couldn't find us in the water. We waited until just the right moment and then moved in for the "kill." Our fire control technician locked onto the carrier, and we reported our position. We had them cold, and they knew it. Had we been an enemy sub in an actual wartime battle, we'd have blown them to kingdom come. We were the bad guys, and we had won.

That was the good news and the bad news. It was a great compliment to the skill of the *Greeneville* crew that we had defeated the carrier group, but it sent off warning flags all over the Surface Warfare Force, U.S. Pacific Fleet (COMSURFPAC) that the *Greeneville* had "sunk" a carrier in a mock battle! The carrier ships were the "good guys," the guys in the white hats; they were the United States Navy. They weren't supposed to lose to a rogue submarine.

When we got back into port at San Diego following the exercises, I paid a courtesy call to the Squadron Eleven commanding officer. He was not happy with me. "You guys really made it hard out there," he said. "The objective was to help them pass."

I was truly surprised. When we got back into port, rather than being commended for outstanding work, we were criticized for being too aggressive in the mock battle. *Too aggressive in battle?* I wondered. *What's wrong with that picture?*

Granted, some people at COMSURFPAC may have thought that we were too aggressive, but at least one high-ranking officer was impressed—Admiral Albert Konetzni, the man who had greeted me when I first passed my engineer's exam back in 1986, and a man who had become a mentor and a friend to me since then, especially since I had come directly under his jurisdiction when I joined the Pacific Fleet.

Admiral Konetzni was a strong proponent of working together with our Japanese allies to maintain a strong U.S. naval presence in the Far East. He had planned a delicate cooperative training exercise with the Japanese Maritime Self-Defense Force, the post–World War II version of the Japanese Navy. The plan was to attach the *Avalon*—a battery-powered, U.S. deep submergence rescue vehicle that can carry one man at a time—to an American sub, and use it to transfer men from the Japanese sub *Hayashio*, which was "stranded" in a mock emergency distress situation on the bottom of the sea, onto the American submarine, or vice versa. The idea was to show that such a rescue could be performed in the middle of the Pacific Ocean. The American sub that Admiral Konetzni wanted to use in this highly difficult and delicate operation was the *Greeneville*.

In November 1999, we set sail from Pearl Harbor with the commander of the Pacific Fleet riding aboard our boat to observe the operation. We went out to a place south of Oahu, called Penguin Bank, ironically about five or six miles from where the *Greeneville–Ehime Maru* incident would take place thirteen months later.

The *Hayashio* pretended to be paralyzed on the bottom of Penguin Bank. The *Greeneville* then went down after her, with the *Avalon* piggybacked to us. It's not an easy chore to maneuver a 360-foot submarine in deep sea water without moving more than plus or minus six inches for a several hours, while another vessel hovers over it, docks, and then locks onto it and transfers one man at a time from one vessel to another. Yet that's what we did.

Admiral Konetzni was so impressed, he actually got in the *Avalon* and made the trek between the *Greenville* and the *Hayashio* himself. The admiral had a bento box lunch aboard the Japanese vessel, and then he came back to the *Greeneville* aboard the *Avalon*. All of this was done on the bottom of Penguin Bank. Admiral Konetzni was blown away by the professionalism of the *Greeneville*'s crew. He heaped praise on the crew and me: "Your people did an unbelievably professional job!"

In April 2000, Jim Hertline, the XO of the *Greeneville*, moved on in his career. I was sorry Jim was leaving, because he was the best XO I'd ever seen, myself included. I met Jim's replacement, Jerry Pfeifer, for the first time at a party in Pearl Harbor. A thirty-seven-year-old Northeasterner, Jerry had just come from the Nuclear Propulsion Examining Board, and now he had been assigned to us. A tall, lean, red-headed fellow, he had a reputation as a good nuke. I may have scared him, though, when I first met him. "I've heard good things about you, Pfeifer," I told him. "But you've got really big shoes to fill." It was a dumb thing to say, and the moment I said it, I wished I could pull the words back into my mouth, but it was too late. I had unwittingly set Jerry up to have to prove himself. As it turned out, Jerry spent most of his time aboard the *Greeneville* challenging my orders. Despite his constant challenges of my authority, I liked Jerry. Maybe he reminded me too much of myself.

Another new officer joined our crew as officer of the deck shortly after Jerry Pfeifer arrived. I first met Lieutenant Mike Coen at the Honolulu International Airport, when I went to pick him up and welcome him upon his arrival in Hawaii. Twenty-six years old and a graduate of Florida State, he was right out of submarine officer training school, and a new husband as well. He and Wendy had just gotten married when they received their orders to head for Hawaii to join the *Greeneville*. A bright, academic sort of guy, Mike was extremely thorough about everything he did. Maybe because of his age, or maybe because he was just conscientious about his job, he was always concerned that he not make any mistakes. The drawback was that he was also extremely slow and methodical in the way he did things, and he often didn't react quickly enough when I switched plans unexpectedly.

My crew regarded me as the consummate politician, consistently going out of my way to serve and to please the people who visited aboard ship. Guests left the submarine satisfied, proud, and extremely impressed at the way the *Greeneville* crew performed.

Some of my guys even joked that I was going to run for political office when I got out of the Navy. They said that I regarded every person who visited our submarine as a potential vote. I laughed right along with them. I'd do almost anything to keep the attitude of the crew positive, upbeat, and moving forward. It was the old cheerleader in me coming out.

My stateroom was adjacent to the control room, and I liked it that way. I had a picture of Theodore Roosevelt on my wall with one of his quotes about leadership. Basically, the leadership style Roosevelt espoused was "Pick the best people you can, and then get out of the way and let them do their jobs."

That was the leadership style I emulated and tried to engender among my officers.

All the while, I wanted my men to know I was ready to help and always there for them. Not one of my junior officers feared me, at least not that I knew of. They respected me and served me well, and crewmembers would not hesitate to ask my advice. Some officers frequently voiced their opinions and sometimes even challenged my decisions, and that, too, was okay with me . . . to a point.

I never wanted to be too far from the bridge of the *Greeneville*. Although my younger officers knew I trusted them, I also wanted them to know that I was always nearby. I didn't want to foster an atmosphere of fear, since I was not a hard-nosed officer. But I wanted to run a tight ship and to encourage an attitude of excellence and confidence, whether the captain was watching or not. My crew knew that I had high expectations of them, that I expected them to be prepared, alert, and diligent, but that I was available in a moment's notice in case of trouble.

My attitude—indeed, the Navy's attitude—was: "A captain is never out of command when he's afloat." A captain is never relieved of the responsibilities that go with command. Even while trying to catch some sleep, a control room microphone fed the sound directly into my stateroom, so I could always hear what was going on next-door. Monitors danced all night long in my stateroom, constantly keeping me apprised of the submarine's vital statistics. At sea or in port, whether aboard the ship or home watching a sporting event on television, twenty-four hours a day, seven days a week, the commander is always responsible for the actions of his crew and what occurs on board his ship.

I also encouraged my crew to develop spiritually. When you're riding in front of a nuclear reactor four hundred feet below the surface, it's a good idea to know where you're going if you suddenly find yourself facing God.

Practicing your faith in the military can sometimes be difficult. It's even more difficult for an officer who is trying to be fair to all the men on the ship, regardless of their faith, or even if they have no faith at all. On board the

Greeneville, I encouraged an atmosphere of spiritual opportunity, while being careful that we didn't exclude those who chose not to participate. That's not an easy thing to do on a submarine, where space is at a premium.

We didn't have a chaplain on board, but we did have a volunteer Bible study leader. That person was never me. When we got together for Bible studies, I didn't want to lead the sessions. I wanted to be a *part* of the study, but not the captain of the Bible study. I never forgot one of the first captains under whom I served early in my career. He preached at his crew from the Bible, and then within a few minutes after we all left the room, he was ripping somebody a new cavity in their body. The inconsistency left a foul taste in my mouth, and when I became a commander myself, I wondered at first, *Should I even try to foster a spiritual climate aboard my ship? Or would it be interpreted in a similar light as what I had felt about my earlier commanding officer?*

I finally decided that the best way I could encourage spiritual growth among my men was to be real with my crew, to let my men know that I was human, with all the same foibles, questions, failures, and sins that they experienced. I emphasized to my crew that the cross of Jesus Christ is the great common denominator. Regardless of a man's rank, be it admiral, ensign, or enlisted man, when we stand before God, we are all on equal ground, and all must come to Him in humble faith, dependence, and obedience.

In the submarine wardroom, the captain's chair is the closest thing we have to hallowed ground on the boat. Nobody sits in the captain's chair other than the captain. If the president of the United States were on board, even though he is the commander in chief, he would not sit in the captain's chair. Once, my daughter, Ashley, was on our boat, and she sat down in my chair. One of the crew immediately told her, "Ma'am, you need to sit in another chair. That's your daddy's chair."

"Oh, he won't mind," Ashley chirped.

"No, that's the captain's chair; you're not supposed to sit there."

"Oh, my dad will say it's okay."

Just then I walked in to the wardroom, and upon seeing her sitting there, I said, "Ashley, get out of that chair!"

But when we had our Bible studies in the wardroom, I never sat in the captain's chair. I left it open. "That's God's chair," I told the guys. "He's here with us today. That belongs to Him."

■ ■ ■

Ironically, our success on the *Greeneville* bred a rather backhanded compliment from our superior officers. The Navy often sent its misfits and miscreant sailors to us, hoping we could salvage their careers and put their intensity and energy to good use. Often we could. The *Greeneville* became known as a ship of second chances. When you've washed out elsewhere, you have a second chance to get it together on the *Greeneville*.

I wasn't put off by a sailor's failure aboard another ship. I rarely rejected a transfer because a man had been a problem elsewhere. I regarded the fact that a guy had messed up and had left another boat as an opportunity. "Hey, you have a second chance here," I'd tell him. "Those guys on your previous boat didn't know what they had in you. And they don't know what they're missing. But they're going to find out. Now let's figure out what you're good at, what you want to do, and how we can harness your energy to do something great."

Many times it was simply a matter of encouraging a seaman to use the gifts and talents he had, rather than trying to plug him into some job he hated. As the captain, I took it upon myself to learn the crewmembers' strengths and weaknesses. We tried to find a good fit for them and then place them in our system where they could best use their talents to become contributing members. It was a thrill for me to see my men find the place where they could be productive. Once they knew somebody believed in them, they started believing in themselves. They just seemed to blossom as they did their work. Consequently, we had very few morale problems aboard the *Greeneville*.

Often a sailor came to me and said, "Captain, thank you for believing in me. Thank you for bringing out the best in me."

"Hey, it was always there," I said. "We just had to see through a bit of tarnish to find the good. None of us is perfect. The only perfect Man who ever walked this earth died about two thousand years ago."

CHAPTER 11
HOLDING TOGETHER

Like so many businesses, the military has a tendency to put people where they need them, rather than where they are best qualified to serve. My careerlong goal was to find the best fit for my shipmates, where the Navy could be best served, but also where the sailor could thrive and grow.

I always tried to be honest with my men about their abilities. As captain of the ship, I felt it was my obligation to be truthful, forthright, and direct with my men. Sometimes that made me the bad guy, or at least the bearer of bad news. If a guy didn't have the proper education or skills to move into a new job, I shot straight with him. If a sailor's estimation of his abilities was inflated, sometimes I'd have to deliver a wake-up call.

I'd say, "I understand that you may not agree with this, but from my observations and my best judgment of your abilities, I don't believe you are qualified for that particular position. Now, let me tell you how you can improve so you can reach that goal." I'd then do all that I could to help the sailor become more competitive.

At times, I'd have to say, "It's not going to happen. You aren't prepared

94

for that position. But here are some things that are a good fit for you, some things that I believe you can do well because of your strengths. Let's consider some of these areas." My goal was always to help my guys get ahead. I never forgot what it felt like to struggle and fail, and when I'd see a guy who was having trouble making it, I'd do all that I could to help him become successful.

During my tenure as captain of the *Greeneville*, only one man came to us who we simply could not use. He was a good man who wanted to serve his country. He tried with all his might to make it on the *Greeneville*, but he just didn't have the academic aptitude to serve aboard a submarine. He was a conscientious, diligent worker, and he was dependable to run errands and do other grunt work, but he was unable to handle the more technical aspects of submarine work.

Unfortunately, in such a compact environment, we couldn't afford the luxury of even one man who couldn't make the grade academically. Every submariner must know the job of every other submariner aboard the boat. This is especially crucial in case of an accident. He has to have an overall understanding of how the systems on a sub work, so he knows how his piece of the puzzle fits into the big picture.

Sadly, as much as we wanted to keep the fellow, we had to let him go. He eventually transferred to a surface ship where he served nobly and effectively.

It doesn't always take a lot of time, effort, or money to make someone feel special. It just takes someone who cares. For instance, when one of the crewmembers aboard the *Greeneville* earned his dolphins, I'd order the boat to the surface, and if possible, we'd make a cell phone call home to the sailor's parents, wife, or other family members. "This is Commander Scott Waddle calling you from the bridge of the USS *Greeneville*," I'd say. "We are at sea, and we just want you to know what a great achievement your son [or husband] has accomplished. He has earned his dolphins and is now a bona fide submariner. We're extremely proud of him here aboard the *Greeneville*, and we're sure you are too. I'll put him on the phone and you can tell him how proud of him you are." It was tough to keep the guy's head from getting big with pride after something like that!

Similarly, when one of our guys' wives had a baby, I'd write a short letter to the child on *Greeneville* stationery, with the notation on the envelope, "Do not open until your eighteenth birthday." Inside, I'd have a glowing letter about the child's father, telling what a hero Dad was, and how he sacrificed many long, lonely hours away from home, living in a submarine under water, so that he might serve, protect, and defend our country.

Besides supporting our own shipmates, I continually encouraged our guys to be supportive of their fellow submariners. When another submarine headed out from port on deployment, I'd muster our entire crew topside to cheer on the departing sub and to give the departing crew a wave. We'd do the same when a ship came back in from deployment, welcoming the crew home.

Any time we were in port, if there was a special ceremony on the waterfront, a retirement, or a change of command ceremony, I had my officers dress in their Navy whites, and we'd attend to offer our congratulations and appreciation.

Besides attempting to improve rapport with our fellow submariners, I constantly sought out opportunities to enhance the camaraderie of our own crew. Simply doing things together rather than as individuals often created more of a team spirit.

For instance, all sailors are expected to exercise and work hard at keeping in shape, but submariners face an especially difficult dilemma. They are on board a ship with extremely limited space, so a regular exercise regimen is tough to maintain.

I recalled a movie I'd seen, starring Clint Eastwood, in which he led his Marine troops in physical exercise. That inspired me, so when I took command of the *Greeneville*, each morning that we were in port, we met at 6:15 at the base gymnasium for group exercise. To further unify our crew, I purchased grey T-shirts that boasted the name and number of the ship on the front printed in blue, with the ship's multicolored logo on the back. When we ran the Hickam trail on base, with sixty to seventy men at a time all wearing the same grey shirts, it was an impressive sight.

People on the waterfront were beginning to notice that we did things differently on the *Greeneville*. In August 2000, in an official evaluation and review, Squadron Commander Dave McCall highly complimented me, commending me as "an outstanding mentor, an inspirational leader, performing flawlessly as commanding officer." I appreciated his commendation and felt it was a victory for my men, as well as for me.

Sometimes, however, I was criticized for being too down-to-earth with my crew, too friendly and easygoing. This showed up especially when reenlistment time rolled around. I'd do almost anything to keep a good man in the Navy and, more specifically, to keep him aboard the *Greeneville*. I always made a big deal about a man signing on to give us four to six more years of his life. If wives, children, parents, or girlfriends were in attendance, I always presented them with a beautiful Hawaiian lei as a token of our appreciation for their sacrifice. The reenlistment of their loved one impacted them profoundly, and I wanted them to know that we honored their commitment too.

Some of our reenlistments were deeply moving. For instance, I'd often take a man right before sunrise to the *Bowfin* submarine memorial, beside the *Arizona* memorial at Pearl Harbor. We'd stand together a few yards from above the water where nine hundred sailors still are entombed. Then just as the sun broke through the sky, I'd read him the reenlistment oath to our country's Navy. The sailor would repeat after me, "I do solemnly swear that I will support and defend the Constitution of the United States of America against all enemies, foreign and domestic, and that I will obey the orders of the president and the orders of the officers appointed over me, in accordance with the regulation and uniform code of military justice." More than a few tough seamen succumbed to tears during those commitment ceremonies as they swore to put their lives on the line to protect the freedoms that many citizens take for granted.

The reenlistment ceremony became one of the strongest magnets that retained men in the Navy. When a man began to waiver, saying, "I don't want to do this anymore," I'd remind him, "But you took an oath before God, your country, and others that you would do this to serve and protect your country. What does that say about you, that you are willing to go back on your word? Just because life is hard does not give us an excuse to compromise our character. Please don't go down a path that you will regret for the rest of your life. Let me show you a better way. I care about you, your future, and the oath that you made. Let's turn this experience into something that is positive. How you deal with this will define your character for the rest of your life."

Many of our reenlistment ceremonies took place in less-than-formal military environments. For instance, I performed one man's reenlistment underwater in scuba gear. Between gasps of air, he raised his right hand and gurgled his recommitment to the Navy. I think he signed up for ten years and didn't know it!

I once did a reenlistment inside Diamond Head, another fellow re-upped at the Aloha Tower at sunset, and another man wanted to sign on at Hawaii's premier surfing spot, the Pipeline, on the north shore. Another man wanted to reenlist while doing a tandem parachuting jump; two shipmates reenlisted while sitting on side-by-side commode stalls aboard the submarine while we were at test depth, the deepest submergence allowed by the Navy except for an emergency. There seemed to be no end to the unique, at times outlandish, ideas for our reenlistment ceremonies.

To me, it was always worth it to go the extra mile to keep a good man on the team. Because of the new attitude aboard the *Greeneville*, our re-enlistment rate was one of the highest in the Navy, more than double the average. Part of that was because we knew how to have fun, but we also knew how to be professional. Still, some of my colleagues feared the worst.

One fellow officer said to me, "Scott, your greatest strengths can be your greatest weaknesses as well. Your aggressiveness could be a flaw. Your ability to engage people, to be gregarious, can sometimes hurt you. It gives the impression that you are running a loose ship."

That was a risk I felt was worth taking.

On the Fourth of July 2000, the *Greeneville* was anchored off the coast of Santa Barbara for the first visit to that port by a nuclear submarine. We had been invited by Dr. Roger Dunham, a physician who had once served on the *Halibut*, and Connie Los, the president of the Santa Barbara Navy League, to take part in the community picnic and celebration on the courthouse lawn. A group of Girl Scouts paraded the American flag in front of several thousand people, and one of the Girl Scouts led the crowd in the Pledge of Allegiance. I was so impressed with her zeal for America that when my time came to say a few words, I asked the young girl to come back to the platform.

I said to the audience, "Folks, this has not been rehearsed, and I hope I don't embarrass this young lady by asking her to come up here, but there's no reason we need to be concerned about the leadership in our country when we have fine young men and women like this."

I looked at the young Girl Scout and noticed the sash on her Scout uniform on which she had pinned several merit badges that she had earned.

I showed the little girl the dolphins I wore on the collar of my uniform. "May I take these dolphins off and pin them on your sash?" I asked her. "I've worn them for a long, long time—almost sixteen years. It would be a great privilege and an honor for me to present these dolphins to you, to represent America's future and our pride in the youth of today and our future tomorrow." I pinned the dolphins on her sash and then saluted my new young friend on the platform, and she saluted me back. The crowd applauded enthusiastically.

"Thank you for having the *Greeneville* here in Santa Barbara. God bless America, and may God bless these young people who are doing such great things today in our communities."

Santa Barbara treated the *Greeneville* crew as though they were American heroes. Indeed, Fess Parker, the man who had played Davy Crockett on television years ago, hosted some of our shipmates at his restaurant and later gave us a replica of "Old Daisy," the Kentucky long rifle. It was great to meet the television version of the man in whose honor the *Greeneville* was named.

Another fascinating person we met that week was Guy O'Neil, a highly decorated World War II submariner, the former captain of the USS *Gunnel*, who had been awarded the Navy Cross by the president. During our conversation Guy mentioned that he was going to San Diego after the event, so I called Admiral Konetzni and received special permission for Guy to ride back to San Diego overnight on board the *Greeneville*. It was a special treat for Guy and an honor for our crew to have the World War II submarine hero ride our boat.

I returned to Santa Barbara in November as the principal speaker at the annual military ball, hosted by Pierre Claeyssens, a local philanthropist and a staunch supporter of the military. During that trip, Jill and I attended a banquet honoring three generations of submariners. I was seated with Captain Ed Moore, who had commanded the infamous *Halibut* during the Cold War, widely credited for performing some of the most dangerous and intriguing spy missions in naval history. Also seated with us was veteran submarine captain Guy O'Neil. During dinner that night, I noticed the many citations Captain O'Neil wore on his tuxedo. He'd brought with him a small, carefully packed box in which he carried the Navy Cross, awarded to him by the president of the United States for bravery in the heat of battle.

He also wore an incredible set of gold dolphins, unlike any I had ever seen. They were absolutely beautiful! They were cast in eighteen-carat gold, different from the dolphins worn by modern-day submariners. On the back of his dolphins was an inscription stating that Guy had received the Navy Cross.

During our conversation, I posed a presumptuous request to Guy. "Sir, I would love to get a cast of those dolphins, so I could have some made to award to the men on board my ship. When they earn their dolphins I could then pin dolphins on their chest that replicate those you earned in World War II."

Captain O'Neil graciously consented, and I gave him my address. A few months later, a package showed up at my door. Inside were Guy O'Neil's dolphins—not a replica, but his actual dolphins—a gift to me from one of the most respected submarine captains I've ever met. Guy included a note: "Scott, I want you to have these fish. Wear these."

I appreciated Captain O'Neil's gift so much, but I held those dolphins in such high regard, I dared not wear them. About as close as I'd come, occasionally, was to get them out just so I could admire them. *Maybe someday*, I'd think. *Someday, for some special occasion, I'll wear Guy O' Neil's fish.*

One day in December, I was walking past Admiral Konetzni's office when he called out to me, "Scott, come on in. Let's talk."

That was the admiral's normal way of operating, so I didn't think anything of it. I walked in his office and sat down. By now, the admiral and I had grown to be good friends. Still, I was somewhat surprised when Admiral Konetzni broached the subject of me possibly coming off the *Greeneville* to be his personnel officer, an extremely important position on the COMSUBPAC staff, or to go to work at the Naval Academy, where I could have a greater influence on young men and women there. We talked for quite a while, and the admiral complimented my work aboard the *Greeneville*, expressing again how much he enjoyed riding the submarine for our training cruise in March, as well as our training operation that we had conducted with the Japanese the year before.

During his ride with us in March, the admiral had given me a mild rebuke. He was genuinely impressed with the *Greeneville*'s cleanliness, professionalism, incredibly high morale, and the general atmosphere of camaraderie among the crew. He loved the way the men answered back formally as orders were called out. "Hey, you're the only one who is informal on this ship," he said to me. It was such a mild reproof, I didn't even remember it, and I would probably not have given it a second thought had it not been thrown in my face dozens of times a year later.

In December 2000, however, my laid-back style reminded the admiral of the way he used to do things when he was a commander, and I took that as a high compliment.

"Keep doing what you're doing, Scott," the admiral said. "You're doing fine. What your fitness report reflects . . ." He paused and nodded toward the file on his desk to let me know that he was referring to my potential future position. "It will move along."

"Thank you, sir," I said. "Admiral, just so you know, my shipmates aboard the *Greeneville* and I would be greatly honored when it comes time for your change of command, if you would consider allowing us to be the host submarine."

The admiral seemed genuinely pleased at my suggestion. "Yes, yes," he said. "That would be a good idea. We can do that."

I left the admiral's office nearly glowing. I knew that Admiral Konetzni would soon be receiving his third star. He was moving on up, and he was inviting me to move along with him. My future looked brighter than ever!

On New Year's Day 2001, Jill and I hosted several of my officers for a relaxing evening to enjoy the Waikiki sunset from the Royal Hawaiian Hotel, one of Waikiki's oldest and most beautiful landmarks. As we were leaving, Jill noticed a handsome couple and their children just coming in off the beach. Hawaii has a constant inflow of celebrities, and seeing high-profile people such as movie stars, musicians, and athletes is rather commonplace. But for some reason, this family looked different. One look and it was apparent that they were not average tourists.

Jill nudged me and nodded in the direction of the attractive family. "Those people are Kennedys," she said quietly.

"What are you talking about? No way!" I responded.

"Right there, that's Bobby Kennedy Jr."

"And what have you been drinking?" I teased Jill. She looked again at the couple and their kids.

"I'm pretty sure," she said.

"I don't think so," I responded, "but it's hard to tell with them just coming in from the beach."

When we got in the car, I called the hotel and asked, "Would you please connect me with the Kennedy party?" Jill looked across the seat at me as though I had suddenly gone wacky.

"One moment please," the Hawaiian voice on the phone replied.

I smiled at Jill and raised my eyebrows. I assumed that the operator was going to come back on the line any second and say, "Sorry, we don't have a Kennedy party here."

But she didn't. I waited on hold for a minute or two, when a female voice with a slight Boston brogue answered the phone.

I really hadn't expected to speak to anyone, so I had to scramble for words. Then I realized I was speaking to Mary Richardson Kennedy, wife of Robert Kennedy Jr. "Who is this?" she asked straightforwardly.

I said, "Mrs. Kennedy, this is Commander Scott Waddle, and I'm the captain of the USS *Greeneville*, a fast-attack submarine based out of Pearl Harbor."

"What do you want? Who are you again?"

I told her my name again. This time she didn't answer me. Instead, she called out, "Bobby, pick up the phone."

"Who is it?" I could hear in the background.

"I don't know, just pick up the phone!" Mary Kennedy said.

A few seconds later, Robert Kennedy Jr. came on the line.

I said, "Mr. Kennedy, this is Commander Scott Waddle, and I'm the captain of the USS *Greeneville*, a fast-attack submarine based out of Pearl Harbor."

My mind was racing a hundred miles an hour now. "I'm aware that you and your family are here in Hawaii for Christmas, and I don't mean to intrude, but knowing your family's interest in ships, I was wondering if you and your family would like to come over sometime while you are in town and tour our boat?" I purposely shied away from telling Mr. Kennedy that we were a nuclear-powered submarine, because I was aware of his strong environmentalist views that regarded nuclear reactors as a dangerous way to produce power. Ironically, the U.S. Navy is one of the most environmentally conscious organizations in the entire world, but most people are not aware of that.

Kennedy was extremely gracious and gladly accepted my offer. We set up a time for him and his family to come over to Pearl Harbor, a short drive from their hotel.

As soon as I hung up with Kennedy, I called Admiral Konetzni, who was relaxing at home. "Admiral, I'm sorry to bother you, but I just thought you might want to know that I'm having the Robert Kennedy, Jr. family over as guests of the *Greeneville*."

"Oh, that's great, Scott," the admiral replied. "Bring him over."

The Kennedys came and toured the boat, along with Mary Kennedy

Cuomo and her children, and we had a marvelous time. Afterward, we went over to Admiral and Missy Konetzni's home, and the group was able to see the old "dungeon" below the admiral's home, which used to house huge gun turrets following World War I.

On our way, Mr. Kennedy asked to drive by the *Arizona* memorial. I pulled the van in as close to the memorial as I could get from the shore, and Kennedy had everyone get out and walk to the shoreline across from the *Arizona*. He then got down on his knees, as did everyone else, and Mr. Kennedy offered a prayer.

Interestingly, I believe we may have even influenced Robert F. Kennedy Jr.'s opinions on the environmental safety of our nuclear submarines. Regardless, I know he and his family were duly impressed with the *Greeneville*.

Perhaps that explains why a few days after the horrible accident on February 9, 2001, I received a FedEx letter from Robert Kennedy Jr. In his letter, he wrote glowingly about the professionalism of the *Greeneville* crew. Then he focused more personally on me. He wrote movingly, as a man who has experienced both personal and public tragedy. "Scott, it's not the outcome that is important, but it is how the man endures the crisis." In the months to follow, I would recall his words again and again, and—along with the Bible and the encouragement of my wife and father—Robert Kennedy Jr.'s heartfelt message helped sustain me through the darkest moments of my life.

On January 10, 2001, the *Ehime Maru*, a Japanese trawler 196 feet in length, weighing more than 400 tons, departed from Uwajima Fisheries School in Japan. It was a floating classroom for students who wanted to learn about professional fishing. The ship traveled to Hawaii where the weather was warm, the fish were plentiful, and the waters were safe.

About the same time, the *Greeneville* headed south from Alaska, on our way to Oakland, California. In late January, while the *Greeneville* was moored in Oakland, I attended a formal Navy function at the Presidio Officers' Club in San Francisco. I was recommending my executive officer, Jerry Pfeifer, for a possible promotion to a position in the office of Admiral Thomas Fargo, the commander of the Pacific Fleet, who would be in attendance. Captain Pete Daly, the admiral's executive assistant, was my neighbor and a good friend.

At the party, I introduced Jerry to Pete, and the two of them seemed to hit it off well. I had high hopes that my executive officer would soon be making his way up the Navy's ladder. I could never have imagined how, within a few weeks, both Jerry's and my hopes of ascending higher in the Navy would be dashed forever.

CHAPTER 12

AN UNUSUAL
MISSION

John P. Craven was the chief scientist of the Navy's Special Projects Office during the Cold War. Craven's highly classified activities make for great movie plots, as he was vitally involved in the planning and execution of America's submarine-based nuclear deterrence and submarine espionage. He was such an enigma to the Soviets, they assigned a full-time KGB agent to spy on him.

After Craven retired from the Navy, he wrote in his book *The Silent War* (Simon & Schuster, 2001), "The Cold War was the first major conflict between superpowers in which victory and defeat were unambiguously determined without the firing of a shot. Without the shield of a strong silent deterrent or the intellectual sword of espionage beneath the sea, that war could not have been won."

Since the conclusion of the Cold War, however, the U.S. Navy's submarine program, like every other branch of the military, has been subjected to draconian cutbacks in funding and in programs, not to mention the building of new subs. During the eight years of the Clinton Administration, the U.S. government carved massive cuts out of the submarine force's budget. Longstanding programs were summarily dismantled and shut down in the mid-1990s, and some naval bases, such as Mare Island, California, were closed completely. It's ironic that our nation's submarine force, perhaps the one branch of the U.S. military service that did more to protect the safety of our shores and win the Cold War against the Soviet Union, has been the hardest hit by these cuts, decimated by the very peace the submariners were so instrumental in winning.

For years we had been the "silent service," but now it was important that people in power understood as fully as possible the value of having a nuclear submarine force. Suddenly, the Navy was in the awkward position of having to validate the peacetime need for its expensive, secretive, silent service. We all recognized this change, especially those in leadership positions.

One day in October 2000, shortly after my squadron commander, Captain Rich Snead, took command, I quipped, "Commodore, it's been three months since you've been in command, and you haven't come down to see our boat yet. The last time you were here was for your change of command ceremony. It would be nice if I could get the boss to meet my crew." Captain Snead and Captain Dave McCall had had their change of command ceremony on board the *Greeneville* in August, and except for our weekly meetings, I had hardly seen him since! Snead smiled and promised to visit soon. He had inherited a mess aboard the nuclear sub *Los Angeles*, and he had been consumed with trying to improve morale aboard that ship. Meanwhile, the *Greeneville* had been receiving rave reviews and was perking along nicely. A pragmatic, native Tennessean, Snead probably felt, "If it ain't broke, don't fix it."

When the commodore finally visited the *Greeneville*, I asked him straightforwardly, "Commodore, what is our mission these days? Some of my crewmembers are asking, and I don't know what to tell them."

Rich Snead knew exactly what I meant. "Our mission is to survive, Scott. Right now we don't have Ivan [the former Soviet Union] to compete against, but our mission is to survive and protect our assets. We have to fight for every dollar, and the drawdown of men and equipment is killing us. Our mission is to survive."

As one of the best ships in the Navy, the *Greeneville*'s crew and I often played a key role in the Navy's mission. We were asked to do a lot of public relations work through what was known as the Navy's distinguished visitors' program. The plan was simple: Take civilians, members of Congress, journalists, or other opinion-makers for a ride on a nuclear submarine, demonstrating its capabilities, all the while subtly reminding the guests of the submarine's importance in maintaining our national security.

The passengers who rode the submarine always came away with a new appreciation for the importance of the U.S. submarine force to our nation's defense. They also came away with a "these-guys-are-good" attitude toward the men handling the ship. Once civilian passengers had been aboard the submarine, we didn't have to lobby them. They became passionate about the submarine force's place in our military culture; they had felt it for themselves and had experienced the incredible capabilities of what these engineering marvels can do.

Having distinguished visitors aboard was not at all unusual for the *Greeneville*. One of the well-known passengers who rode the *Greeneville* in February 1999 was Tipper Gore, wife of then Vice President Al Gore. Tipper Gore and the *Greeneville* had a longstanding relationship. She was the ship's sponsor and had commissioned the *Greeneville* in 1996.

In 1999, Mrs. Gore actually sat in the helmsman's seat during a distinguished visitors' cruise in which the *Greeneville* crew expertly demonstrated "angles and dangles" and an emergency main ballast tank blow, a maneuver that would make the *Greeneville* famous . . . or infamous.

After meeting with the crew, Mrs. Gore was outspoken in her praise of the *Greeneville*. "I've so enjoyed being aboard the ship, and I am so proud to be the sponsor," she gushed. "This crew is really special to me, and they do a wonderful job under great leadership. I am truly honored to have taken part in your operations today."

Another celebrity who rode the *Greeneville* during a training mission was James Cameron, the Oscar-winning director of the movie *Titanic*.

In late January 2001, shortly after George W. Bush had been inaugurated as the new president of the United States, the *Greeneville* was docked at Alameda, near San Francisco. I received a call from the Submarine Squadron One operations office in Hawaii, asking me if I could take a group of distinguished visitors on a demonstration cruise arranged by retired Admiral Richard Macke for February 9, 2001. The cruise would embark from Pearl Harbor, Hawaii, and Admiral Konetzni, commander of the Pacific Submarine Force, and Admiral Macke might even join us.

I doubted seriously that Admiral Macke would make the trip, but Admiral Konetzni's office was in Pearl Harbor. Call it pride or whatever, but I wanted to take Admiral Konetzni for one last ride aboard the *Greeneville*. It had been nearly one year since the admiral had ridden with us, back in March 2000, and he had been incredibly impressed then. I couldn't wait to show him how much our crew had matured.

Perpetually outgoing, gregarious, and upbeat, Admiral Konetzni was my mentor in the Navy. Besides being a highly competent military man, Konetzni had led the way in improving morale among submariners in the "new" Navy since the draft had been done away with. He had recently announced that he'd be giving up his Pacific command to transfer to Norfolk, Virginia, as the deputy commander in chief of the Atlantic Fleet, and he had said that he would like to hold his change of command ceremonies aboard the *Greeneville*.

As captain of the ship, it would be a feather in my cap to be involved in the ceremony for the popular head of the Pacific Fleet. I loved any opportunity to show off our boat and our crew, and the ebullient admiral's change of command ceremonies would showcase us in an extremely favorable light. Personally, I wanted the privilege and pleasure of having the admiral experience the *Greeneville* at sea one more time before he left us in Hawaii. The distinguished visitors' excursion might be our last chance.

"Yep, we'll do it." I said. "As long as we get to take Admiral Konetzni and Admiral Macke, we'll be glad to help out."

On Wednesday, February 7, I went to the COMSUBPAC public affairs office to pick up some information concerning the distinguished visitors' cruise I was to conduct on Friday. While there, I received some bad news. "I'm sorry, Scott," I was told, "but Admiral Konetzni will not be riding with you on Friday. Nor will Admiral Macke. Admiral Konetzni's chief of staff, Captain Robert L. Brandhuber, will be accompanying you, though."

My heart sank. I was sorely disappointed. I had been excited about doing the distinguished visitors' cruise because I thought I'd have another chance to get the admiral out to sea with us. Now it was going to be just another afternoon of schmoozing. Was I ever wrong!

The *Greeneville* had already had a busy year. We had been through a four-month dry dock selected restricted availability, an intense period of servicing and updating the submarine, similar to a 100,000-mile checkup on a truck. Then we were out to sea for a month to do acoustic trials off Alaska, down to California to thaw out, and then back to Hawaii. We had only been in port for a week before we received news that we were going back out to sea for the distinguished visitors' program. About 30 percent of our 140 crewmembers were in training. We were gearing up for a six-month deployment, heading out to sea in June and not returning home till right before Christmas. As we always did before a long trip, we analyzed our strengths and weaknesses, and we sent some of our guys back into the classroom for retraining.

We had planned some classroom training for some of our crewmembers around this time. Following our monthlong deployment, and well before the February 9 distinguished visitors' cruise, the *Greeneville*'s sonar chief petty officer reported, "Captain, we need some remedial training for our sonar operators." We had taken a number of new guys on board, so it was normal procedure for our new sonar operators to receive retraining on sonar-search procedures before departing for such a long deployment.

"Okay, fine," I said. The remedial training meant that part of our regular sonar men would be off the ship for the day, including our sonar chief petty officer, but I wasn't worried about being understaffed. Submarine crews are in a constant state of continuing education. It wasn't considered unusual for a third of our crew to be in the classroom at any one time. No big deal; we could do the distinguished visitors' cruise and operate fine with the crew we had. Sure, there may be different crewmen at the controls, but all of the men were highly qualified. First Class Petty Officer Edward McGiboney was a seasoned submariner and a phenomenal talent. First Class Petty Officer Rayes was another highly talented sonar man. A young broadband sonar operator named Bowie was another top-notch submariner. It never crossed my mind that anyone on the *Greeneville* crew might not be competent to perform.

I spent most of Thursday, February 8, going over final preparations regarding Friday's distinguished visitors' cruise. When I left the ship shortly after 5:00 P.M., everything was in tip-top shape, and we were ready to go to sea. I went home and indulged in one of my secret pleasures—cooking dinner for my wife and daughter. After dinner, Jill and Ashley and I sat outside and talked leisurely about Ashley's eighth-grade school day. As I relaxed with my wife and daughter, I couldn't help thinking, *Life just can't get much better than this.*

Later on Thursday evening, I went out to a little shop located off the naval base in the small Hawaiian town of Aiea. I bought some miniature flags to decorate the dining table in the *Greeneville*'s officers' wardroom on Friday. This wardroom is separate from the crew's galley and is about the size of an average-priced cabin aboard a luxury cruise ship. Although the officers' wardroom has a few perks, such as a television video monitor and stereo system, it is far from luxurious. It is simply decorated with a few pictures and plaques on the walls, and one large table in the center that serves as a dining table, desk, and conference table. Ten people could be seated at the table: four on each side and one on each end.

This was where I planned to have the distinguished visitors eat lunch. Any time we had guests aboard, I tried to do something special to make them feel at home. In this case, I wanted to decorate the tables with an American flag, some Tennessee flags—because the *Greeneville* was named for Davy Crockett's birthplace in Greeneville County, Tennessee—and some Texas state flags, since fourteen of the sixteen visitors hailed originally from Texas.

Escorting the distinguished visitors, COMSUBPAC Chief of Staff Robert L. Brandhuber was scheduled to be on board that day too. With Admiral Konetzni away from the base, visiting in Yokosuka, Japan, Brandhuber was the ranking staff officer for the entire Pacific Submarine Force. In the admiral's absence, it was unusual for the chief of staff to be out of the office, especially going out to sea, but Brandhuber wanted to see his son-in-law, Tyler Meador, our ship's engineer, perform at sea. After all, we were just going to be cruising around Hawaii, so technically Brandhuber would still be in position.

I wanted to get a flag honoring Brandhuber as well, so I asked Tyler, "Where did your father-in-law go to school?"

"Purdue," Tyler answered. For some reason, I thought Purdue was located in Ohio. I didn't give it a second thought, and I bought the Ohio state flag. Imagine how embarrassed I was when Brandhuber later told me that Purdue is located in Indiana!

If that had been my worst mistake during that trip, I'd still be in the Navy.

Jill and I watched an episode of *Seinfeld* on television, followed by the late news, before heading off to bed around midnight. We had no sooner fallen asleep than the telephone in Jill's and my bedroom rang. "Captain, the engineering watch section is on board, and we are ready to commence a normal reactor start-up." I recognized Tyler Meador's voice. Before the *Greeneville*'s nuclear reactor could be fired up, the ship's engineer was required to check in with the captain . . . regardless of the hour. "Here's the specific data you need to know concerning the reactor start-up," Tyler said. The ship's engineer rattled off the current information regarding the status of the

Greeneville's nuclear power plant. Following his report, he asked, "Do I have permission to commence a normal reactor start-up, sir?"

Getting a nuclear submarine ready for departure and underway, even for a short trip, is not as simple as turning the ignition key, revving the engine, and backing the family minivan out of the garage. It is a mammoth undertaking involving dozens of highly skilled men, and it takes more than twenty-four hours! The nuclear reactor, the primary source for energy on the ship, has to be started several hours before departure. It takes that long to get the nuclear reactor critical, so in the case of our scheduled trip on February 9, the reactor was started in the wee hours of the morning. Once the reactor was critical and we were generating our own power, the crew would disconnect the ship from our power source on the pier, and we would be on our own.

"Permission granted," I mumbled. "Commence a normal reactor start-up." I hung up the phone, rolled over, and went back to sleep.

I awakened around 5:30 A.M. and crawled out of bed, trying not to disturb Jill. This was going to be a short, out-and-back trip, planned carefully as a five- or six-hour event, after which I'd return home from work like a normal family man. There was no need for any prolonged good-byes. Saying good-bye was always tough for Jill and me anyhow. We had planned to have a quiet, romantic dinner that night.

I dressed casually in a pair of shorts, an oxford shirt, and dock shoes. My uniforms were already in my stateroom aboard ship, so I often went to work dressed as though I were going sailing . . . which, in a way, I was!

As I stepped out into the morning air, the incredible beauty of our surroundings struck me for about the zillionth time. How fortunate Jill and Ashley and I were to be stationed here in Hawaii! The Hawaiian Islands are a favorite place for submariners to be stationed for many reasons. The natural beauty of Hawaii is unparalleled anywhere in the world, and the weather isn't bad either. From a seafaring standpoint, Hawaii far exceeds the East Coast locations, or even the West Coast ports, where a submarine has to travel for hours to clear the shallow water of the continental shelf and reach waters deep enough to conduct submerged operations. In Hawaii, just forty-five minutes away from the dock usually found us in really deep water. It was a submariner's dream.

It was still dark, but the sun was beginning to peek through the clouds above the Koo Lau mountain range to the east. It was a gorgeous Hawaiian morning, the sweet smell of tropical flowers drifting in my direction, wafted gently by the ever-present trade winds. *Another day in paradise*, I thought as I hopped in my 1985 blue Honda Prelude, my "island car," and headed toward the waterfront. Looking at the glint of sun just making its way into the sky, I said to myself, "It's going to be a great day!"

One of the luxuries of living on base at Pearl Harbor was that I was only a few minutes away from work. Usually, I'd drive to the ship, but some mornings, I hopped on a bicycle and pedaled the three miles over to the three-hundred-foot, billion-dollar machine I got paid to "drive."

On the way to the boat, I detoured long enough to sweep through the McDonald's drive-through to pick up an Egg McMuffin and a fresh cup of coffee. I was slightly overweight, and these early-morning breakfast stops weren't helping much, but I wasn't worried. *I'll have plenty of time to work out later this afternoon, after we get back*, I thought.

I pulled the car into my reserved parking spot in the captains' parking area at the head of the pier. Only four crewmembers received such special parking privileges: the captain of the ship, the executive officer, the chief of the boat, and the sailor of the year. I walked across the dock to the *Greeneville*. The ship looked absolutely majestic in the morning light, high-lighted by an array of lights dotting the waterfront. From a distance, I noted the topside sentry guarding the ship. The *Greeneville* was, after all, a nuclear fast-attack submarine—an awesome weapon of war that many rogue countries would love to get their hands on, or possibly even destroy. We dared not let down our guard, even for a moment.

The ship was already bustling with activity. The engineering team had been working since midnight. The duty section, the guys who keep the ship running even while in port and comprised of about 20 percent of our 140-man crew, had gone home or gone forward aboard ship to catch some sleep after midnight. The fresh watch team replaced them for the reactor start-up.

For a long moment, I let my eyes run up and down the *Greeneville*. To the uninitiated, it may have looked like a large hunk of blackened steel, but to me, it was a work of art. As I often did before getting underway, I walked the pier in humble awe, checking details on the ship, noting things that needed to be cleaned up on the dock before departure, but mostly just admiring the three-hundred-foot *Los Angeles*–class vessel I commanded. I loved looking at the boat. *What a spectacular piece of machinery!* It seemed almost a waste to be taking her out to sea today. Our sole mission was to entertain a group of distinguished visitors. We had no other reason for going to sea that day.

CHAPTER 13
NO VISUAL CONTACTS

"Good morning, Skipper," the topside sentry called as he saluted.

"Good morning, shipmate," I responded. I talked with the sentry for a minute or so and then passed on over the brow of the ship. As I did, I heard the announcement over the ship's general communication system, "*Greeneville* arriving."

Greeneville was me, and the crew was always informed of my whereabouts when I came aboard or departed the ship.

I swung down the ladder of the forward escape trunk, stepped down about six feet to the level below, and walked down to my stateroom, where I changed into my submarine coveralls, affectionately known by sub guys as a "poopy suit." I started going through the stack of paperwork on my desk and the navigational charts for today's trip. Within five minutes of hearing the announcement, "*Greeneville* arriving," the food service attendant—affectionately known as our "mess crank"—arrived with a fresh cup of coffee. Now that they knew

I spent my early years in Japan, while my family lived overseas, and am told my first words were in Japanese. This is me at age 2.

May 27, 1981—Graduation day from the Naval Academy at Annapolis, Maryland. With me are (L-R) my mom, Barbara, and my dad, Air Force Lieutenant Colonel John Coe.

Jill and I on our wedding day, December 31, 1986. We left the chapel and headed for Naples, Italy. Pictured left to right are Jill's parents, John and Loretta Huntington, me and my beautiful new bride, and my mother, Barbara, and dad, John Coe.

Just married!

My father, retired Air Force Colonel and pilot Dan Waddle, on board my boat.

Ashley and Jill on the periscope, August 16, 1992.

Rear Admiral Konetzni was the keynote speaker at my change of command ceremony on March 19, 1999. He spoke of the importance of people, engagement, and efficiency.

Jill and I on one of the biggest days of our lives.

The crew and shipmates of the USS *Greeneville* in November 2000 while the sub was in dry dock. The boat looming above us gives you an idea of how enormous these magnificent machines are.

Three different views of the *Greeneville*. It would take nearly half an hour to bring this billion-dollar boat to the surface. PHOTOS BY DEBBIE OQUIST

The view from the bridge.

Master Chief Petty Officer Doug Coffman, the *Greeneville* chief of the boat, one of the finest sailors I've ever worked with. PHOTO BY DEBBIE OQUIST

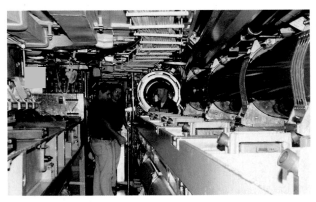

Inside the torpedo room.
PHOTO BY DEBBIE OQUIST

A day at the office. This is me in the control room.

A relaxed moment in the sonar room after anchoring off Santa Barbara, California, in July 2000. PHOTO BY DEBBIE OQUIST

Although extremely cramped, my stateroom was a combination office and living quarters. Even when I was resting, monitors kept me in touch with the control room. PHOTO BY DEBBIE OQUIST

Captain Guy O'Neil, decorated submariner, awards the coveted gold dolphins to Lieutenant Matt Dukette as Executive Officer Lieutenant Commander Jerry Pfeifer (middle) looks on.

A view of the bridge from the deck.

The *Ehime Maru* after the accident, two hundred feet below the surface.   U.S. NAVY PHOTO

The damage to the *Greeneville* appeared minimal, but actually required more than two million dollars to repair.   U.S. NAVY PHOTO

Exiting the court of inquiry with Jill and my attorney, Charlie Gittins, after a tough day of hearings.

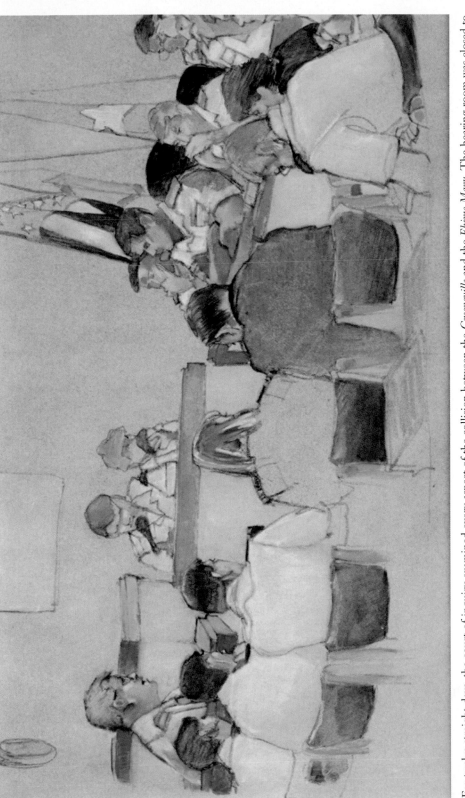

For twelve straight days, the court of inquiry examined every aspect of the collision between the *Greeneville* and the *Ehime Maru*. The hearing room was closed to the media. ARTIST: © LYNN MATSUOKA 2001

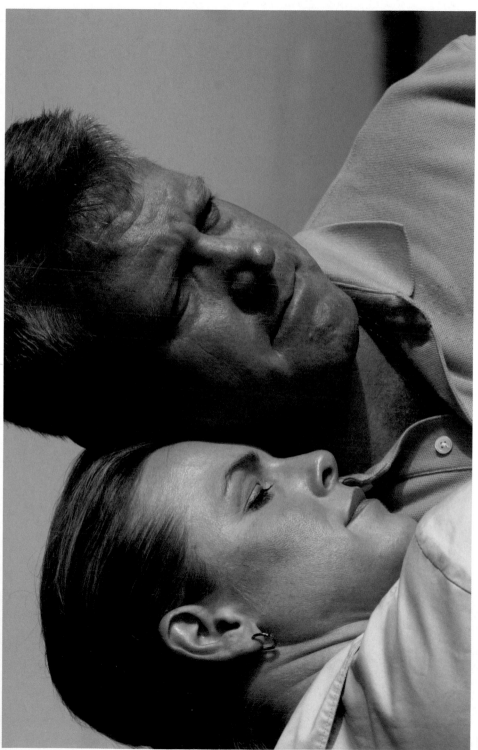

Jill never stopped believing in me throughout the ordeal.   PHOTO BY STEVE LISS

I saluted the *Greeneville* as it went to sea for the first time after the accident. In a moment I will never f

en on the bridge waved and sounded the boat's whistle.   PHOTO BY STEVE LISS

I knew my life would never be the same. PHOTOS BY STEVE LISS

There's a time to be silent, and a time to speak up for what is right. I had to take responsibility and let the chips fall where they may. It's the right thing to do.   PHOTO BY STEVE LISS

Three things sustained us in this ordeal: our faith in God, the unconditional love of family, and the help of our friends. When I look at my daughter, Ashley, I know the future holds great promise.   PHOTO BY STEVE LISS

my routine, the ship's cooks never missed with my morning coffee. I was always glad to see them each morning, too, since it gave me a few minutes to talk with the cooks about how things were going in the galley. When you're at sea for six months at a time, the one group you want to be happy is the group in charge of preparing the food!

Just before 7:00 A.M., Lieutenant Commander Keith Sloan, who had been serving as the ship's duty officer for the previous twenty-four hours, came to my stateroom with a status report. "Captain, the AVSDU is not working."

I could feel my countenance fall, and Keith picked up on it. "Sorry, Captain." Keith knew that with visitors coming on board, I wanted everything working perfectly, and when I'd gone home the night before, it had been. The crew of the *Greeneville*, like that of any nuclear-powered sub, constantly cleaned, repaired, and serviced every piece of equipment aboard the submarine, meticulously making sure that we could operate safely at sea. You don't want to push a button, press a computer key, or pull a handle six hundred feet below the surface and find out that some vital piece of equipment is not working.

Fortunately, the AVSDU was not considered vital, at least not in my mind. The AVSDU is the analog-video signal display unit, located in an overhead console forward of the periscope area in the control room. It served as a repeater system, which means that it is basically a backup, sort of an extra computer screen, displaying information from the three sonar stacks and screens forward of the control room. The sonar screens on the *Greeneville* were only a few feet away from the periscopes. While the AVSDU was a convenient way for me or the officer of the deck to quickly check the sonar screens, it was not a crucial piece of equipment . . . or so I thought.

"Any other problems?"

"No, sir. Everything else is ready to go." Keith handed me his morning reports to review.

"All right, fine." We entered the broken AVSDU in our "green book," our trouble-log, knowing that the monitor would be fixed upon our return

later that afternoon. It irritated me that the piece of equipment wasn't working, but I downplayed its importance in my mind. Looking back now, I wish
we'd have taken the time to repair the AVSDU before embarking. It may
have helped us avoid the nightmare that was coming.

Lieutenant Commander Jerry Pfeifer, my executive officer, came to my
stateroom to brief me. "Captain, we're ready to get underway. Here are the
'welcome aboard' pamphlets for you to sign for our sixteen guests, plus one
for Chief of Staff Brandhuber."

"Thank you, XO," I replied.

I made the rounds of the ship, receiving informal status reports from
various system operators as I walked. Everything was functioning properly
. . . everything except the AVSDU.

"Station the maneuvering watch!" came a voice over the general
announcing system. That announcement meant it was time for all personnel
to be in their places. The ship's divers headed topside to keep an eye on the
line handlers, the crewmembers in charge of disconnecting the submarine's
mooring lines from the pier. The divers were dressed in rescue gear and
shorty wet suits, just in case somebody should fall overboard and they'd be
called upon to help rescue the embarrassed sailor or pierside line handler. I
headed back to my stateroom to freshen up before greeting our guests.

Our distinguished visitors arrived about thirty minutes before our
scheduled 8:00 A.M. departure time, and I climbed out of the boat and
crossed the brow to meet them. On my way, I met Chief of Staff
Brandhuber, who had also just arrived. Although I knew him from our regular Wednesday staff briefings and had chatted with him occasionally at the
Friday afternoon happy hour at the officers' club, we were not close friends.
I greeted the COMSUBPAC's chief of staff as I would any senior officer—
cordially.

Brandhuber responded warmly as we shook hands. "Scott, you look
great! And the crew looks great. I'm excited to be here."

"Thank you, sir," I replied. "Welcome aboard."

I walked further up the pier to where our sixteen distinguished visitors
were waiting. I didn't recognize most of their names and had no reason to

wonder about their motives for making this trip. Two of the visitors, a sportswriter and his wife, had actually taken a tour of the *Greeneville* the day before. I'd met them and struck up a conversation with them. Knowing that we were going out to sea the next day, I invited them to join us as my guests.

As for the fourteen Texans, I knew little about them. I'd heard that several of them were visiting Hawaii to participate in a golf tournament benefiting a project restoring the retired battleship *Missouri*, but I wasn't even certain of that. Nor did it matter to me. All I knew was that the Navy wanted to impress them. My goal for the day was to provide them with a short voyage they would never forget.

I greeted the civilians collectively and then went person to person to shake hands. "Good morning. I'm the ship's captain, Commander Scott Waddle, from Austin, Texas, and this is our chief of the boat and senior enlisted man on board, Master Chief Doug Coffman. The *Greeneville* is glad to have you here. Welcome aboard. I'll be seeing each of you a bit later, and will be glad to answer any of your questions. Right now, however, please excuse me, as I have to get up to the bridge."

Standing on the bridge as the *Greeneville* slipped out of Pearl Harbor's channel that morning, I noticed the sky was a bit overcast, which was not unusual in Hawaii. A haze, similar to the June-gloom in San Diego, seemed to be hovering over the sea. But the weather report looked good. *It's a bit hazier than normal, but I'm sure this will burn off,* I mused. *It's Hawaii, where the sun always shines.*

We were slightly late getting to our dive point, where we prepared to submerge the ship. It was nearly 9:30. Our visitors watched and listened in rapt attention as I rattled off orders and the crew responded expertly. Before the visitors knew it, we were going under the sea. By the time the dive was completed and we were cruising comfortably, it was approaching 10:00. By 10:30 we were ready for our first lunch sitting.

Lunch aboard a submarine must be served in two sittings. We can serve about forty guys in the crew's galley, and about ten comfortably in the officers' wardroom. We seated eight of the guests at each of our two lunch sittings in the officers' wardroom, the first lunch sitting scheduled to run from

10:30 to 11:30 in the wardroom, followed immediately by the second sitting from 11:30 to 12:30. After lunch, we planned to put on a display of the sub's abilities, showing how to avert being hit by an enemy's torpedo, as well as several other challenging maneuvers. All of this was planned to give our guests the maximum bang for their bucks and still get them back to shore by 2:30 that afternoon.

At about 12:45 A.M., I was still in my stateroom, autographing souvenir photos of the ship for the distinguished visitors with whom I had eaten lunch during the first sitting, when the XO popped his head in the door and said, "Excuse me, Captain, but we're running a little late. We need to get this thing moving."

I wanted to say, "Lighten up, XO. We're the only ship out here. It's Friday afternoon and the tugboats will run in Pearl till 4:30. We have lots of time. If we run a few minutes behind, so what?" On the other hand, I knew Jerry was right. In our posted Plan of the Day, we were scheduled to be at "Papa Hotel," a point in the ocean at the entrance to Pearl Harbor, at 2:00 P.M. We had announced our time of arrival back at the pier to be between 2:30 and 3:00, and if we were late, we'd probably inconvenience a lot of people. I certainly didn't want to do that.

I nodded to Jerry and said, "I know what I'm doing, XO," letting him know that I was aware of the time. "We'll deal with it."

"Yes, sir," Jerry Pfeifer replied. The XO entertained the guests during the second lunch sitting, which ran until after 1:00 P.M. I was a bit concerned about the time, but I was confident that we could perform all our planned maneuvers and get back into port before late afternoon.

Before beginning our afternoon maneuvers, I stopped in sonar to check on the surface situation, to see what nearby boats they might be tracking. Petty Officer McGiboney reported several contacts, but all were distant. I walked over to the fire control technician of the watch and looked over his shoulder at his screen, to see what he was tracking. Between the two, I got a clear picture that we had three and sometimes four vessels in our general vicinity, none of which was within miles of us. Our closest contacts seemed to be a small merchant craft, about seven miles to the northeast, going west along the coast of Oahu. Another vessel appeared to have stopped in the water; apparently it was a fishing boat.

I continued on to the periscope area, where I acknowledged Mike Coen, our officer of the deck. Mike had been driving the boat while I had been at lunch. Mike had worked with me aboard the *Greeneville* for more than eighteen months, and I had complete confidence in him. He was slow and methodical, but he always did his job by the book, to the letter. I had no reason to doubt that Mike was fully aware of all other ships in close proximity to us. I knew that if he had any concerns that something might be wrong, he'd let me know. But Mike Coen didn't say a word.

The maneuvers I had scheduled for that day were not simple. They were designed to train the crew to evade an enemy and to operate in shallow water, making high-speed, full-rudder, thirty-five-degree turns, side to side, as well as "angles," rapid up-and-down movements in the water to practice the submarine's ability to change depths quickly. We also practiced high-speed maneuvers, operating at speeds up to twenty-five knots and reversing course while submerged, turning the submarine around 180 degrees in less than twenty-five seconds. Most submarine crews are proficient at such maneuvers in deep water, but I trained my men to perform these drastic maneuvers in shallow water, only a couple of hundred feet deep, within a five- to ten-foot depth band, so we could change course quickly to get out of trouble in a wartime situation. My motto was still, "We train like we're going to fight, because we will fight like we have been trained."

The *Greeneville* crew performed with precision that day, putting the submarine through its paces, negotiating the maneuvers as though they were driving a car through the cones on a test track. The submarine pitched from side to side and up and down as we went through our "angles and dangles," and the distinguished visitors were loving it! Everyone was enjoying the ride and having fun, and one of the guests was taking pictures as his fellow guests hung on as though they were on a ride at Universal Studio's Islands of Adventure theme park. I could barely suppress a smile as I watched the expressions of joy and amazement on the faces of our distinguished visitors. Even Captain Brandhuber seemed to be impressed.

We were on a good roll, so I decided to push the crew a bit further. Anyone who has ever watched a World War II submarine movie has a mental image of what happens aboard a sub when the captain commands, "Dive! Dive! Dive!" Consequently, no cruise aboard a nuclear sub would be complete without a similar scenario. Nowadays, however, the "emergency deep," as the dive is called, is much more sophisticated.

Before calling for the emergency deep, I ordered the *Greeneville* back up to periscope depth, a keel depth about sixty feet below the surface. Mike Coen, our young officer of the deck, echoed my orders to the crew with the usual intense expression on his face. I had only given him five minutes to prepare, and to Officer Coen, that was hurrying!

Coen put up the scope and then I visually scanned the sea to make sure there were no other ships, buoys, or other dangerous obstacles on the surface. We were still catching waves in the periscope's glass, so I ordered the ship to go up to fifty-eight feet so I could get an unobstructed high view of the sea. I trained the scope on the area where our sonar and fire control technician of the watch had reported contacts previously. I peered intently into the lens and saw only blue water against a grey-white sky. Little did I know that somewhere in that haze, a large white ship was heading in our direction.

"I have a good feel for the contacts," I said. Before initiating any type of underwater maneuvers, a three- to five-minute scan of the surface was normal. But I also knew that we were in open water and that our officer of the deck, Lieutenant Mike Coen, a notoriously methodical and deliberate watchstander, had just scanned the sea and found "no contacts" within any reasonable distance. Neither had Patrick Seacrest, the ship's fire control technician. Petty Officer Carter, the electronic surveillance measure watch manning the gear that detects the presence of radar signals, reported "no threat contacts"; Petty Officer McGiboney, the supervisor in the sonar room, said the same thing. Besides, we were running behind schedule on our planned maneuvers.

Rather than the usual three-minute scan, I did an 80-second, 360-degree sweep. I went to high-powered magnification. When I turned the scope toward the open sea, I saw nothing but blue water. When I turned the scope back toward Oahu, I could see the island's volcanic mountain peaks all the way from Mount Tantalus to Diamond Head.

The afternoon sun was beginning to droop in the winter sky, and a white haze seemed to hover over the water. I thought, *That's strange. That haze has been with us all day.* I swung the periscope around one more time, just to make sure there were no contacts nearby. I had a good feel for the contact surface situation and said so. The coast was clear. There were no objects within miles of us.

"I hold no visual contacts," I announced to my crew. I turned and smiled at the distinguished visitors, several of whom had gathered around me near the periscope to watch what I was doing.

Off to my right, with the visitors standing between us, Patrick Seacrest sat staring at the ship's fire control console, a computer screen showing the relative position, bearing, and speed of any contacts in the area. A fourteen-year veteran at his job, Seacrest had served admirably aboard the *Omaha* and the *Buffalo*. He had been aboard the *Greeneville* less than a year and had earned my respect and trust as a fire control technician, handling sensitive equipment used to target and launch weapons and to process sonar information. Patrick Seacrest had taught the younger fire control technicians on his previous ships and was the career counselor on board the *Greeneville*, which meant he was the sailor I trusted to help me reenlist the talented guys and keep them in the Navy. On his screen, Seacrest saw not one, but three contacts: Sierra 12, Sierra 13, and Sierra 14. Seacrest was concerned because he didn't have a clear read on Sierra 14, and he was absorbed in trying to get a lock on that contact. Meanwhile, he failed to notice the computer solution indicating that Sierra 13 was only about two miles away and heading in our direction, closing on our position. Although none of us knew it at the time, Sierra 13 was a sixty-yard trawler named the *Ehime Maru*.

I had a standing order on the *Greeneville* that any military contact within ten thousand yards, about five miles, should be reported to the XO, the officer of the deck, or the commanding officer. Any nonmilitary vessel within four thousand yards was considered a threat to our ship and should be reported.

Seacrest trusted me. His computer screen showed that we had a contact at about four thousand yards and closing. But when Petty Officer Seacrest heard me say there were no visual contacts in the area, he knew that a contact within two miles of us would certainly be visible through the ship's periscope. He deduced that there was only one possible solution: His computer screen must be showing dated information. The contact must have already passed or moved off in a different direction. Patrick Seacrest "outspotted" the contact, changing its distance from four thousand yards to a distance of nine thousand yards, and hit *enter* on his computer. Had he looked more carefully at the screen next to him, Patrick may have realized that he had programmed a physical impossibility. The contact he had just listed showed a speed of ninety-nine knots! Anyone with common sense knew that not even a speedboat could travel that fast. But Patrick Seacrest didn't notice the absurdity. He was more concerned with getting a fix on Sierra 14. Seacrest updated the plot on his computer screen to reflect that there were no close contacts.

But Patrick Seacrest was wrong, and so was Mike Coen . . . and so was I.

CHAPTER 14
THE RIDE OF MY LIFE

The emergency deep is an evasive maneuver that thrusts a submarine far below the surface in a hurry, which was exactly what I wanted to do, since we were running short on time. I couldn't linger any longer. My crew had had an adequate, though not an abundant, amount of time to search for contacts, and we all had come to the same conclusion: *No visible contacts.* Nobody challenged me when I had reported no contacts in the area. We were ready to dive. Sure, I was probably pushing them too fast, but I always pushed our crew. I was confident in their abilities, and I was confident in myself. Besides, I was eager to further impress our guests, so I called the emergency deep. "Hang on, everybody," I said to our visitors.

"Emergency deep!" the chief of the watch's voice rang out through the ship's communication system, as though this were the real thing. As far as the crew was concerned, it was! I never told them in advance, "Now, guys, this is just a drill." Quite the contrary, we always trained as though it were an actual emergency.

I raised the training handles on the periscope and lowered the scope.

The helmsman increased the speed to "Ahead full." The cavitation bell rang three times, telling the throttle man back aft in the engine room, "This is serious! Let's get going! Give us some speed quickly!"

Water flooded into the variable ballast tanks to help the ship dive more quickly, but the most important factors in the emergency deep maneuver were the ship's plane, angle, and propeller speed. Done all together, in the right combination, the ship zoomed downward. The special guests' eyes widened as though we were on a roller coaster ride and dropping fast.

Although the crew may have assumed that we were just showing off, that this emergency deep was just a drill, they responded as though it were a real emergency. Finally, I picked up the phone and made the official announcement, "The emergency deep was initiated as a drill for training." The crew collectively breathed a sigh of relief.

We leveled off at about four hundred feet below the surface and cruised for a few minutes at a speed of fifteen knots. Running underwater is better than riding in the most quiet, smooth-driving, luxury automobile. Once the boat is trimmed and level, it's even smoother than an airplane ride at thirty-five thousand feet. There is little sensation of movement, and it is easy to walk around normally, though it feels a bit like walking through a basement of a building. You're on solid footing, but you know there's a world of activity above you, and in the sub's case, a world of activity below you as well.

About nine miles off the coast of Pearl Harbor, as I often did when we hosted distinguished visitors aboard the *Greeneville*, I invited two of our guests to operate the submarine's controls, under the close supervision of our crewmembers.

We had already done a series of "angles and dangles," large dolphinlike sweeping motions, up-and-down movements at moderate speeds combined with quick turns, demonstrating for our guests the nuclear sub's incredible handling capabilities under the sea. We had done the emergency deep, the dive our guests would always remember. Now, for a finale, I decided we'd perform a drill certain to thrill our passengers.

I ordered an emergency main ballast blow, the procedure that would shoot the seven-thousand-ton *Greeneville* from a depth of about four hundred feet to the surface in a matter of seconds. It was the ultimate roller coaster ride, a life-or-death desperation order that every commander hoped he'd never have to implement in reality, yet a procedure we practiced occasionally to make sure we were prepared. Each of the twenty submarines operating in the waters near Hawaii practiced an emergency blow at least once a year, either for training or to verify that the ship's emergency systems worked correctly or for demonstration. Today, our blow would be for all three purposes, but mostly for show.

I addressed John Hall, one of our guests. "Sir, would you like to take the position to initiate the emergency blow?"

"Me?" he responded nervously.

I forced a chuckle back down my throat. "Yes, sir. Don't worry. We'll explain all that you have to do. It will be easy, and I'll have a crewmember standing right with you, just in case." I smiled broadly. "It's a piece of cake."

"Well, okay . . . yeah, sure! I'd love to."

I turned to Jack, the sportswriter whom I had just met the day before during the ship's tour. "Sir, would you like to sit in the helmsman's seat and help steer the ship?"

"I'd be honored, Captain," Jack gushed.

My selections of the guests to help operate the sub were completely arbitrary. They were just people who happened to be standing in the control room, near the helmsman and planesman controls.

I explained the maneuver to all our guests, while our crewmembers made certain that everyone was safely situated in a position where they could hang on. I was standing in the submarine's control room to the right of the officer of the deck when I gave the command, "Initiate emergency blow, now!"

The guests sitting at the planesman and helmsman's aircraft-style control panel threw the two plunger-shaped levers, and high-pressure air rushed into the sub's main ballast tanks, simultaneously blowing the water out of the tanks. The ship instantly began to become buoyant, rising rapidly toward the surface. Once the emergency blow was initiated, there was no reversing it. We were headed up . . . fast, and there was no way to stop. All we could do was hang on for the ride!

"The ship is now at four hundred feet," I announced, "achieving a twenty-degree up angle, proceeding toward the surface."

I continued to calmly call out the ship's progress. "The ship is now at two hundred feet, proceeding toward the surface. Steady at the helm." Our steel tube as long as a football field was hurtling through the water, rushing toward the surface.

I mentally noted the time; it was precisely 1:43 P.M. "The ship is now . . ."

Suddenly, I heard a loud *BANG!* It sounded as though I was standing inside a fifty-five-gallon metal drum, and somebody had taken an aluminum baseball bat and whacked it as hard as they could. I felt a jolt, more of a shudder that jarred the entire submarine, and we seemed to slow down for a moment and then we lurched forward.

"What was that?" I shouted. Another noise and a second shudder shook through the sub.

"All stop!" I called to Mike Coen, the officer of the deck. "I need to get this periscope raised!" I grabbed the periscope, pulled it up, whipped it around into position, and peered intently through the eyepiece. The *Greeneville* had broken the plane of the water and was still moving away from where we'd felt the impact, so I turned the scope around to look back "over our shoulder." To my horror, I saw a ship!

I had thought that perhaps we had hit a buoy or some ocean debris, but this was a *ship!* A white trawler, a large vessel about sixty yards long, lay dead in the water. The back of the ship was already starting to list astern to starboard. I squinted hard through the scope, and on the back of the ship, just above the water's surface, I caught a glimpse of the words, "HIGH SCHOOL." I couldn't make out the name, but it looked like UWAJIMA HIGH SCHOOL.

Oh, God! I thought, *We've hit some kids!* A picture of my own thirteen-year-old daughter, Ashley, flashed through my mind. *These are kids!* I increased the periscope's magnification and watched as what looked to be teenagers scrambled forward, toward the front of the ship, as the stern began to dip deeper into the water. "No!" I wanted to scream. "Don't run for higher position; get off the ship!" Could they not see what was happening? *If they can't see what's happening, I can! They're going down! Get away from the ship, so you don't get sucked under! She is going down . . . and you don't have a lot of time!*

I fought desperately to control my emotions and maintain my composure. "All ahead full!" I called into the *Greeneville's* communication system. "The captain has the con. Right full rudder!"

I wanted to turn the *Greeneville* around to where I knew the survivors in the water were going to need some help. The beautiful blue waters off the coast of Hawaii already glistened with diesel fuel oil surging from the trawler.

As I looked on, horrified yet helpless to do anything about the awful sight, I cried aloud, "God! Get them off the ship! Get them off that ship *now!*" The stern listed further, the bow came out of the water, and the entire ship stood vertically for a few seconds . . . and then the ocean swallowed the trawler whole. The vessel disappeared beneath the sea.

Part of me died as I watched that ship sink.

Aboard the *Greeneville*, pandemonium reigned. Stark terror flushed the faces of our civilian passengers. People were yelling loudly and crewmen dashed back and forth, instinctively racing to get to their battle stations.

We train like we're going to fight, because we'll fight the way we have been trained.

"Quiet!" I shouted loudly to the people around me. I quickly gathered my composure. Despite the near-panic that threatened to overwhelm me, I struggled to calm my emotions. *The captain has to keep his composure, no matter what.* "Be quiet," I repeated in a much calmer, quieter tone. I spoke evenly and directly to the crewmen. "Gentlemen, a horrible thing has happened, but we're prepared for this. Let's calm down. Everybody take a deep breath. Let's do our job. We're trained to handle this. Let's operate the way we've been trained, and we'll work through this." I made a similar announcement over the ship's communication system informing the remainder of the crew. Suddenly all our many hours of training began to pay off. Most of the men snapped to quickly and automatically began performing their assigned tasks.

Captain Brandhuber nudged me away from the periscope. "Get off the scope; I need to see," he said. I stepped aside in a daze. Brandhuber peered into the periscope and simply said, "Oh, God." He let go of the scope and hurried to the radio communications area to place an emergency distress call. Fewer than five minutes had gone by since the impact.

Jerry Pfeifer immediately rounded up the visitors and herded them out of the control room and down to the wardroom. We had no idea whether the watertight integrity of our ship had been compromised, so the crew raced into action, checking compartments, computer screens, life-support and back-up systems in an attempt to assess damages.

Meanwhile, I tried to maneuver the *Greeneville* close to the people in the water, some of whom had made their way to the trawler's life rafts. Others flailed wildly in the water, diesel fuel burning their eyes. Although the emergency blow had whisked us to the surface by rapidly displacing about 70 percent of the water in the ship's ballast, I knew it would normally take another half an hour for the ship to pump the remaining 30 percent of the water out of the ballast tanks. In the meantime, the sub was a seven-thousand-ton steel tube floundering on the surface, bobbing in the sea. With every bob below the surface, we displaced an enormous amount of water, creating waves that threatened to capsize the survivors who had made their way to life rafts. The closer we got, the worse the waves. Still, I felt we had to try to render assistance. But as we approached, huge swells of water threatened to flip the survivors out of their rubber rafts back into the thick diesel fuel. *Back off, now!* I thought. I ordered the *Greeneville* to move away from the survivors before we killed them. We stayed close so we could maintain visual contact with the survivors, but we dared not attempt any rescue from the sub. Later, we would be accused of driving off, running away, callously "leaving the scene of an accident," but such was not the case.

As soon as I felt it was safe enough to do so, my executive officer and I went up to the top of the ship's bridge to get a better look. The wind whipped against my face and the pungent smell of the diesel fuel filled my nostrils. The sight I saw sickened me. The trawler was gone without a trace. Eight or ten orange life rafts bobbed in the waves and the diesel fuel. A few of the rafts were empty; others were crowded with Japanese young men, several of whom looked to be teenagers.

Two members of our ship's scuba diving team quickly assembled their gear and hurried topside, prepared to go into the water if we found any survivors not already in life rafts. I knew that sending our divers into the water under these conditions could easily be a one-way trip for them. The rounded shape of the *Greeneville* pitching up and down in the water created precarious waves slapping violently against the ship's sides, and an oil slick from the trawler's diesel fuel had already formed over much of the area. The late-afternoon sea was now heaving six- to eight-foot swells almost as high as our sail. Several waves came close to pouring over the chest-high wall of the sail, threatening to flood the bridge and compromise the watertight integrity of the *Greeneville*. It would be extremely dangerous for anyone diving off or trying to climb on board the ship that day.

Besides, the water temperature off the Hawaiian Islands was in the high seventies, so we knew there was no danger of the survivors succumbing to hypothermia. From the bridge, we could see that the survivors had all made it to life rafts and were safer there than they'd be if we attempted to rescue them. Better to be floating in a life raft than for a bruised or bloody survivor to be flailing about in the water. For all its tropical romance, the deep seas off the Hawaiian coast possess their own potential perils. Sharks, barracuda, and other flesh-eating fish could be rapacious. Not to mention the sun, salt, and diesel fuel. Fortunately, the sun was going down, but a large, black splotch of fuel oil covered the water like an ominous, viscous blanket, sticking to anything it contacted. The survivors who got it in their eyes or nasal passages cried from the pain, exacerbating the problem further by rubbing their eyes, trying to get the slimy, foul-smelling liquid off them. Those who swallowed the salt water with fuel oil vomited ferociously until it seemed their stomachs were turned inside out.

Consequently, we concluded the survivors in the life rafts were in the safest place they could be right now. We had immediately alerted COM-SUBPAC following the impact, and no doubt the Japanese vessel had sent off some distress signals as well. Help was on the way. All we could do was to stand by and wait.

A Coast Guard helicopter was on the scene within fifteen minutes of our distress call. Media helicopters arrived in less than forty minutes, having heard the distress calls on shortwave radio bands. A U.S. Coast Guard vessel approached about a half-hour later, making the trip from Honolulu Harbor in just thirty-six minutes. We watched from a distance as the Coast Guard crew pulled the survivors from the sea. When all the life rafts had been evacuated, I spoke by radio with the Coast Guard's on-scene commander, Robert Schmidt.

"All twenty-six are accounted for," the commander told me.

"Thank you, Jesus," I said instinctively. I thought the commander meant that the trawler carried only twenty-six passengers and crewmembers, and all had been rescued. I started to breathe a sigh of relief.

"Captain . . ." the commander spoke quietly.

"Yes, sir?"

"Sir . . ."

"Yes?"

"Sir . . . the captain of the trawler says nine people are still missing and presumed to be dead."

NO! I silently screamed. I suddenly felt like my heart was being ripped out of my chest.

CHAPTER 15

TEARS AND FEARS

On the afternoon of February 9, Japanese Prime Minister Mori had been playing golf when he was first informed about the accident. Apparently, he didn't realize the importance of the message, because he continued his round before giving the matter any further attention. His apparent indifference to a tragedy of this magnitude eventually led to his ouster as prime minister. He would not be the only person whose life was thrown into disarray as a result of my mistakes.

The search-and-rescue operation continued all afternoon and into the night. At first, the captain of the Japanese trawler, Hisao Onishi, had reported ten people were still missing, but in the shock and confusion, he had forgotten to include himself among the ranks of the survivors. He later revised the number still missing to be nine, several of whom were students.

The accident had occurred shortly before 2:00 in the afternoon. It was 4:00 P.M. by the time the Coast Guard felt certain that all the survivors had been plucked from the sea, and dusk had already begun to envelop the island of Oahu. It would be nightfall by the time the *Greeneville* could get back in to Pearl Harbor. Since submarines do not normally travel the narrow port channels after dark, Admiral Fargo made the decision in conjunction with the command onshore to keep the *Greeneville* out at sea all night.

I didn't understand the decision to keep us out all night, but orders were orders. I would have rather brought the sub in that night. To me, the darkness was not that big of a deal. Submarines operate in the dark under the sea all the time. We depend on our electronic "eyes and ears" to navigate. More importantly, I wasn't certain to what degree our boat had been damaged in the collision and wouldn't be able to ascertain any potential danger until we got back to the pier. Beyond that, I had sixteen traumatized visitors on board a submarine. Moreover, had we come in at night, we could possibly avoid some of the media frenzy that certainly would accompany our arrival in broad daylight.

No doubt, part of this decision was a public relations ploy, intended to give the impression that the *Greeneville* was actively involved in the search-and-rescue attempts. In truth, however, the ocean was entirely too rough to attempt to get anyone on or off the submarine that night. Even our sixteen distinguished visitors were forced to stay with us. We'd just have to try to make them as comfortable as possible.

I climbed down the twenty-foot ladder from the upper area of the bridge and walked down to the wardroom to speak to our guests. They were huddled together in a state of shock, their faces pale and their expressions sullen and filled with disbelief that this nightmare was happening. Several of the women were sobbing when I walked in.

"This certainly wasn't part of our scheduled events," I spoke softly to the group. "A horrible accident has occurred. Apparently, we have hit another vessel. I can't tell you what is going to happen next. But I can only ask you to do this," I paused and took a deep breath. "Tell the truth. Remember what you saw," I implored everyone. "Remember what you heard. Don't embellish anything. If there's anything you don't understand, then just stick with the facts as you know them." I paused again momentarily, looked down at the floor, and said, "And I am so sorry."

The silence in the room was almost palpable. Finally, one of the visitors spoke up and said, "We're sorry too."

Tears flowed freely from men and women alike. I hated to do it, but I had to inform the passengers that we'd be staying out overnight.

One young woman nearly panicked. "How are our families going to know that we're okay? I've got a mother who has a heart condition. If she finds out that I'm on a submarine that's had a collision, she might have a heart attack!"

Another woman sobbed, "My babies! My children are going to be worried about me."

"I'm so sorry," I repeated about a thousand times. "We've been directed to remain out overnight to assist in search-and-rescue efforts. We have asked COMSUBPAC to notify your next of kin, to let them know that everyone on board is okay. We must stay here tonight, and we'll get you in as soon as possible in the morning. My crew will do all we can to make you comfortable. Please try to understand. I'm so sorry this has happened." I could resonate with the guests; I longed to be home with my wife and daughter and away from the shadow of death around us, but I had eighty-five other men on board, all of whom had family members or friends who were expecting them home that night. There was no way to notify them all. They'd find out what had happened soon enough.

Later, I went to John Hall privately. I could tell he was especially shaken. John was the civilian who had actually pulled the emergency blow lever, with the help of one of our sailor's hands interlocked with his. I could see the awful look of despair in John's face. I sensed he was thinking, *I've done this horrible thing. It's my fault. I'm responsible.*

I understood all too well the tormenting thoughts haunting John, so I went to him and said, "Look, John. This was not your fault. Once the emergency blow begins, it doesn't really matter who is at the controls. The submarine is going up. Your presence there didn't cause this accident, nor could you have changed the outcome. It didn't matter who was in that chair, who was standing at the controls, or who initiated the action. I called for the emergency blow; I'm responsible. This is not your fault."

John thanked me for attempting to console him, but I could tell it was going to be a long time before he could put this tragedy behind him.

I went to my stateroom adjacent to the control room, sat down at my desk, and buried my head in my hands. By now, I had learned the name of the ship we had struck—the *Ehime Maru*, a large four-hundred-ton teaching vessel operated by a Japanese fisheries school, apparently in conjunction with Uwajima High School. In addition to the crewmembers, the people on board were students and teachers, most of them male, most of them young.

I replayed every sequence of the day's events over and over in my thoughts. Questions pummeled my mind. What had gone wrong? How had this happened? One question nagged relentlessly: *How could that Japanese ship have closed the distance between us without the crew of the* Greeneville *knowing it? Why had I not seen it? Why hadn't I known the vessel was there?*

At several points through the night, Captain Brandhuber came to my stateroom to check on me. He put his hand on my shoulder and asked, "How are you holding up, Skipper?" The chief of staff looked down at me pensively. "What are you thinking?"

"I'm not," I hollowly replied.

"Are you okay, Skipper?" he asked.

"Yes, sir. I'm fine," I lied.

"Are you going to hang in there?"

"Yes, sir. I'll get us safely back into port." Everything within me was screaming to die, but I spoke quietly, "Captain, I just don't know how I missed this guy."

"I don't either, but we'll figure it out," Brandhuber replied, looking down at the floor.

I really didn't expect Captain Brandhuber to offer much encouragement. After all, nothing like this had ever happened in the history of the U.S. Navy's submarine force. Collisions had occurred before. Admiral Chester Nimitz, the World War II commander in chief of the Pacific Fleet, and himself an early submariner, had once suffered a collision, but it was at wartime. We were not. During the Cold War, our submarines had collided with the Soviets a time or two. Then in Guam during the mid-1980s, we had a tugboat that lost power and drifted backward while performing a personnel transfer with a Trident submarine. One of the sub's stern plane vertical stabilizers caught under the tug, gashing a hole in the vessel, and it sank, killing two men. The entire catastrophe had been caught on videotape by the crew, so the submarine captain was exonerated. The Navy was accustomed to accidents. But never in U.S. naval history had a collision between a nuclear submarine and a civilian vessel caused the loss of so many lives.

Sometime during the night, John Hall came out of the officers' wardroom and looked into my stateroom. I was still sitting in the dark at my desk, with my head in my hands. The always-on, red gas-plasma screen adjacent to my bunk that showed the latest data on the ship's position, course, speed, and other vital information cast an eerie red glow over the room.

I didn't know at the time that John was looking at me, so I didn't say a word. John backed out of the doorway, went back to the wardroom, and wept. He later said, "At that moment, I didn't know how the captain was going to live with this awful burden."

Neither did I.

CHAPTER 16

THE END OF THE LINE

I didn't sleep more than a few minutes on Friday night. I laid awake in my bunk listening to the emergency distress communications on channel 13, monitoring the rescue efforts but knowing in my heart and mind that it was hopeless to think that any additional survivors would be found. I knew within ten minutes of the accident that any people who were not in the *Ehime Maru* life rafts were not likely to be alive.

By the time the sun rose on Saturday, February 10, I had already been up for several hours. Under other circumstances, I'd have been excited about getting back to port. It was a bright, beautiful Saturday morning, and the sandy beaches of Oahu were beginning to fill with sunbathers. Looking out to sea, the cloudless blue sky melded into an unalloyed turquoise and dark blue ocean. Viewing the tropical paradise from the bridge of the *Greeneville*, it was hard to believe that the horrors of yesterday had occurred. But when I glanced at the *Greeneville*'s sail and saw the damaged metal, the grim reminders were all too real.

The ship's cook prepared a makeshift breakfast for the distinguished visitors, so I met with them one last time that morning in the wardroom before they were to be transferred to a "torpedo retriever," a small vessel used to transfer passengers on and off submarines moored in Pearl Harbor. I had not finished signing all the pictures of the *Greeneville* for our guests, so as we waited for the transfer vessel, I sat down and signed the remaining photos. It was an innocuous gesture of kindness on my part that was later thrown back in my face when my critics taunted, "Even at the end, Scott Waddle didn't have the ability to turn off the public relations persona."

I wanted our guests to understand that what they had experienced was a rare accident, an aberration. I told the visitors, "You came here for a visit, and I'm sorry it didn't turn out the way we all anticipated." I handed out some of the photographs, along with the Texas state flags from our lunch table. "We also have some saltwater samples that we collected for you when we were down at test depth. This obviously didn't end the way we wanted it to. It has really been a tragic event, but I appreciate the fact that you came out. I'm so sorry things have happened the way they have."

The visitors expressed their appreciation, awkward as it may have been. None of them refused the pictures or tokens of our trip. No one appeared cognizant of the historic implications of what we had experienced together.

As we headed in toward Honolulu Harbor, suddenly a large Japanese fishing vessel cut right in front of the *Greeneville*, challenging us. I could hardly believe my eyes! The ship was almost identical to the *Ehime Maru*, the ship that we had hit the day before. It was obvious that whoever was driving that vessel was making a deliberate statement by cutting across our path. I ordered a "back emergency bell" to immediately stop the *Greeneville's* forward motion, and we backed down quickly to avoid colliding with the Japanese ship. This incident was a preview of coming attractions.

Just inside the Pearl Harbor channel, we were met by the torpedo retriever, the smaller vessel that had come out to pick up our passengers. Commodore Rich Snead and Catholic Navy chaplain Commander Dick Pusateri accompanied the transfer vessel and boarded the *Greeneville*. I stood on the bridge, along with the officer of the deck and a lookout, and watched as the small boat transfer took place, allowing the civilians to disembark from the submarine onto the torpedo retriever.

After our distinguished visitors had disembarked, Commodore Snead climbed up to the bridge of the *Greeneville* for the short ride into Pearl Harbor pier. Snead was particularly somber and stoic. He didn't say a word, but stood with me, looking straight ahead. Ironically, this was the only time my boss had ever ridden aboard my ship.

As we rounded the bend at Hospital Point in Pearl Harbor, I could see my house over to the right, but the sight that greeted me caused me to wince. A swarm of television cameramen, print photographers and journalists, and other members of the media were camped within seventy-five feet of our front yard! I later learned that Commodore Snead had called Jill at home to inform her of the accident. Jill and Ashley had already been whisked away from the madcap scene. Almost instinctively, before leaving the property, Jill had pulled down the name plaque in front of our house, so the media didn't know that they were waiting right in the front yard of the *Greeneville*'s skipper.

Helicopters hovered overhead as the *Greeneville* slowly glided into port, with television news crews vying for the best camera angles. I knew this was going to be my last landing, and it better be a good one, because millions of people were likely to see it on their evening newscasts. A lot of people were likely to be interested in how the *Greeneville* did business.

A tugboat met us, and I asked the tug's captain to stay on the right side of us—between the shore and our ship, shielding my men who were topside from the media cameras—during the final few hundred yards of my final trip. Ordinarily, the families and friends onshore share the excitement of the submarine coming in to the pier, but today, the mood was somber. This was not a celebration. We were not coming in as heroes. We were coming in as a "killer sub," the notorious *Greeneville* that had just blasted through a Japanese trawler, killing nine civilians. This was not a time to stand tall and proud, though as American seamen, we tried to maintain the best Navy decorum we could muster.

I caught a glimpse of my wife, Jill, and our thirteen-year-old daughter, Ashley, who had come to watch my return. They were standing on the pier, along with the other family members of the crew. On a better day, I would have waved to them, but not today. Memories of the many happy reunions we had shared upon my return from duty through the years flooded my mind. They were always exuberant, happy occasions. But this was different. This was like a death dirge. Wives and children onshore were somber; some were already in tears. Everyone knew what this meant.

We moored at 10:00 A.M. As soon as the crew tied up the ship, one of the first people to come aboard was Admiral Konetzni, commander of the Submarine Force, U.S. Pacific Fleet. The admiral was his usual upbeat self as he addressed the crew over the ship's communication system. "We'll get through this," he said. "This is a tragic thing, but don't worry, we're going to take care of the tribe." The crew listened respectfully, but everyone knew that life aboard the *Greeneville* would never be the same. After the admiral addressed the crew, I spoke over the ship's communication system what would turn out to be my last personal message to my crew. "Tell the truth," I encouraged them. "Remember what you saw here. We need to figure out what happened so the men who lost their lives will not have died in vain." It was one of the most stomach-wrenching speeches I'd ever given.

I went to my stateroom to meet with the admiral. He was dressed in his khakis, and as soon as I walked in, he stood up, grabbed my shoulders, and said, "How are you, buddy?" We talked briefly, and I said, "Admiral, I am so sorry. I don't know how this happened."

"You need to go see your bride," the admiral said, nodding toward the shore where Jill was waiting. "Then come back and see me." There was no admonition from the admiral to be careful of what I said, and no effort on his part to create some sort of spin control for the media.

"Yes, sir."

The admiral spoke flatly, "Scott, I need to see you in my office in about an hour and a half."

"Yes, sir," I saluted, as Admiral Konetzni turned to leave.

Commodore Snead echoed, "Stop by my office before you go to see the admiral."

"Yes, sir," I replied.

I climbed up the forward escape hatch, walked off the ship to the pier, and met Jill and Ashley on the shore. We hugged tightly, and I whispered to Jill, "I am so sorry. I know this is going to be hard. This was an accident. I don't know how it happened."

"It'll be all right, Scott. I'm sorry it happened. Don't worry. We'll be okay," Jill tried to reassure me. We were both near tears, and I knew if I stayed much longer, I was going to lose my composure completely. "I've got to go back to the ship. There are some things I need to do," I said.

Jill nodded. I gave her a quick kiss, hugged and kissed Ashley, and turned to go.

I was dog-tired and emotionally exhausted, but when I returned to the ship, Captain Fred Byus, the commodore of Submarine Squadron Seven, was waiting for me in the officers' wardroom. Along with him were a representative of the National Transportation Safety Board (NTSB), a couple of Coast Guard officers, and Barry Henson, a Navy JAGC officer.

"We need to get a statement, Scott, while everything is fresh in your mind," Captain Byus said. "Sit down. Tell us what happened out there. What do you remember?"

I sat down at the table and willingly answered all of their questions, never once thinking that perhaps it might be unwise to do so. Nor was I informed that anything I might say could be used against me in a court of law. Nor was I told that Captain Byus's job was to determine whether a preliminary Navy inquiry should be conducted. I was simply fulfilling my obligation to the Navy. My superior officers were asking questions, and I tried to answer them as best I could. "I don't know what happened, sir, but here's what I saw. Here's what I did." The officers grilled me for nearly an hour. When they were satisfied I'd given them as much information as I knew, they dismissed me and called in my executive officer, Jerry Pfeifer, and the officer of the deck, Mike Coen, and questioned them outside of my presence.

My chief of the boat, Doug Coffman, drove me over to the Squadron office, across the street from the COMSUBPAC offices, and, as ordered, we went first to the office of my squadron commander, Commodore Rich Snead.

Doug remained in the van, while Commodore Snead and I walked across the street to the admiral's office in the Pearl Harbor complex. Commodore Snead waited outside Admiral Konetzni's office while I went in to meet with him privately.

I glanced around the admiral's spacious office as I waited. Many items of Navy memorabilia were displayed on the admiral's walls, including numerous hats from the various ships he had been aboard, and items from foreign allies in the Pacific. The room had a heavy scent of cigar smoke. Although, technically, smoking was not allowed in government buildings, the admiral could smoke wherever he wanted . . . and did so.

The gravity of the situation weighed heavily on me—an American submarine ramming a Japanese vessel near Pearl Harbor, of all places! Yet, while I was concerned how the Navy might handle the mess, I wasn't worried about me or my job. Silly me! I thought sure that the Navy would see this incident for what it was, a freak accident. Awful as it was, it was not an intentional dereliction of duty or some other punishable offense. Anyone could clearly see that it was an *accident*. The *Greeneville* had done everything right. Surely the Japanese vessel must have been dead in the water; otherwise we'd have heard it. It certainly had not been emitting any fish-finding signals. If it had been, my crew would have known it was there. There was no possible way that I could lose my command.

Admiral Konetzni was a two-star admiral, and he was my boss; but more than that, he was my mentor. I looked to him as a father in the Navy, and he had often said that he looked at me as a son. I had no fear about meeting with the admiral. I was nervous because of the seriousness of the situation, but Admiral Konetzni was my friend.

I sat down across from the admiral's desk, and he sat in his chair behind the desk. He was straightforward. "Scott, this is something I don't want to do." He pushed a piece of paper across the desk in my direction. I leaned over and picked up the official-looking document. The words hit me like a sledgehammer to the stomach: "Effective immediately, you are hereby detached for cause as commanding officer of the USS *Greenville*." For the first time since the impact, I suddenly realized that I was being fired. The paper effectively relieved me of my command *immediately*. Captain Tony Cortese, a friend of mine, would be the interim commander of the *Greeneville* until a permanent replacement was assigned.

I had expected to be reprimanded, disciplined even. I had, after all, just smashed up one of the most expensive military machines in the world. The Navy wasn't going to pat me on the back and say, "Bad break. You really need to improve your driving." People had died because of my decisions!

Intellectually, I understood the seriousness of my mistakes, but in the back of my mind, I assumed the Navy would consider their investment in me worth salvaging. I'd even considered that perhaps the Navy might put me on some sort of administrative leave for a while, similar to a police officer whose actions are investigated when someone is killed by one of his bullets. After a reasonable amount of time, I had hopes of returning to my ship. But as the admiral slid that paper across his desk, I realized there would be no reprimand, no leave of absence. As far as the Navy was concerned, I was history. I was gone! Adding insult to injury, the Navy had misspelled the name of my ship. In the order dismissing me from command, the *Greeneville* was misspelled as *Greenville*. Regardless of the spelling, the message was undeniable.

Twenty years of hard work suddenly flashed before my eyes, and I could see it swirling to the bottom of the ocean. Twenty years of trying to be a good leader, an upbeat spokesman for the Navy, a mentor to hundreds of men; twenty years of working to be the best naval officer I could possibly be. It was all wrapped up in that paper the admiral slid across the desk.

"You'll be temporarily assigned to my staff," the admiral said. "We'll get you a desk job doing something until the completion of this investigation. You'll report to Captain Al Gonzales to work there." Tears glistened in Admiral Konetzni's eyes as he acknowledged that my naval career was over. "I love ya, buddy," he said, discarding any semblance of formal military language and attitude.

I looked back at him through my own tears. "I love you too," I replied. "And I know this is tough. It's tough on me, and I know it's tough on you." We stood and shook hands, and I walked out the admiral's door.

Doug Coffman was waiting for me in a Navy van. When he saw me approaching, holding the paper, he broke down and cried. Doug drove me back to the *Greeneville*, where I gathered a few boxes and went to my stateroom. I pulled out my duffel bag and started packing my belongings. Several of my men came by, and in an effort to be consoling, yet not knowing what to say or do, they just stood outside my stateroom. "Can we give you a hand, Captain? Is there something we can do for you, sir?"

"Fellows, thanks, but no thanks," I replied. I continued cleaning out my desk, carefully handling each item as memories flooded my mind. Each article I packed into the box held special significance for me. A few pictures, plaques, awards—the stateroom on a submarine does not allow space for a lot of excess materials. As I removed each article from the stateroom and packed it in a box, I felt as though I was tightening down a vice grip on my heart. Within thirty minutes, I had packed up the mementoes of my naval career and walked off my ship.

Doug drove me to my house. We said little as we unloaded the boxes, and then my chief of the boat and I shook hands. Neither of us knew what to say, but there was no need for words. With tears welling in his eyes, Doug hastily headed to the van.

I walked inside the house where Jill was waiting for me, concern written all over her face. "Oh, Scott . . ." she blurted as the tears welled in her eyes. We instinctively fell into each other's arms and simply stood there in the doorway for the longest time, just holding onto each other. Words refused to come.

People outside the Waddle family had lots of words for me. Our telephone rang incessantly. At first Jill tried to field the calls, accepting the kind, consoling words of friends, much as a family member would when someone in the family has died, and shielding me from the more intrusive callers. Before long, members of the media began calling from all over the world, particularly from Japan.

I didn't want to talk to anyone. Finally, I just said to Jill, "Turn it off. Pull the phone line out of the wall if you have to, but shut it off!"

I slumped down onto the couch and turned on the television. My face was all over the screen. The *Greeneville* accident was now national news. I quickly turned off the television.

Ashley bounded down from upstairs. "Hi, Dad!" she called cheerfully. She knew better than to try to talk with me just then, so she went on outside, calling out to me as she went, "Love ya, Dad!"

"I love you, too, Ashley." I didn't move from the couch.

I just didn't want to see anyone right then, so I went upstairs and checked the e-mail on my home computer. I was inundated with notes from friends around the world. I tried to read a few of them, but the enormity of the accident and attempting to make sense of it was impossible to express in a brief response to friends who had sent notes, offering encouragement or asking questions. I turned off the computer.

Later on Saturday afternoon, I called my father. A retired Air Force colonel, he had been planning to come to Hawaii from his home in Austin, Texas, to spend a few days with me on Maui, playing golf and enjoying some all-too-rare time together. I figured I'd better call him to let him know there'd been a change in plans. I could tell from the moment that he answered the phone that my dad wasn't concerned about golf; he'd seen the news reports and was concerned about me. We talked about the accident, and I dropped my guard. "Dad, why did this happen? Why did God allow it to happen?"

A lifelong Christian, my dad heard the cry of my heart. "I don't know, son," he answered. "But God didn't make that ship, and God didn't make the sub. Man made those ships, and when the two of them collided and nine people died, that was not God's doing, but man's. And God wept. But God has a purpose in everything, and if He allowed this tragedy to occur, sooner or later, you will discover what His plan is."

Then my father told me of his 1959 jet fighter plane crash in northern Japan that narrowly avoided any loss of life. I was struck by the irony that a few months after I had been born, my dad had nearly killed some Japanese schoolchildren in a freak accident.

"Dad, are you sure you still want to come to Hawaii?" I asked him.

"Yeah, now more than ever," Dad replied.

Dad gave me some good advice and wise fatherly counsel. "We'll get through this, son. Scott, I love you. Take care of your family, and be sure to give your wife and daughter a hug."

"I love you, too, Dad. Thanks. I'll look forward to seeing you."

I later called my sister and my stepdad, and they expressed similar sentiments. I talked with them, but I was numb. I was mentally and physically exhausted. The atmosphere around our home felt as though we had experienced a death in our own family. Jane Daly, wife of Pete Daly, the executive assistant to Admiral Thomas Fargo, the man before whom I'd eventually have to give an account, prepared all sorts of delicious food and brought it to our home. Tracey Davidson, whose husband, Phil, was the special assistant to Admiral Fargo, did the same. We received incredible support from the Navy community in which we lived.

But nothing anyone could say or do could bring back the nine lives that had been lost at sea.

I tried to sleep on Saturday night but kept waking up in a cold sweat, reliving the accident over and over. Finally, at about 4:00 in the morning, I crawled out of bed, trying not to disturb Jill's sleep. I went downstairs and walked past our coffee table, on which was sitting a small statue with a ceremonial Russian naval officers' dagger. I glanced at the dagger and stopped short. I stood there staring at the dagger, and suddenly I felt an attack worse than anything I'd ever have experienced in the military. Evil seemed to flood my soul, as my mind entered one of the darkest caverns I'd ever known.

It would be so easy to take that dagger, I thought, *and to go upstairs and put Ashley down and then take care of Jill, and then myself. Then our family wouldn't have to endure any more of this ugliness and pain.*

I shook my head hard, as though snapping out of a trance, and said aloud, "What are you thinking about? That is so *wrong!* Where did that come from?"

I had never before thought of suicide under any circumstances, and I had even questioned the courage and intelligence of those who had taken that route. Yet now it seemed like a logical solution to a problem that was going to haunt us for the rest of our lives. I suddenly felt overwhelmed with incredible compassion for people who felt so hopeless and helpless, and for the first time, I understood a little of their plight. But I also knew such thoughts were coming right out of the pit of hell, and I rejected them.

I walked out to a bench near the water, the same spot that had been lined with camera crews that morning. I sat down, staring blankly out at Pearl Harbor. I was lost, devastated, and for the first time in my life had no idea what I was going to do. The water looked peaceful and tranquil. For a long time I sat there, just thinking, praying, and reflecting. "God, why has this horrible thing happened?" I cried.

Eventually, I walked back inside and climbed the stairs to Jill's and my bedroom. I crawled back in bed and waited for the dawn.

CHAPTER 17

SPIRITUAL STRENGTH

On Sunday morning I asked Jill, "Honey, do you want to go to church?"

Jill, who was still weary and emotionally wounded from the ordeal, said, "Scott, I don't think I can handle going to church this morning. I'm sorry. I don't want to leave the house today."

I understood, so I didn't press it. I was physically and emotionally exhausted myself. I hadn't slept now for two nights, and my entire body and mind were simply numb. Nevertheless, I felt that I needed to be in the company of other believers that morning; I needed the fellowship and consolation of our spiritual family. So I got dressed and drove over to St. George's Episcopal Church, near Hickam Air Force Base, in time for the 9:20 A.M. service. Our church family in Hawaii had been an integral part of our lives for many years. I had attended St. George's as a teenager, when my sister and I had spent the summer of 1976 with my father and my stepmother. Jill and I had attended St. George's during my two previous tours of duty in Hawaii, and now that we were back, it was natural that we should return to worship with that same congregation. Our daughter, Ashley, was an acolyte in the church, and I was a lay reader. Anytime I was in port, I was glad to read the Scripture during our church services.

People appeared genuinely surprised to see me at church that morning. "Where's Jill?" they asked. "Where's Ashley?"

"They didn't want to come this morning," I answered honestly.

The congregation of St. George's was comprised predominantly of military families, so I didn't have to say anything more; they understood.

One of the first people I saw when I walked in the back door of the church was Joe Diana, Ashley's Sunday school teacher. Joe was the aide de camp, the number one assistant, to Admiral Dennis Blair, the commander in chief of Pacific Command, the commander of the entire U.S. military force in the Pacific theater, including the Army, Navy, Marines, and Air Force. Joe grabbed me and gave me a big bear hug. "I feel so bad for you," he said.

"Joe, you don't know. I feel so bad too. Nine people are dead."

"I know, Scott. Come on, let's pray." Before I even walked into the service, Joe prayed for me that I might have strength and that I might represent the Lord well in whatever I said and did. We prayed for the families of the victims, and we prayed for strength for my family, that we could withstand the attention that was sure to be focused on me during the aftermath of the accident.

"Joe, please tell the admiral I am so sorry," I said.

"He knows, Scott, he knows," Joe said. "Admiral Blair is a pretty smart guy."

"Do you think I could have his home number so I could call him?" I asked. Ordinarily, Joe would never give out the admiral's phone number, but these were not ordinary circumstances, and Joe must have seen the desperation in my eyes. He took out a pen and scribbled the number on a scrap of paper. I called the admiral later that day and apologized to him personally. Admiral Blair accepted my apology and expressed his own regrets and understanding of how I felt.

The church was relatively small, only about twenty rows of people. Jill, Ashley, and I almost always sat near the front, in the second row, on the outside edge near the wall. On this Sunday, though, I was by myself, and I wasn't

sure that I wanted to be so visible. Instead, I was tempted to find an incon-
spicuous seat in the back of the congregation. But then I thought, *No, this is
where I belong. I know these people and they know me. They are my spiritual family.* Church was the one place where I felt safe. As I walked into God's house,
I immediately was overwhelmed by feelings of peace, calm, comfort, solace,
and support. I could feel it the moment I walked in. I walked to the area
where my family ordinarily sat and sat down by myself.

Pastor Liz Beasley's sermon was fitting that day, as she talked about the
tragedies in life and what happens when they hit home. Of course, she
included the *Greeneville's* accident in her message. Liz acknowledged that
many sincere believers experience unexplainable tragedies and crises in life,
yet even in the midst of those times of devastation, if we allow Him to do so,
God will bring good out of them. During the sermon, Liz alluded to the Old
Testament character Job, a good man who had lost everything he'd ever held
dear because of an attack of Satan. I could relate. I had never read the entire
story of Job in the Bible, but as I listened to Pastor Beasley's message that
morning, I promised myself that I'd read it soon.

By early Sunday afternoon, February 11, the United States government was
doing everything in its power to apologize to the Japanese government and
its people. President Bush led the way with an apology. On national television, the president said, "I want to reiterate what I said to the prime minister of Japan: I'm deeply sorry about the accident that took place; our nation
is sorry." Secretary of State Colin Powell expressed his apologies as well. So
did Secretary of Defense Donald Rumsfeld. The U.S. ambassador to Japan,
Thomas S. Foley, apologized twice, once to Japanese Prime Minister Mori,
and once to the emperor.

As noble as those efforts to express our national regret may have been, I
knew that the Japanese people, and especially the families who had lost loved
ones, were waiting to hear from the man who was responsible for the accident. In Japan, an apology is a matter of honor; in the United States, an apology is often regarded as an admission of guilt. I understood that, but I still

felt that I wanted to express my sorrow to the Japanese people in some formal manner. I wasn't looking to make a big show of my apology; it was simply the right thing to do.

After church on Sunday, I called Commander Dave Warner, the public
affairs officer of COMSUBPAC, and offered to apologize to the Japanese
families who had lost loved ones in the accident. Dave knew me well, and we
had worked together often on Navy public relations events such as the distinguished visitors program, personal tours of the *Greeneville*, and other
informal requests. The public affairs office always knew they could count on
me whenever they needed to entertain visitors or when last-minute opportunities came up. We had a good relationship, so I felt no qualms about calling him.

"Dave, what's going on over there?" I asked. "I saw on television this
morning that the families of the victims arrived in Honolulu late last night
and that Admiral Fargo is going to meet with them this afternoon to give
them a report and an apology. Is that right?"

"Yes, Admiral Fargo is going downtown to meet with the Japanese families, and he will apparently offer an apology."

"Dave, would you call his office and see if I can accompany him? I would
like to go down to meet with the families and to apologize."

"Ah, well . . ." Dave hedged. "I don't know, Scott. I've got to clear it
through the CINPAC Fleet public affairs office; I'll have to get back to you."

"Dave, when do I get to apologize? The president has apologized, Colin
Powell has apologized, Secretary Rumsfeld and who knows how many others have apologized. The guy the Japanese families really need to hear from
is *me.*"

"I'll get back to you, Scott."

I waited all day Sunday, hoping for Commander Warner to call me back.
He never did. Nor did anyone else from his office call me back that day.
Later that afternoon, I called the public affairs office again and was told that
it wasn't possible for me to join Admiral Fargo in apologizing. Perhaps they
felt the matter was too sensitive or the timing wasn't right or that emotions
were running too high.

That night, I watched the television newscasts and saw clips of Admiral Fargo spouting sound bites for the media about how sorry the U.S. Navy was for this tragedy. For whatever reason, we missed an important opportunity to express the captain's remorse to the victims' families. It was a mistake that would be repeatedly thrown in the face of America in the weeks to follow.

CHAPTER 18

IT'S HARD TO SAY "I'M SORRY"

On Monday morning, Jill, Ashley, and I got up and tried to pretend it was a normal day—with Ashley getting ready for school and me getting ready for work. I reported to Admiral Konetzni's office for my assignment, but I really had no job to go to. I was assigned to Captain Al Gonzales, Admiral Konetzni's deputy chief of staff who handled personnel issues within the Pacific submarine force. Captain Gonzales readily admitted that he had no idea what to do with me. "Here's an empty desk where you can set up camp," he said, nodding to a cubicle in the office complex. "We'll get you some projects to get started on before long."

"Thanks, Captain," I said. "I don't know how much good I'm going to be to you. But I'm told this is where I'm supposed to work. I do know that I've got to get some legal help, so would it be okay if I went over to legal services?"

"Sure," Captain Gonzales replied. "Take what time you need, but if you want to take time off, be sure to fill out leave papers." Whether the captain was encouraging me to seek help or he was just glad to have me out of his hair for a while, I'm not certain. It didn't matter to me. I realized that I needed legal counsel, so I decided that since I was going to be in the COM-SUBPAC office area anyhow, I'd stop in and talk to someone in the naval legal counsel office.

Interestingly, by Saturday, February 10, the Navy had already initiated a full-fledged internal investigation into the incident, based on the recommendation of Commodore Fred Byus, who had spearheaded the preliminary investigation. Admiral Konetzni assigned Admiral Charles Griffiths, commander of Submarine Group Nine, the Trident ballistic missile submarines in Bremerton, Washington, as the investigating officer, arranging to fly him in from the state of Washington. Admiral Griffiths immediately dropped what he was doing and flew to Hawaii from Seattle. The U.S. Department of Defense officials had been in contact with the Japanese government; the U.S. Navy and Pacific Command were working with the Japanese consulate in Hawaii to provide medical care, lodging, and transportation back to Japan for the survivors of the *Ehime Maru*. About the only person involved in the accident not being addressed was me. In a culture so predominantly governed by orders from a superior officer, I was surprisingly all alone, cut loose to fend for myself. Nobody from the government or the Navy had given me any advice about anything. I didn't know what I should or shouldn't do; I didn't know if I was free to talk about the incident or if I should just keep as low a profile as possible. I honestly didn't have a clue what the Navy wanted me to do.

I was hoping the Navy judge advocate general's corps office could help give me some direction when I stopped in on Monday morning. There I met Lieutenant Commander Kimberlie Young, a bright, articulate attorney. I told Commander Young my story of what had occurred aboard the *Greeneville* on Friday. She listened attentively, wrote down some notes, and seemed genuinely interested in helping me. That's why I was surprised when she responded so cautiously.

"I don't know that I can form an attorney-client relationship with you,"

Kimberlie said. "I'll have to find out. But then again, since we've already talked about the event, perhaps we already have. This is a unique situation for me."

"Me too," I replied. "I've never had to seek legal counsel before. I wasn't even sure where to start. That's why I came here."

"Well, this isn't our normal sort of case . . ." she said.

I knew what Commander Young was implying. The majority of her cases dealt with relatively minor offenses—serious matters, but usually not earthshaking. As a member of the JAGC, she mostly defended young enlisted men and women who had gotten into some sort of trouble driving under the influence of alcohol, roughhousing during leave, drug problems, and other discipline issues—but nothing portending the potential international storm or the personal consequences to me that the *Greeneville* accident represented.

But I liked Kimberlie's style and her personality. She was well organized and very businesslike, yet she was also extremely personable and charismatic. She seemed to march to her own drumbeat, and I related well to that. Most importantly, I trusted her.

"Let me make some phone calls, and we'll see what we can do," she said, standing and shaking hands, indicating our conference had concluded.

I went back to my nonexistent job at the admiral's office. For the next few days, I lived in limbo, going through the motions of being a naval officer. The one place I felt accepted and secure was down on the pier. Everywhere I went, sailors on the waterfront called out to me, "Hey, Skipper! How're you doing? We're pulling for you, sir." The guys at the sub piers knew me; they knew that I cared about them, and they cared about what was happening to me.

Meanwhile, Admiral Griffiths, incorporating information gathered by Captain Byus and others, completed the preliminary inquiry into the *Greeneville's* collision with the *Ehime Maru*. On February 16, the report was turned over to Admiral Thomas Fargo, commander of the Pacific Fleet. The following day, Admiral Fargo announced that the Navy would convene an official court of inquiry, the Navy's highest form of an administrative hearing.

The court of inquiry is similar to a grand jury investigation in civil court in that it provides legal safeguards for the affected parties, as well as complete subpoena power for witnesses to be called and their testimony heard publicly. It also provides that the affected parties be afforded their due process rights, including their right to be represented by counsel.

The court of inquiry is slightly different from a grand jury, since it is a military administrative investigation and there is no judge. Three admirals make up the court, and it is their job to find the facts and make a report. It is not a court-martial, but it could lead to court-martial, conviction, and imprisonment.

Admiral Konetzni could have nixed any further investigation of the incident after the preliminary inquiry. But because the *Greeneville–Ehime Maru* incident was stirring up such an international ruckus, he turned the matter over to Admiral Fargo. Moreover, Admiral Konetzni was anxious to show that no one other than the sailors on board the *Greeneville* was culpable and that he and his staff were exonerated of any responsibility. By deciding to go forward with the court of inquiry, Admiral Fargo was indicating to the world the seriousness of the incident, and just how seriously the U.S. Navy viewed my role and those of Executive Officer Jerry Pfeifer and Officer of the Deck Mike Coen. All three of us were named as "parties to the inquiry"—in other words, defendants.

In a press conference at Pearl Harbor on February 17, Admiral Fargo explained, "The court will be constituted of three U.S. Navy flag officers and will be led by Vice Admiral John B. Nathman, the commander of naval air forces in the U.S. Pacific Fleet; Rear Admiral Paul F. Sullivan, the director of plans and policy at the U.S. strategic command; and Rear Admiral David M. Stone, the commander of Cruiser/Destroyer Group Five."

It seemed clear to me that Admiral Fargo was pulling out the "big guns" for this duty.

Then the admiral shocked the world of jurisprudence. "We also intend to invite Japan to send a Japanese Maritime Self-Defense Force flag officer to participate as an adviser," said Admiral Fargo.

Whether the press caught the significance of the admiral's statement is a matter of opinion, but it meant that for the first time in naval history, a Japanese naval officer, with no allegiance to the United States and no oath to uphold the Constitution of the United States, was going to be sitting in as an adviser in a U.S. naval court of inquiry! To me, this was not good news. Moreover, the admiral said, "I expect this court to convene on or about Thursday, February 22, in Pearl Harbor, Hawaii."

Thursday, February 22! That was only five days away!

In the meantime, Kimberlie Young heard from her boss, headquartered in Yokosuka, Japan, ironically the location of the U.S. Navy's Pacific legal service department. Her boss told Kimberlie, "Stop what you are doing immediately. You do *not* have an attorney-client relationship with Commander Waddle. We are sending out an assigned officer, Commander Jennifer Herrold, to represent him as his lead counsel."

When Kimberlie told me what her boss had said, I was upset. "I don't want anybody else to represent me," I said. "I want you."

"I'm sorry, Scott. I can't do it."

"But I want you, not someone I don't even know! Who's this Herrold person, anyhow?"

Kimberlie gave me some background information on Herrold, the military lawyer on her way from Japan to be my defense counsel in what would certainly be an emotion-packed case involving the deaths of nine Japanese civilians. Jennifer Herrold was the officer to whom Kimberlie reported, and Kimberlie admitted that there was no love lost between Jennifer and her. Herrold was a "by-the-book" JAGC, and Young was one who liked to push the envelope. The Navy permitted me to retain Kimberlie on my defense team, but Commander Herrold was directed to be my lead counselor.

Oh, great! I thought. *I'm being assigned a JAGC I'm unsure of, and one who doesn't have a good working relationship with the attorney I've trusted. How are these women going to work together effectively on my behalf?*

I appealed to the Navy's senior legal officer and requested to be represented by Chris Reismeyer out of Norfolk, a well known JAG with formidable experience in representing commanders who had gotten in trouble. Indeed, Reismeyer had been so successful at defending Navy captains against charges leveled at them, it was rumored that he had been passed over for promotion because he had done his job too well. I really wanted Reismeyer to handle my case.

"No," I was told, "according to Navy rules, your legal counsel has to come from within a one-hundred-nautical-mile radius of your command."

A hundred miles? There's nothing but water within a hundred miles of Hawaii! I was puzzled; the Navy JAGC officers representing Jerry Pfeifer and Mike Coen came from San Diego and Mayport, Florida. Captain McDonald, the lead prosecutor for the court, was coming from Bremerton, Washington. Another attorney hailed from Washington, D.C. Clearly a double standard was in play. There was no legal or logical reason that I could not have Chris Reismeyer defend me.

I began to wonder, *What's going on here? This isn't fair. This is going to be a widely publicized case. Why wouldn't the Navy want the best possible counsel to represent me? Why are these guys with whom I have worked for all these years suddenly turning on me, and treating me as if I were some sort of pariah?*

Although I protested vehemently, my request for Chris Reismeyer to represent me was denied. I was reminded again that the closest judge advocates to Hawaii were located in Japan, and the only one available was Jennifer Herrold.

From the moment I met Jennifer Herrold at the airport later that week, I had an uncomfortable feeling about our ability to work together. Married to another military lawyer, Jennifer was about my age or a few years younger than me. Shorter in stature, she looked fatigued when she disembarked her flight. I assumed she was tired because of her long flight, but she looked and acted the same way the following day.

Sports teams call it chemistry; it's either there or it's not. In the military, we think in terms of esprit de corps, camaraderie, and an almost innate sense of who works well together and who does not. If that secret ingredient is missing, it doesn't matter how qualified, talented, or brilliant your people are; the team is not going to click. Jennifer and I did not have it. In fairness to her, she was not feeling well physically, and the spur-of-the-moment trip from Japan to Hawaii didn't help matters. She had served on other legal staffs, and had performed well, but had not recently been involved in litigation in the courtroom.

Not surprisingly, from the beginning, we had differing opinions about how we should prepare for the court of inquiry. Being a stickler for details, I wanted to meticulously describe every little thing about what the *Greeneville* did and how we did it. Jennifer was content with the broad picture. More importantly, I wanted a plan of action, but after three days, Herrold still did not have a detailed plan. I panicked; February 22 was only days away, and it was clear to me that my attorney—if she had a plan—couldn't communicate what she intended to do.

I knew I was in trouble.

In the meantime, I was getting blasted on a daily basis by the local news media in Honolulu. They wrote again and again of the *Greeneville* "ramming" the *Ehime Maru* or "slamming" into the Japanese fishing boat. The local press rarely used the term "accidental collision" and instead portrayed the incident as though the *Greeneville* had overtly, recklessly, almost willfully collided with the Japanese vessel.

I was raked over the coals by the local media. They were not supportive; quite the contrary, most of their reports were hostile, anti-U.S. Navy, and pro-Japanese. Had I not known better, as I watched the television interviews on newscast after newscast, I'd have thought I was watching an English translation of Japanese television.

Jennifer Herrold accompanied me when Admiral Griffiths sent for me to make a statement during his preliminary investigation. "We're going to decline to answer any questions or make any statements," Jennifer told me before we went.

"Good idea," I said. "I agree. We'll decline."

By now the National Transportation and Safety Board investigators had arrived at Pearl Harbor and had set up their offices in the squadron staffing rooms on the base. The NTSB called me as a witness to provide information to them. Jennifer accompanied me to the hearing. We sat at inquiry tables, forming a U, with microphones to record the conversations. Jennifer and I sat to the left, some Coast Guard officials sat in the middle, and the NTSB officials sat at the right table. Shortly into the meeting, I looked to my right and noticed that the NTSB had reconstructed the *Greeneville*'s track, the path on which the boat had traveled the day of the accident, and the ship's movements prior to the collision. It was information that we didn't have.

Without saying anything, I tried to call Jennifer's attention to the NTSB material, but she never caught on. When we left the room, after declining to say anything, I was irate. "Didn't you see what was on the table?" I asked.

"No. What was it?"

"It was the track!" I said. "They have the tracks of the two ships. Somehow, they have figured out the geometry of the collision between the *Ehime Maru* and the *Greeneville*, taken from the ships' course changes. How could you miss that? We need that information!"

"What? I don't know what you're talking about." It seemed that, to Jennifer, it was an irrelevant piece of material.

Soon the NTSB was holding its own press conferences, releasing bits and pieces of information to the media, which then went national and then global, serving only to fan the fires of Japanese antipathy toward the United States in general, and toward me in particular. My position was becoming more perilous every day, because I had no solid plan how I could defend myself, and my lead counsel seemed unwilling or unable to provide one. I felt as though the jaws of the abyss were opening wider and wider, and I was dangling by a thread above the flames.

After about another week or so, I grew weary of Jennifer's inability to communicate a plan of action and her lack of understanding of submarine operations. To her, it seemed, I was just another open-and-shut case, a guy who had made a dumb mistake. Beyond that, Jennifer and Kimberlie didn't get along.

I needed help. I especially needed a technical expert, somebody whose professional opinions the Navy admirals would respect. But who? All of the guys most qualified to speak about how and why certain things are done aboard a nuclear submarine were in the Navy themselves. Beyond that, my technical expert would be in the awkward position of having to inform and explain material to some of the most highly respected military leaders in the world. Worse yet, at times he'd be forced to challenge their presuppositions or their misguided information, and possibly even their conclusions. It would take a man with extraordinary courage, someone willing to lay his own career on the line, to go to bat for me in such a situation.

I could think of no better man than a classmate of mine at the Naval Academy, Commander Mark Patton. Mark had completed a tour as captain of the *Topeka*, and he was now a squadron deputy at Squadron Three, stationed in Hawaii. Mark had gained international recognition during the New Year's Eve celebration ushering in the new millennium. As the calendar changed from one century to the next, Mark's ship was hovering over the International Date Line, with part of his ship on one side of the line and part on the other side of the line. For a short time, ostensibly, a person could literally walk back and forth between the centuries and between the millenniums by walking back and forth between the front of the boat to the back.

Two weeks after the *Greeneville* accident, I walked over to Mark's office and said, "Classmate, I need some help."

"Certainly, Scott. What can I do?"

"Well, I have these two attorneys, neither of whom understand submarining. You're an expert. I need someone who will serve as my technical expert during the court of inquiry. Would you be willing to risk it?"

I knew Mark stood to lose a lot. As a popular, talented, up-and-coming naval officer, he was in a position to rapidly ascend through the ranks. Yet by asking him to challenge the Navy's data on the *Greeneville* accident, I was asking him to challenge the very admirals who might possibly hold his career in their hands. Jesus once said there is no greater love than for a man to lay down his life for his brother, and both Mark and I recognized that was precisely what I was asking him to do. And what did he have to gain?

Absolutely nothing.

"Well," Mark paused, "I'd really like to help, but I need to check with my boss to see if I can do it." Mark looked back at me, and said quietly but firmly, "If I can, I'll do it. I'll help you, Scott."

I wanted to hug him! I appreciated the fact that Mark would even consider helping me at great peril to his own career.

Later, unknown to me, Mark sent an e-mail to Admiral Konetzni and asked him, "Admiral, if I help Scott Waddle, am I going to get in trouble? Will I be across the breakers with the submarine community?"

"No, you'll be fine," Konetzni assured him. "You'll be doing your classmate a great service. You'll be protected."

Unfortunately, the admiral may have been too optimistic. When word got out that Mark Patton was going to serve as my expert witness, he received a phone call from an officer with whom I had once served. "Be careful, Mark," the officer warned. "Don't forget where your loyalties lie. Watch yourself."

Clearly, in some people's minds at least, the *Greeneville* incident divided us. Where a few weeks ago, we had been close friends, comrades, and colleagues, now we were not. To some people, the *Greeneville* investigation was turning into an "us versus Scott" battle, which was ludicrous. I was still one of them . . . or so I thought.

About that same time, I learned that Admiral William J. Fallon, vice chief of naval operations, was heading to Japan as a special envoy to offer apologies for the *Greeneville* incident on behalf of the president, the U.S. government, the U.S. Navy, and the American people. I was profoundly disappointed. For the past two weeks, I had waited for someone in the Navy to contact me about an opportunity to apologize to the victims' families. No invitation came. Quite the contrary, it seemed that the Navy—or someone above the Navy—simply wanted me to take my medicine, shut up, and go away quietly. Meanwhile, anti-American sentiments grew stronger every day in Japan because the captain of the ship had not apologized. Making matters worse, the Japanese press stoked the fires of anger by implying that the *Greeneville* had not done enough to rescue survivors of the *Ehime Maru*. The Japanese family members, who were already grieving the loss of three crewmembers, two teachers, and four students, became incensed. The distraught families began referring to me as "the most terrible criminal of them all."

Although not an expert on Japanese culture, I knew the president's message would fall on deaf ears if I didn't get an apology to the families first. I had to do something, but what? How?

Jill and I talked about it and came up with a plan. I would write a personal apology and deliver it to the Japanese consulate located in Hawaii. We were excited about the idea, but when I ran it by my legal counsel, I was advised against putting anything in writing just yet.

"I have to do something," I protested. "Those families need to hear those words coming from me. I'm the person responsible."

"Don't you realize that you can jeopardize your case before the court of inquiry if you say anything that can be used against you?"

"I don't know about all that. All I know is that an apology is the right thing to do."

"Well, choose your words very carefully." I was glad I wasn't paying too much for such profound advice.

I purchased beautiful parchment paper and drafted a personal letter of apology tailored especially to each of the family members, the crewmembers, the captain of the *Ehime Maru*, the principal of Uwajima High School, the Japanese prefecture of Uwajima, and to Prime Minister Yoshiro Mori. I carefully sealed each letter with a wax seal, and then Jill bundled them together with ribbon.

I dressed in a dark business suit, so anyone who saw me would know that I was not acting on behalf of the U.S. Navy, and took the letters to the Japanese consulate. I had called earlier for an appointment, so when I arrived, I was courteously ushered to the office of Yoshio Mochizuki, the Japanese consulate general. I was extremely nervous, not sure of what to say or how to say it. But when it came time to speak, I stood before the vice minister and bowed low in front of him, as a sign of respect and humility. He rose and bowed slightly in return

I held the letters in my hand and offered them to the consulate general. Large tears dropped from my eyes as I apologized for the horrible accident that had taken the lives of nine Japanese people, four of whom were teenagers. I begged him, "Please pass these words to the Japanese families, and tell them that when the time is appropriate, I will meet with each one of them in person and give them my personal apology."

The consulate general accepted the letters, and I was escorted out of the embassy offices. When I walked out to my car and arrived at the parking lot, members of the Japanese consulate's staff stood single file to the left of my car as I got in. To my amazement, the Japanese staff members saluted me. I returned the hand salute and drove my car through the gates out into the traffic. At that moment, I felt a heavy burden lift off my shoulders, and I wept in the car on the way home.

What's going on here? I thought. *I'm a career naval officer. I'm supposed to be a leader of men, one of the tough guys. Why can't I keep these tears from falling from my eyes?*

I didn't have an answer. All I knew was that big teardrops continued to form. I blinked hard so I could see as I drove the car, and the tears spattered my perfectly pressed suit pants, leaving large, dark spots of moisture.

Songwriter Gordon Jenson once said, "Tears are a language that God understands." If that's so, and I believe it is, God and I were communicating very well. The tears just kept on coming. I couldn't stop them, and after a while, I no longer wanted to.

CHAPTER 19

THANK GOD FOR CHARLIE!

Adding to my own tension, I was growing increasingly frustrated with Jennifer Herrold as my judge advocate general legal counsel. I considered firing her, but she was the senior Navy JAG available in the Pacific at the time. To fire Jennifer would leave me either bereft of legal counsel or with someone of lesser experience in her place. Neither option would have been wise.

Jennifer had been assigned to me by the Navy free of charge, but that didn't mean I had to listen to her. On the other hand, if I wanted outside help, I had to pay the legal fees myself, and I wasn't sure that I could afford a civilian attorney. More and more, however, I began to feel that the price might be worth it, regardless of the cost.

For her part, Jennifer was dropping not-so-subtle hints that she was fed up with me as well. She even told Kimberlie that if I wanted to fire her, that was fine with her. She was ready to go back home. Finally, one day, I went to Jennifer and asked, "What are some names of other civilian attorneys who are available?"

Jennifer was more than willing to refer me to several civilian attorneys who had experience handling military cases. I decided to give them a call, starting with a lawyer in Washington. He knew who I was, and we briefly discussed my case. Almost immediately the discussion turned to money. "I'm interested in hiring you," I said, "so could you tell me what I might be able to expect in regard to your expenses?"

"Sure, I'd be glad to," the lawyer replied. He quoted me an astronomically high initial retainer fee. He went on to describe his hourly fee, which sounded to me like a week's pay. He also demanded that I pay for his travel and lodging in a hotel in downtown Honolulu, plus all meals and entertainment, administrative support, long-distance telephone calls, personal expenses, and provide a means of transportation.

Clearly, I couldn't afford the attorney on my U.S. Navy salary and savings, so I decided to try another tack. "In view of the fact that this case is gaining a lot of international exposure, and you'd be getting a lot of additional notoriety and attention, would you be willing to cut me a bit of a break on your charges?" I asked.

The lawyer shot back, "I *am* giving you a break."

"Thank you," I replied. "I don't think I will be retaining your services."

"Well, good luck to you," the lawyer replied coolly.

The next name on my list was Charles Gittins. I didn't know Charles Gittins any better than I did the previous lawyer, but I figured it was worth a call. What did I have to lose? I dialed the number, and a male voice answered the phone. "This is Gittins."

"Mr. Gittins, this is Scott Waddle."

"What took you so long?" the lawyer asked cheerily.

I knew instantly that I had found not just a great lawyer, but a great buddy.

"Mr. Gittins . . ." I began.

"Charlie."

"Charlie?" I repeated slowly.

"Yeah."

"Charlie . . . I need your help."

"I'm here for you."

"Mr. Gittins, er, I mean, Charlie . . . what cases have you represented in the past?"

Charlie rattled off a few of the high-profile cases in which he had been involved, including the Navy Tailhook scandal, where he represented former Commander Bob Stumpf and the Army's Sergeant Major McKinney against sexual harassment charges. In both cases, Charles Gittins's clients were found not guilty of the charges against them. McKinney was later charged with obstruction of justice and took a fall for that.

I recognized those cases, and I suddenly realized who the man was to whom I was speaking!

"And, well, I need to know how much this is going to cost."

"Don't worry about the money," Charlie chirped. "We need to worry about saving your butt."

"But, I don't have any . . ."

"Don't worry about it. Money is not an issue. Let's worry about saving your butt first, and then we'll talk turkey."

That was the beginning of an incredible attorney-client relationship. Over the next few weeks, I came to love Charlie Gittins as a person and respect him immensely as the consummate professional legal strategist.

I told Charlie that I wanted to apologize publicly to the Japanese families who had lost loved ones in the *Greeneville–Ehime Maru* accident, so he helped me draft a letter expressing my sorrow. He cautioned me against going as far as apologizing, since in America an apology was tantamount to an admission of guilt, and that could seriously jeopardize our ability to mount a valid defense in the court of inquiry. Nevertheless, Charlie and I went as far as we dared at the time.

I wrote, "It is with a heavy heart that I express my most sincere regret for the accident. . . . I know that the accident has caused unimaginable grief to the families of the *Ehime Maru*'s missing students, instructors, and crew members . . . and to all of the Japanese people."

Charlie sent the letter to the Japanese public television network, NHK, where it was broadcast nationwide. Unfortunately, the letter fell on deaf ears. Many of the family members refused to see the intent of my heart in sending the letter. They did not regard it as an apology and continued to insist that I had not done enough to express my remorse.

The announcement that I had hired Charles Gittins to represent me sent shock waves throughout the Navy. Within military circles, Charlie was known for his thoroughness and his keen strategy. Outside the military, Charlie was known as a legal shark because of his aggressiveness and his dedication to his clients. "Oh, no! Not him," a number of people groaned. "He got Sergeant Major McKinney off at Tailhook; he'll be a pain to work with on this case."

I talked with Charlie frequently by phone over the following few days. He was finishing up on a case at the time of my initial call, so he couldn't come to Hawaii for two weeks until the case on which he was working was completed. Charlie immediately wrote to the court of inquiry asking for a stay so he could have more time to prepare, having just been hired as my lead counsel. The stay was granted, and the inquiry was rescheduled to convene in two weeks, during the first week of March. *Whew!* It wasn't a lot of time, but hopefully it would be enough to allow Charlie to get up to speed on the case. He had seen the news footage of the *Greeneville* floundering on the surface on February 9, after we had conducted the emergency blow and struck the *Ehime Maru*. At the time, he told his wife, "I feel for that guy. He is in real trouble."

Later, when I told him that Captain Robert Brandhuber had been aboard the submarine at the time of the accident, Charlie was ecstatic. "You're kiddin' me! That's a blessing from above," said Charlie. "You've got a senior officer present on board your submarine, who was in the control room, watching your maneuvers, yet who obviously didn't intervene to do anything. That is great! If he didn't see anything that was wrong, how can anyone cite you? There's no way the Navy can find you criminally negligent

and culpable without finding him culpable as well." I wasn't quite as confident as Charlie, but if Charlie had hope, so did I! I was beginning to think
Charlie Gittins was a godsend.

Charlie Gittins arrived in Hawaii the afternoon of March 4, the day before
the court of inquiry was to convene. I first met the man who had my life in
his hands at the Honolulu International Airport. I had no idea what he
looked like, so I had gone on-line to search the Internet and find a picture
of him so that I'd recognize the man I was to pick up. Charlie needed no
such help. My picture had been all over the media in the past few weeks.

As I walked down the open-air concourse, I noticed a television camera
crew set up at the gate where Charlie was to arrive. It didn't take a genius to
figure out who they were waiting for. Fortunately, I hadn't worn my Navy
whites. Instead I had dressed casually in an Aloha shirt, shorts, and sunglasses.
I looked like a thousand other tourists and locals at the airport that day.

I stood behind the smoked-glass partition trying to remain as inconspic-
uous as possible. Just about the time Charlie's flight eased up to the ramp, a
reporter looked over at me. He looked away, and then he turned and looked
at me again. He looked at me a third time, and I thought he had surely recognized me, so I decided to head him off at the pass. "Can I help you, pal?"
I growled as belligerently as I could muster.

"Oh, I'm sorry. I thought you were someone else." The newsman shuffled
off in a different direction.

A few minutes later, Charlie Gittins got off the plane. A solidly built,
bespectacled, happy-go-lucky man in his early forties, I guessed, Charlie
looked to me like an ordinary, everyday guy, rather than a man who had
earned a notorious reputation as a cutthroat legal shark. His eyes quickly
darted around the concourse, obviously looking for someone who was supposed to meet him. I walked over toward him, and Charlie greeted me
warmly. "Hey, how are ya?" he called.

"Hi, Charlie," I said. "Nice to meet you. Welcome to Hawaii." The two
of us quickly hustled away from the television cameras.

"Did you see the cameras back there?" Charlie asked.

"Yeah, I saw them, but they didn't see us," I said with a laugh. Charlie laughed uproariously. He was a reporter's dream, always good for a quote or a sound bite, but he also knew how, when, and where to use the media to his advantage. On the news that night, the local reports told of Charlie's arrival, placing a shadow around Charlie's picture as he was getting off the plane, but nobody had scored an interview with him.

Anyone who has ever flown to Hawaii directly from the East Coast knows what a grueling trip that can be. Charlie had left home around 5:00 A.M. and traveled all the way from Washington, D.C., so we quickly got a rental car for him, and I led him back to the base at Pearl Harbor, where he had agreed to stay. As a reserve Marine lieutenant colonel, Charlie was permitted to stay on the base in the bachelors' officers quarters, right across from the Navy Legal Service Office. Charlie charged me for his legal services, but because of his gracious attitude, he did not require the many perks other hot-shot lawyers had demanded. The fact that Charlie was willing to stay in the spartan military accommodations rather than a fancy, five-star Waikiki resort hotel saved me literally thousands of dollars in hotel and food bills during his prolonged stay for the inquiry.

Charlie even had simple tastes when it came to food. Earlier in the week, in anticipation of his arrival, I called and asked him, "Charlie, what do you like to eat for breakfast?"

"I'm a simple man," Charlie responded. "Blueberry yogurt and Diet Coke."

"Okay," I said with a smile, "what do you like for lunch, or to snack on?"

"Peanut butter, jelly, and wheat bread," Charlie rattled off his requests as though he were quoting baseball statistics.

"Are you serious?"

"Yeah, I've been trying to lose some weight."

It was already past 5:00 in the afternoon by the time I got Charlie settled into his living quarters. I knew he had to be dog-tired, but he wouldn't take a minute to rest. "I need to see a submarine," Charlie said, "and I want to meet with the JAG officers you've been working with."

We went over to the legal services office, and I introduced Charlie to Kimberlie and Jennifer. They both seemed delighted that Charlie was on the scene. Meanwhile, I called Russ Janicke, a friend and commander of the *Greeneville*'s sister submarine, the *Louisville*.

"Russ, I need to get Charlie Gittins, my lawyer, on board a submarine. I know I can't get him on the *Greeneville*, but I'd like to bring him down and walk through your boat to give him a feel for where everything is located on the ship."

"Sure, Scott. Anything I can do to help," Russ replied without a moment's hesitation.

We went down to the waterfront, and Charlie and I spent about three hours going through Russ's ship, defining terms and explaining the way things worked. Charlie had a military background, and had graduated from the Naval Academy a year before I did, but, like most Americans, he had little knowledge of how a nuclear submarine operates.

When Charlie was finally content that he had a rudimentary understanding of the submarine and how the accident aboard the *Greeneville* had happened, we went back to my home, where I cooked dinner for him. I introduced Charlie to Jill and Ashley, and it was obvious from the start that Charlie was going to be a fourth member of the Waddle family. Jill and Ashley loved him!

It was during dinner that Charlie first expressed his adamant conviction that I should not take the witness stand during the inquiry without immunity. "Over my dead body will I let you take the stand without immunity," Charlie joked. "I'll kill you before I let you take the stand! It isn't happening, not unless we get you immunity so anything you say can't be used against you."

"Mm-hm, okay, Charlie," I said with a mouthful of pasta. "Whatever you say."

We talked for several more hours, told stories, and laughed together. For a brief but precious time, we were almost able to put out of our minds the reason that we were all gathered together.

"We better get some sleep, Charlie," I suggested after a while.

"Yeah, you're right. Tomorrow's going to be an important day."

Important? How about *life-changing?*

CHAPTER 20
ODD MAN OUT

The following morning, March 5, Jill and I awakened around 5:30 A.M. Jill dressed in a classy business suit, and I dressed in my Navy whites. I had to fight back the tears as I started to place my gold dolphins on my shirt. I picked up the dolphins that were given to me by Guy O'Neil, the highly decorated World War II submarine captain. They were a priceless treasure, given to Guy by the secretary of the Navy on behalf of the president of the United States when Guy was presented a Navy Cross for bravery in battle. The priceless gold dolphins had commemorated the presentation of the Navy Cross.

Ever since Guy had given me his dolphins after the event in Santa Barbara, I had cherished them, but I had never worn them. I always wore my own dolphins, having purchased a new pin after giving mine to the patriotic young Girl Scout. But this morning was like no other I'd ever faced in my naval career. I needed all the moral support I could get. I wasn't superstitious, but Guy O'Neil had worn those dolphins into battle and had come out victoriously. Maybe having Guy's dolphins on my uniform would provide some extra impetus for me to stand strong in the battle for my life.

Jill and I met Charlie at 7:00 A.M. at the bachelor officers' quarters parking lot on the base. We rode in Charlie's rental car, with Charlie driving and Jill and me riding in the backseat, to the Navy Legal Service Office where the inquiry was to be held, a mere four hundred yards away from where Charlie was staying. Charlie was extremely conscious of appearances, and he didn't want to give the impression that Jill and I were divided in any way.

When we arrived at the inquiry, we received our first hint at what sort of treatment to expect. There was no designated parking space for us. Everyone else involved in the case had an assigned parking place; the admirals all had theirs, and the litigators had theirs. Only the principal parties to the case were left to go searching for a spot to park a car on the extra-crowded, busy base. It was a minor inconvenience, and only a short walk from the lot where we found a parking place to the inquiry room, but with a full complement of media cameras and microphones ensconced in front of the building, waiting for our arrival, and my heart pounding like a jackhammer, the overlooked parking place sparked extra tension that we didn't need.

Working our way up the sidewalk through the maze of reporters' microphones and cameras was like running a gauntlet. Jill and I walked together hand in hand, cordially acknowledging the members of the media but not stopping to talk. Many reporters called out specific questions as we made our way to the door. Others simply said, "Good morning, Commander. Do you have any comments?" Cameras clicked constantly, and flashes went off in our faces as we walked by.

Charlie had coached us the night before to be friendly, but not too accessible. "Acknowledge them, but don't say anything. Just keep looking straight ahead and keep moving toward the doors," Charlie instructed. That's what we did.

Members of the media were provided an audio and video feed in a separate room off base. They were permitted to monitor the events, make notes, and write their own observations, but they were not allowed to record or transcribe the witnesses' testimonies during the court of inquiry. There were no members of the media in the courtroom.

We went through the large, double-glass doors to the legal services building. Once inside, for security purposes, everyone entering the courtroom was required to go through a metal detector. Jill, Charlie, and I made a sharp left and went upstairs to meet with Jennifer Herrold and Kimberlie Young, to go over last-minute strategy details from about 7:15 till around 7:50. We then walked downstairs to the courtroom. That became our pattern every morning.

The courtroom itself was a stark white-walled room, with additional tables and chairs set up for the admirals and a separate table for each of the defendants—Jerry, Mike, and me—and our separate legal teams. I was the only one of the three "parties" to have a civilian lawyer at my table.

"Are you ready for this?" Charlie asked before we entered the room.

"I'm ready, Charlie. Let's do this thing."

When I walked into the room, I was shocked. There, sitting right behind the place where Charlie and I were to sit, were all the Japanese family members of the victims. Jill was seated across the room, far from me.

Seated directly across from my table were the three American admirals and a Japanese two-star, Admiral Isamu Ozawa, sitting on the court in an advisory role. Ozawa was permitted to ask questions during the inquiry and would sit in on all deliberations of the judges. The only thing he could not do as part of the inquiry judges' panel was vote.

Charlie immediately lodged a written protest to the court, challenging the presence of Admiral Ozawa on the judicial panel. Ozawa was not a U.S. citizen, he had no responsibility to the U.S. government, and he had not sworn allegiance to our country or an oath to uphold our Constitution. His opinions could not be challenged in a higher court, if ever there was a need for that. The court accepted Charlie's protest without comment and moved on—entering it in the official record as "Exhibit A" and then ignoring it completely.

After a brief introduction of all the admirals and judicial advocates, the court explained the protocol and procedures. Interestingly, the admirals did not read any charges against me. "This is to be an information collection process," one of the admirals said.

I'll bet, I thought, as I sat there staring at the U.S. flag standing in the front of the room. I had served my country for twenty years, twenty-four if I counted my time at the Naval Academy, and now here I was sitting in this room as the odd man out. It was a strange, unfamiliar feeling.

The first witness called was Admiral Charles Griffiths, who had conducted the preliminary investigation of the *Greeneville* accident and turned in the report upon which Admiral Fargo based his decision to proceed with the court of inquiry. Admiral Griffiths and I had sat together at a Baltimore Orioles baseball game years earlier when I had been a Prospective Commanding Officer student in Washington, D.C. and he had just learned that he had been promoted to flag rank. He was a friend whom I had always respected as a fair man.

Charlie was champing at the bit. "This is great!" he whispered to me under his breath. "It's been a long time since I've mopped the floor with an admiral!" True to his word, Charlie calmly but firmly ripped gaping holes in the information presented by Admiral Griffiths. The three admirals bristled at Charlie's willingness to confront them. This was not going to be a pretty affair.

CHAPTER 21

INQUIRING MINDS

The court of inquiry was emotionally and physically draining. Just walking in each morning and seeing the Japanese families sitting behind me was gut-wrenching. Many of the Japanese visitors didn't understand English, so they listened to a translator on a headset. They took their cues from Admiral Ozawa, the Japanese adviser on the judicial panel. Ozawa understood English perfectly, but he also listened on a headset to the Japanese translator. Every time anybody mentioned anything about the victims, Ozawa scowled, raised his eyebrows, or flinched in some way. Ozawa's gestures evoked heart- rending, emotional responses from the victims' families. At first, it was unnerving; then after a while it became irritating.

The inquiry itself was tedious and taxing. We started each morning at 8:00, and I sat there all day long listening to testimony that was sometimes inaccurate, often misleading, and at other times laced with false presuppositions and innuendoes. It was extremely difficult to remain silent, and at times, immunity or not, I wanted to jump up and say, "That just isn't so! That's not the way it was on board our ship!"

From the beginning, I hoped to shield my crewmembers as much as I could, similar to the way a parent would try to protect a child. I knew that things had gone terribly wrong aboard the *Greeneville* on February 9, and as important as it was that we dig into the details of the accident, after a day or two, the ponderous who, what, and why questions grew rather redundant and irrelevant to me. The responsibility for the tragic accident all came back on my shoulders. I didn't mind shouldering the brunt of the burden if it could help save one of my guys' careers. The dilemma was, *How can I protect my guys and still try to protect myself from court-martial as well?*

There was an awkward, invisible barrier that had been erected between myself, my executive officer, Jerry Pfeifer, and the officer of the deck, Mike Coen, since the day of the accident. No longer were we a team working together; now the inquiry system forced us into an "every man for himself" posture, something that was totally foreign for the three of us. Before or during the inquiry, we didn't compare notes, try to make our stories gel, or speak about our defense. We hardly even talked to each other. Jerry and Mike had not hired civilian attorneys, but were relying on the Navy JAGC officers to defend them. That was fine, yet I knew that we needed to present a united front to the court. When we spoke at all, I encouraged Jerry and Mike to have their attorneys talk to Charlie, Kimberlie, Jennifer, and Mark just to make sure we were all on the same page.

Each of the admirals on the panel seemed to focus on one aspect of the accident, apparently, by design. Admiral Stone seemed most interested in operational risk management—the priorities in which we performed our duties—zeroing in on the speed at which we did our maneuvers on the day of the accident. Admiral Sullivan was locked up over the watchbill issue, that nine of thirteen crewmen were not in their designated positions at the time of the accident. Admiral Nathman focused on my situational awareness, whether my crew and I truly had done a good job of checking to make sure no other ships were near us before initiating the emergency dive and the fateful emergency blow. The inquiry also thoroughly examined the impact the distinguished visitors may have had on the accident. The admirals came to the conclusion I was hoping they would: The guests aboard the ship had no bearing on the accident.

The inquiry spent a great deal of time discussing the shortness of my periscope search the day of the accident. What could I say? I had not performed a three- to five-minute sweep of the water according to the general guidelines I had established for my own crew in standing orders; I had done an eighty-second sweep and seen nothing anywhere near us. By examining the tracks of the two ships, the inquiry determined that I had at one point looked directly into the haze at the *Ehime Maru* in the scope, but I didn't see it. How could that be? Only one explanation makes any sense: It was a white ship with a narrow aspect—which means it was pointed in our direction, coming straight at us—against the background of a hazy sky on a February afternoon in Hawaii. Had the *Ehime Maru* been moving across the plane of our vision, I'd have seen it, but the white ship against the white horizon was difficult to see two miles away, and I simply missed it. There was no other explanation.

Imagine, if you will, how easy it is to make a similar mistake. The next time you are swimming in the ocean, allow your body to be submerged up to your chin. With the waves rolling toward you, look out at the horizon and try to pinpoint an object two miles away. It is not as easy as it seems, even with a high-powered lens.

That in no way makes up for the fact that I missed the *Ehime Maru* in my visual search. Nor does it explain why we didn't catch it on our sonar screens, radar intercept equipment, or other high-tech equipment on the nuclear submarine. I walked back to the sonar controls twice during the afternoon of February 9, and I did not see the contact approaching us at a speed of about fifteen knots, a contact that turned out to be the *Ehime Maru*. To this day, that remains a perplexing enigma to me.

One of the most exasperating testimonies during the proceedings was that of Captain Hisao Onishi, the captain of the *Ehime Maru*. Onishi refused to look at me face-to-face during the time he was on the stand. He would not even make eye contact when Charlie Gittins, sitting next to me at our table, asked him questions. Apparently, something in the Japanese code of honor prevented him from looking at me. Onishi's testimony was also laced with contradictions. Perhaps the one misrepresentation that bothered me most was his claim that he was swept overboard by a wave, tossed far from the *Ehime Maru*, and therefore unable to help the crew and passengers of his own ship. I doubted the veracity of Onishi's claim.

Nevertheless, I felt compelled to search out Onishi after his testimony. Through an interpreter, I apologized to Captain Onishi, captain to captain, as best I could. I told him that I realized how severely the loss of his crewmembers and several of his passengers had affected him. He seemed genuinely surprised at and appreciative of my expressions of sorrow and remorse.

The victims' families were not quite so amenable, which was understandable considering their tragic losses. Each day when I entered the courtroom, before sitting down at our table, I bowed to the Japanese family members seated behind Charlie and me. At first, the hot glares I received in return could have seared through steel. Several days into the inquiry, however, I had an opportunity to speak to two groups of Japanese families. It didn't turn out as I had hoped. When I finally was able to apologize to the family members, one of the fathers stood and screamed at me. I had no idea what he was saying, but it wasn't hard to figure out.

"I'd like to extend my sincere apology," I told the family members through an interpreter. "I can't ask for your forgiveness. This is a burden I will carry to the grave. I am accountable for the incident."

As I spoke, I bowed my head before the relatives, while teardrops flooded my eyes and spattered on the floor. Ryosuke Terata, whose seventeen-year-old son had died aboard the *Ehime Maru*, spoke emotionally to me in Japanese. "Why didn't you apologize earlier?" she wanted to know.

Another grieving woman, Mikie Nakata, mother of one of the teachers who had died, told me, "I carry a photograph of my son with me while I watch the inquiry every day," she told me. "Please tell the truth in court," she urged.

"I will," I replied, "when the right time comes."

The father, Kazuo Nakata, said he appreciated my tears but implied that he wouldn't be totally convinced until he heard me testify before the inquiry. "Tell the truth to prove your tears are real," he told me.

"I will," I promised. "I will speak truthfully, and you will hear my side of the story."

Before doing an interview for a Japanese television network, a friend helped me prepare my entire apology in Japanese. I memorized the speech phonetically so I could speak to the victims' families in their own tongue. I wanted them to hear my message from me personally, rather than in the disjointed fragments necessary when speaking through an interpreter. If nothing else, the extra effort convinced the Japanese family members of my sincerity. What the speech lacked in finesse apparently was made up for in sheer intensity.

My father arrived after the fourth day of testimony. He accompanied us and sat with Jill in the courtroom each day. Dad had spent his life in the military and had retired as an Air Force colonel. He knew the potential and the pitfalls of military power. He also understood the intense pressures political correctness placed on such proceedings as we were experiencing. It was a tremendous boost of moral support just to see him in the courtroom every day. It was also a blessing for Ashley to have "Grandpop" around for a while.

Somehow, even in the middle of this nightmare, I discovered that life goes on all around us. People get up each morning, go to their jobs, and do all the normal things that must be done every day, most of them unaffected by the heartache around them. Everyone has their own concerns, and except for the occasional stare or whisper, most people didn't pay much attention to me outside of the courtroom. Jill and I tried to maintain some semblance of normalcy during the inquiry as well. Several afternoons during the inquiry, we'd hustle away from the reporters, race home, change into casual clothes, and head out to watch Ashley play one of her junior high school basketball games. Every other evening, Charlie Gittins and I would change out of our courtroom clothes, throw on shorts and T-shirts, and go for a run out along the Pearl Harbor channel and waterfront.

It helped a lot that throughout the process, Patti Smith, Claudia Prince, Nancy Scardon, Jane Daly, and other Navy wives frequently got together to prepare meals for my family, as well as for Jerry and Tannie Pfeifer and Mike and Wendy Coen, plus the attorneys working on our case. They'd just show up carrying mounds of food! Despite the awkwardness of being at the center of the nationally publicized case, the real Navy, not the hierarchical system, rallied around us as family.

Perhaps the most difficult moment for me during the inquiry came most unexpectedly. While a Coast Guard officer was on the stand, describing the recovery efforts, the admirals ordered the lights dimmed and video footage shown of the rescue scene. The video had been taken from a Coast Guard helicopter shortly after the *Ehime Maru* had gone down. I sat horror-stricken as I watched again the orange life rafts dotting the rough sea and the *Greeneville* floundering on the water, and there I stood atop the sail, harnessed into the bridge, unable to do anything but wait for help. As I watched, my stomach began to roll with the waves. For a moment, I thought I was going to throw up. The Japanese families sitting behind me wailed loudly. I could feel my body begin to shake. As hard as I tried to control myself, I could not. The tears welled in my eyes again, spattering loudly on the papers in front of me on the table. I leaned forward and tried to wipe the tears and the scene from my mind. The tears could be cleansed, but the scene of those people in the rafts, and the *Greeneville* heaving in the ocean, was indelibly impressed in my mind forever.

Admiral Nathman looked over and noticed that I had lost my composure. I whispered to Charlie Gittins, "Charlie, I need a break."

Charlie interrupted the proceedings and said, "Excuse me, Admiral, my client needs a recess."

Admiral Nathman didn't dispute the obvious. He called for a twenty-minute recess. I got up and hurried out the doors into a side briefing room, not speaking to anyone. As soon as I exited the room, I burst into tears. I stumbled up the stairs toward the sanctuary of our meeting room in Kimberlie's office, Jill, Charlie, and the rest of team gathering behind me.

■ ■ ■

Another day when it was hard to remain silent was when Admiral Albert Konetzni, commander of the Submarine Force, U.S. Pacific Fleet, testified. Admiral Konetzni was extremely complimentary of me. The admiral told the court that he loved me "as a brother, if not my son." He confided that he had held high hopes for me, that I had the right stuff to one day move up in the ranks of COMSUBPAC. In what to me seemed like a high compliment, Admiral Konetzni told the court that I reminded him of himself when he was a young captain. "I wanted this man to be what I have become," he told the admirals. "This man was running a good ship."

Admiral Konetzni also reminded the court of inquiry that the *Greeneville* had one of the highest first-term sailor retention rates of any ship in the Navy, 65 percent, double the average Navy ships' rate. Beyond that, we had only a 5 percent attrition rate, the admiral told the court. "This ship was unbelievable!" said Admiral Konetzni.

The admiral also vehemently defended the fact that even during a distinguished visitors' cruise, the crew of the *Greeneville* was engaging in training. "It wasn't a joyride," he stated emphatically. "I detest that word. It was training."

Yet Admiral Konetzni's words were not all flowery. He soundly criticized me for failing to delegate responsibility to my senior officers, for taking the ship's controls twice during the time before the accident, and especially for not taking more time to make certain no ships were approaching us before engaging in the emergency deep and the emergency blow. "He has the obligation to make sure the area above is clear," the admiral told the court.

Konetzni continued to drive home his point that I had moved too rapidly on February 9. He didn't say that I had performed poorly; he simply said there was "inappropriate, inadequate, and improper backup." The admiral blamed the accident on my failure to give my crew and myself enough time to accurately determine whether there were any other ships in our vicinity. He summed up the situation, saying, "The backup on this situation was time, and he told time to go away." When you make the choices that I did, he said, "then you better be right."

When asked about the nature of my mistakes, Admiral Konetzni said, "Let's face it. The honest thing is that this commanding officer would not have gone down to do an emergency blow if, in his brain, in his heart, in his soul, he knew that there was a surface ship there. The issue is, What could he have done to ensure that he knew better what was up there?"

Perhaps the admiral's most damaging comments had to do with a caution he recalled giving me a year before the accident, in March 2000. The admiral said that he had told me, "Hey, slow down. Give the crew the opportunity to grow. You're smart, but give them the opportunity. Don't run too fast; let them catch up."

In summing up his testimony, the admiral said of me, "I know he is not a criminal. . . . But due to some unbelievable, fateful things . . . that I call fateful decisions, this accident occurred. You couldn't replicate this accident in a million years, you just could not."

Looking over at me from the stand, Admiral Konetzni commented, "The tragedy of this thing is we have nine people who are dead. But you know, equally as tragic . . . I know this human being. I know this man. He's a dear friend. He will be my friend forever. . . . He can't let this go. And it breaks my heart."

In a statement that was later widely reported out of context, Admiral Konetzni looked over at me and said, "I'd like to go over there and punch him for not taking more time."

It was clearly a statement intended to separate the admiral and his staff from me and from the incident. As serious as the moment was, I couldn't suppress a smile. It was typical Konetzni bombast, and I loved him for it.

Patrick Seacrest's testimony, on the other hand, was extremely troubling. The fire control technician aboard the *Greeneville*, Seacrest testified under a grant of immunity. In light of his testimony, that was probably a good thing.

Patrick Seacrest had not been scheduled to sit at the fire control panel on February 9. But another sailor had some personal matters to take care of and had asked Seacrest to fill in for him. Nevertheless, Seacrest was one of the best fire control technicians we could have had on duty. He was in charge of weapons launch consoles, target motion analysis, and high-tech equipment that helps process sonar sensor information to determine what the Navy calls a fire control solution. The information Seacrest handled could be used to target Tomahawk cruise missiles, Mark 48 advanced capable torpedoes, and mines.

On February 9, since we were conducting a distinguished visitors' cruise, it was highly unlikely we'd be calling upon Seacrest to target any weapons. Instead, his job was to monitor the surface picture on the computer screen and through the perivis, a black-and-white videocamera mounted in the periscope, with monitors aboard ship in tandem with the sonar operators. By combining the information, he could develop a possible computer analysis to show a detailed picture of any vessels in the area, including their direction and speed. Yet with all the information at his disposal, Patrick Seacrest missed the *Ehime Maru*. How he could possibly have made such a serious mistake was a question the court of inquiry returned to repeatedly.

On the stand, Patrick Seacrest admitted that he failed to warn me that there were three contacts on his screen, one of which was labeled "Sierra 13," the Japanese fishing trawler, *Ehime Maru*. Contact Sierra 13 was only four thousand yards away from the *Greeneville* at the time we did the emergency deep. Seacrest also admitted that it was his responsibility to warn the officer of the deck, Mike Coen, of such contacts, but he did not. He simply assumed that we knew the contacts were there.

Earlier in his testimony before the National Transportation Safety Board, and in his pretrial preparation with Captain Bruce MacDonald, Seacrest had hinted that the distinguished visitors aboard the *Greeneville* on February 9 had interfered with his ability to communicate information to me. But in the court of inquiry, he reversed his position and stated that the guests had not impeded his performance or his ability to get information to me. In fact, he admitted, he usually didn't pass along information to me, but rather to his watch supervisor, the officer of the deck.

MacDonald severely criticized Patrick Seacrest for not updating the contact evaluation plot, a chart on the opposite side of the submarine's control room. Unquestionably, the civilians stood between Seacrest and the tactical chart, so he allowed it to go unattended.

Captain MacDonald zoomed in for the kill. "You got lazy, didn't you, Petty Officer Seacrest?"

"Yes, a little bit," Seacrest replied sheepishly.

"A little bit . . ." MacDonald repeated.

One of the most disconcerting aspects of Seacrest's testimony concerned the timing of when he outspotted the contact, Sierra 13. Seacrest stated that he changed the position of Sierra 13 from two thousand to nine thousand yards away just before the collision between the *Greeneville* and the *Ehime Maru*.

Captain MacDonald wasn't buying it. He provided data from the *Greeneville*'s sonar logger, equipment that maintains constant updates of sonar information, similar to a black box on an aircraft. The sonar logger recorded that the position of Sierra 13 was changed within fifteen to thirty seconds *after* the collision. When asked to explain the discrepancy, Seacrest had no plausible answer. At that point, I was glad Patrick Seacrest had received testimonial immunity.

After listening all day long to Patrick Seacrest testify before the court, I actually *wanted* to talk to the media. Every other day, as we'd leave the inquiry, I was inundated with questions as we made our way to the car. "How do you think it's going, Commander? Do you have any comments, Commander Waddle?"

As Charlie had instructed, I acknowledged the members of the media and kept right on moving.

Following Seacrest's testimony, though, I really wanted to make a statement. I tried to make eye contact with various reporters as we exited the inquiry, but not one of them asked me a question. What was up with *that?* I wanted to talk, and nobody in the press asked me! Every other day, they asked me for statements. Now for the first time, I was ready and willing to say something and nobody asked!

I mentioned the curious change in the media's demeanor to Charlie. "Yeah, I know," he said nonchalantly. "Let me take care of it. Tomorrow morning, when we get out of the car, Sarah Frueman, a producer for NBC news, will be among the members of the media waiting to ask you for a comment." I looked at Charlie quizzically. "Trust me," he said. "She'll ask you to say something. Look for her and head straight for her cameraman."

Sure enough, the next morning as I made my way through the throng of reporters and cameramen, I heard Sarah's voice. "Commander Waddle! Do you have anything to say?"

I detoured slightly from my direct path and walked in Sarah's direction. "Good morning," I said.

I suddenly felt as though I was starring in an old E. F. Hutton commercial. Reporters gathered around and jammed microphones everywhere they could find a spot. I felt amazingly calm as I spoke. "I just want to let it be known that I am very proud of Petty Officer Patrick Seacrest. In command, accountability and responsibility are absolute. I am personally responsible, personally accountable for the actions that led to the tragic collision and sinking of the *Ehime Maru*. No one else should be punished; no one else should be held responsible. I alone am responsible for this accident." Nobody was asking any questions; the media members were just standing there in amazement, listening. I quickly brought my comments to a close. "I just wanted to say that. Thank you."

I hurried on into the building, Charlie guarding my rear.

This was my last chance to set the record straight.

CHAPTER 22

THE BUCK
STOPS HERE

At the end of the eleventh grueling day of testimony, our legal team gathered, as we did each afternoon, in Kimberlie Young's office to review the day's court session and to talk about our plans for tomorrow—the day designated by the admirals for final summations and closing remarks. We were all tired and a bit dejected, sorely disappointed that Admiral Fargo had just denied me immunity for the fourth time.

Mark Patton, our technical expert, sat in the corner of the room, holding his head in his hands. In a quiet voice, Mark looked up and asked, "Charlie, is Scott going to take the stand?"

"No!" Charlie replied adamantly. "Didn't you hear what went on in there today? Testimonial immunity was denied for the fourth time! They won't give Scott immunity, and it's too risky for him to testify without it. I'm not going to let him take the stand."

"I know, I know," Mark spoke softly. "But Charlie, the guys on the waterfront really think Scott should take the stand. They expect him to. Charlie, you know it's the right thing for Scott to do."

That's all I needed to hear. The guys on the waterfront . . . my friends and coworkers, the guys who believed in me, trusted me, prayed for me . . . the guys with whom I had served my country, *they* thought I should testify. I interrupted my famous lawyer's response to Mark. "Charlie, I gotta take the stand," I said. "I promised those Japanese family members I met with that at the proper time they'd hear from me. I promised them that they'd get to hear my side of the story, that I'd tell it like it was. I promised them that I would do this. I've gotta do this. Now is the time."

"Bull! You're not doing it! I'm not going to let you do it."

"Charlie," I insisted, "I have to do it."

For a long moment, Charlie Gittins stood silently, just staring at me, as though he was trying to figure out what made me tick. Then he threw his arms up in the air and nearly shouted, "Okay!" He dropped his hands to his side. "Okay. You want to do it, you can do it. But before you take that stand tomorrow morning, we're going to grill you. Mock questions, mock cross-examinations, the works. Kimberlie, what do you think?"

Kimberlie looked at me and raised her eyebrows slightly. "I don't know," she replied. "It's risky, but I think he should do it."

"Jennifer, what do you think?" Charlie asked.

"I think it's a bad idea," Jennifer replied emphatically, "but it's your call."

"All right, let's meet tonight at Scott's house at 7:00."

"Charlie, why don't you all just come over for dinner and we'll get an earlier start," I suggested.

"Sounds good to me," said Charlie.

That night after dinner, for nearly four hours, Charlie, Mark, Jennifer, and Kimberlie threw the book at me, asking every possible sort of question about the accident. "Well, Commander, what about this? What about that? Why did you do things that way? Why didn't you do things differently?"

I sat in a chair without moving and answered as though I were on the stand. Charlie and the others listened carefully and offered suggestions.

"Okay, Scott, slow down your answer; this is complicated material. Don't rush through it."

"Scott, that's too confrontational. Don't say that! Remember, these are admirals to whom you will be speaking. Make sure you give them proper respect. Instead of putting it that way, state your case this way."

It was difficult work, but it was well worth it. When I finally went to bed that night, I felt confident that I could handle any question the panel of admirals tossed at me.

"Get some sleep, Scott," Charlie said. "Jill and I are going to do another interview." Nearly every night of the inquiry, Jill and Charlie had to stay up until the wee hours of the morning to do "live" television interviews from Hawaii. With the five-hour time difference, the interviews seen in New York at 7:00 A.M. were done at 2:00 A.M. Hawaiian time.

A major brouhaha raged in Japan over the *Greeneville–Ehime Maru* incident. People were literally marching in the streets of Tokyo carrying placards denouncing the United States, the U.S. Navy, and especially me. Many people there wanted my head.

Naturally, the media covered those incidents as well, and they had new questions on a daily basis for Charlie and Jill. Charlie was fantastic at dealing with the legal questions, and Jill did an incredible job of letting people know that we were real people, a real family. I was not a cold-hearted killer; I was a highly trained, skilled seaman who knew how to drive a ship and who had served my country for more than twenty years with an unblemished record. More importantly, I was a husband and father who loved my wife and daughter. In a weird sort of way, thanks to Jill's and Charlie's appearances, many people began to feel that I was being victimized almost as much as the people struck by the *Greeneville*.

Many Americans were outraged that I was being made such a spectacle. After all, I had expressed my deepest regrets. Wasn't that enough? After all, the Japanese have never apologized to the United States for the horrific sneak attack on Pearl Harbor on December 7, 1941. Nearly twenty-three hundred of our best and brightest young men were literally blown to bits, burned to death, or otherwise slaughtered while they slept. Why, within a stone's throw of the house where Jill and I lived on Hospital Point, lay more than nine hundred men who were buried alive on the USS *Arizona*; fifty-eight more remain trapped and entombed in the battleship *Utah* to this day, another little-known fact of Pearl Harbor history. Nobody ever apologized to them or their families! Why were we making such a big fuss about what was clearly an unfortunate accident? People I'd never met were angry that our government was bending over backward to pacify the Japanese, offering my head on a platter to placate them.

I didn't exactly share those sentiments. I understood that since World War II, the U.S. and Japan had become strong allies. Japan was our lynchpin in the Pacific, politicians and military leaders often reminded us. I recognized the importance of Japan to the United States, politically, economically, and militarily. Yet I wasn't completely immune to the martyr syndrome. At times, I did feel sorry for myself. At times, I did feel that I was getting a raw deal. Maybe that's what led me back to the Book of Job.

Captain Kai Repsholdt, the COMSUBPAC deputy chief of staff, had piqued my interest in Job's story shortly after the *Greeneville* accident. Captain Gonzales and I agreed that it might be better if I worked in Captain Repsholdt's office, so I reported to work in Kai's office every day between the time of the accident and the beginning of the court of inquiry. During that time, Kai Repsholdt reached out to me not only as a fellow naval officer, but as a concerned Christian.

Kai had been on board the *Greeneville* on two occasions, and we had a mutual respect for each other. One Sunday shortly after I had started working in his office, Kai called and invited me to join him for breakfast. We went to Annie Miller's, a small coffee shop in Aiea. While we ate and talked, Kai brought up the biblical account of Job. "Have you ever read the Book of Job in the Bible, Scott?"

"No, not really." I was vaguely familiar with the ancient story, but I had never before read the full account.

"Well, let me tell you about it." Kai explained to me that Job was an extremely successful guy. Then one day, Satan went to God and said, "You're protecting that fellow. Just let me have a shot at him, and before long, he'll curse You and walk away from You."

God said, "Okay, you can do anything you want to him; just don't take his life."

Before long, Job came under intense attack from the enemy, Satan. He lost everything he had. His children died, his possessions were wiped out, and his reputation among his friends and peers was besmirched. Almost overnight, nearly everything that he'd ever held as dear was gone. Physically, he became sickly and could barely move because of the grotesque boils on his body. It got so bad that his wife encouraged him, "Why don't you just curse God and die!"

Job's answer was classic. "Shall we indeed accept good from God and not accept adversity?" he asked (Job 2:10). But Job maintained a steadfast faith in God.

"Scott, you're going to be tested," Kai said matter-of-factly. "And this is going to be a very difficult time in your life. So be aware that there was a man before you who endured awful pain, humiliation, and tragedy, but he continued to trust in God. In the end, Job persevered."

Job's story intrigued me. Kai and I talked further about the similarities between Job's story and mine, and I made a mental note that I wanted to read the story for myself.

In the grim weeks following the accident, I periodically picked up the Bible and read certain favorite passages. But right before the last day of testimony, I turned to the Book of Job and read the entire story. I found it fascinating to discover the hardships, trials, and tribulations that Job went through. Worse yet, Job knew in his heart that he hadn't done anything wrong. Yet some of his friends advised him, "Just admit you have sinned, and take your punishment." As I read, I could identify with Job's losses, what he gave up, but more importantly, I was amazed at what he received, what he found. At the conclusion of the story, it is obvious that Job gained far more than he lost because he gained a fresh realization of who God is.

There lies the secret to what has gotten me through this tragedy.

More than any other thing, that helped me get through this process, maintain my integrity, and not make excuses. How easy it was to mumble to myself, "Hey, this was not my fault. The fire control technician had the information and the solution on his computer and could see it in front of him, but he didn't give it to me. It's his fault! Although the information was there, I wasn't challenged when I said there were no visual contacts."

But the captain is responsible, so I knew then and I know now that the buck stops here.

CHAPTER 23

RIGHTS VERSUS RIGHT

The night before the final day of the inquiry, I tossed and turned, trying to rest. Nevertheless, I still probably got more sleep than Jill or Charlie that night. They were still up doing interviews.

The incessant sound of the alarm clock jolted us out of bed at 6:00 A.M. As we had done every other morning of the inquiry, I dressed in my Navy whites, and Jill dressed in a conservative business suit. We kissed Ashley good-bye and headed off to meet Charlie. But when we arrived at Charlie's quarters, shortly before 7:00, Charlie was nowhere to be seen. We waited a few minutes and he still didn't come. By 7:10, I was getting fidgety, and still there was no sign of him.

"Oh, no!" I groaned aloud. "Don't tell me that on this last day of the inquiry Charlie overslept!"

Around 7:15, I was just about to go pound on Charlie's door, when the cagey lawyer came bounding out to the car.

"Hey, Charlie, what's up? Are you okay? Is everything all right?"

"Oh, yeah, I'm fine. Sorry to be late. I've been working on your opening remarks. I just finished them." Jill and I left our car there behind the building and got into Charlie's rental for the short trip to the Navy Legal Service Office building.

When we arrived at the inquiry, Charlie and I went upstairs to Kimberlie's office as usual, and Charlie handed me a file folder with some handwritten notes inside. "Here, read this," he said. "This is what I want you to say when you take the stand this morning." Charlie headed downstairs to inform the admirals that I would take the stand—even without testimonial immunity.

I sat down, opened the folder, and began to read. I could hardly believe my eyes! Charlie's five pages of scribbles were absolutely brilliant! He had written with just the right touch of respect and military honor, but he had also expressed my feelings of remorse, as well as my irritation with Admiral Fargo for not granting immunity because my testimony was deemed unnecessary. They were Charlie's words on paper, but they expressed my heart.

I studied the three pages until Charlie came back, at about 7:45. Charlie was grinning from ear to ear. "You're not going to believe this," he crowed.

"What?" I asked.

"They are completely caught off guard. They are in a panic down there! They can't believe you want to take the stand without immunity."

"Great," I replied and went back to reading my opening remarks one more time.

Just before 8:00, we entered the inquiry room for the last time. As always, I bowed to the Japanese family members sitting behind me and they bowed in return. I looked over at Jill to give her some sign of reassurance, and took my seat. Charlie sat next to me; Kimberlie and Jennifer took their positions to the far left and far right of me, and Mark Patton sat directly behind Charlie and me.

The three admirals—Sullivan, Nathman, and Stone—sat at the front of the room, along with Admiral Ozawa, the Japanese adviser. Admiral

John Nathman called the session to order and asked if there were any procedural matters to be addressed. The counsel for the court, Captain Bruce MacDonald, presented two exhibits: Admiral Fargo's denial of my testimonial immunity request and my signed Privacy Act statement, both of which were entered into the court record. That done, Admiral Nathman looked at Charlie, and said, "Okay. Counsel for Commander Waddle, you can proceed."

Charlie looked at me, then back at the court, and said, "At this time, we call to the stand Commander Scott D. Waddle, to provide testimony under oath."

I started to get out of my chair, but Captain MacDonald intervened. "I'm going to have to warn Commander Waddle of his rights. Mr. Gittins, do you wish me to do that outside of court, or do you want me to do that in here?"

I saw a glint of a smile sneak across Charlie's face.

"I wish you to read Commander Waddle his military rights in this courtroom, in front of the public, sir," Charlie replied.

Charlie hadn't warned me ahead of time about this part. He wanted me to be surprised when I heard the charges, and I was. He also wanted everyone else, the media included, to be aware of just how serious these proceedings were, and what a risk I was taking by testifying without immunity.

"Very well," Captain MacDonald said. In a voice reminiscent of a television police drama, the counsel for the court began reading aloud the charges against me. And his words were bone-chilling. "Commander Waddle, you are suspected of having committed the following offenses under the Uniform Code of Military Justice: dereliction of duty; improper hazarding of a vessel; negligent homicide. You have the following rights: You have the right to remain silent. Any statement you do make may be used as evidence against you in trial by court-martial . . ."

I'm sure Captain MacDonald read the remainder of my Miranda rights, but I don't remember hearing them. My mind was stuck on those first few statements. Negligent homicide . . . evidence against you in trial by court-martial. It was the first time since the accident that the charges against me were actually presented in my presence. It was also the first time since the accident that my Miranda rights were read to me. I sat stoically listening, trying to keep my stomach from jumping up into my throat.

"Now, do you fully understand your rights as I've explained them to you?" Captain MacDonald's voice interrupted my thoughts.

"I understand them, sir."

"Counsel, you may proceed," Admiral Nathman said to Charlie.

MacDonald interrupted again. "Just a minute, sir! I need to go through the waiver of rights." Nathman nodded, and Captain MacDonald looked at me. "Do you expressly desire to waive your right to remain silent?" The silence in the courtroom was nearly palpable.

I looked back at MacDonald and spoke emphatically, "I desire to waive my right to remain silent." Captain MacDonald went through a litany of questions to make sure I understood that I was giving up all of my rights except to breathe. Finally he asked, "Is this waiver of rights made freely and voluntarily by you, and without any promises or threats having been made to you, or pressure or coercion of any kind having been used against you?"

Now there was a loaded question if I'd ever heard one!

"It is, sir," I answered.

Finally, the court gave the floor to Charlie, who promptly turned toward me and said, "We call Commander Waddle."

I got up, walked to the stand, and was sworn in. I took a deep breath and waited for Charlie's cue.

"Scott, do you have a statement you'd like to make to this court of inquiry?"

It seemed the courtroom itself contracted and held its breath, the next gulp of air contingent upon my answer.

"I do. Yes, sir."

Whooosh! Everyone exhaled quickly and took another fast breath as though afraid of sucking the remaining air out of the room.

I took out Charlie's notes and began to slowly read the speech he had written for me. "Admiral Nathman, Admiral Sullivan, Admiral Stone; as I indicated publicly yesterday before court, I accept full responsibility for the actions of the crew of the USS *Greeneville* on 9 February 2001. As the commanding officer, I am solely responsible for this truly tragic accident. And for the rest of my life, I will live with the horrible consequences of my decisions and actions that resulted in the loss of the *Ehime Maru* and nine of its crew, instructors, and students. I am truly sorry for the loss of life and for the incalculable grief that those losses caused the honorable families of those lost at sea."

I paused and looked straight at the admirals. I wanted them to hear this next part. "I have always assumed that the purpose of this investigation would be to ascertain the cause of this accident for the Navy, for the submarine force, and, most importantly, for the families of those lost on the motor vessel, the *Ehime Maru*. To that end, I have always been willing to provide the information I possessed about this accident, consistent with protecting my legal rights and my family's future. I understand the realities of this accident and the substantial international and diplomatic implications it has had on the United States' bilateral relations with Japan. Prime Minister Mori's visit today could not make those considerations more plain."

The admirals were well aware that even as I spoke to them, the Japanese prime minister was in Honolulu, preparing to lay a wreath at the site where the *Greeneville* struck the *Ehime Maru*, about nine miles off the shores of Oahu. The trip "just happened" to coincide with the last day of testimony at the court of inquiry.

I looked straight at the admirals again as I said, "I am also aware and understand the real potential that those political and diplomatic pressures might exert on the military justice system where those decisions are made at various senior levels." I wanted the admirals to know that I sympathized with their dilemma in dealing with me, but I also wanted them to recognize that how they handled their responsibilities would show whether they had any starch besides that in their uniforms.

"Therefore, on the advice of my three very competent and qualified counsels, I requested testimonial immunity from Admiral Fargo to assure a full, fair, thorough, and complete investigation by preserving my rights and taking reasonable precautions in the event the international and political environment dictated that I be sacrificed to an unwarranted court-martial."

In my peripheral vision, I noticed the admirals shifting uncomfortably in their seats, but I didn't look up. This was my one shot, and I wasn't going to miss the mark. I continued, "I have been informed by counsel that this court's recommendation was that the testimonial immunity should be denied for me because my testimony, quote, 'is not essential or material to the conclusion of the court's investigation,' unquote. Counsel has informed me that since you consider my testimony unnecessary, that I should not provide it. I have, however, decided, with the advice of my counsel, that your determination that my testimony is not essential or material is wrong."

Whaaap! If I'd have smacked the admirals with a steel pipe they wouldn't have looked more taken aback.

"And I have decided to testify under oath, subject to cross-examination."

I didn't intend to sound confrontational, but I wanted the admirals to know upfront that Admiral Fargo's stubbornness in refusing immunity was unnecessary, and that their insistence that the testimony of the captain of the ship was not material to the case—that they could somehow make an accurate and valid determination of what happened that day without consulting me—verged on being ludicrous.

"When I was assigned as a commanding officer and as commanding officer of the USS *Greeneville*, I assumed an awesome responsibility. I have no less of a responsibility to stand up and explain the exercise of my judgment as commanding officer, and I am prepared to do so. I've given my entire adult life to the Navy. I have served the Navy faithfully and honestly. For my entire career, including the day 9 February 2001, I have done my duty to the best of my ability. I am truly sorry for this accident and the loss of life that it caused on the ninth of February. I was trying my best to do the job that I had been assigned. If I made a mistake or mistakes, those mistakes were honest and well intentioned. I'm truly sorry for this accident. It has been a tragedy for the families of those lost, for the crew of the USS *Greeneville*, for their families, for the submarine force, for me, and for my family. I understand by speaking now I may be forfeiting my ability to successfully defend myself at a court-martial.

"This court and the families need to hear from me," I said, turning to face the victims' family members as I spoke, "despite the personal legal prejudice to me . . . and because it is the right thing to do." The wives of two of those who died on the *Ehime Maru* brushed tears from their faces.

I paused, looked up at the admirals, and spoke clearly. "Gentlemen, I am prepared to answer your questions and address your concerns."

For a few seconds, there was a long, awkward silence in the courtroom. Finally, Admiral Nathman leaned forward and addressed Charlie, "You have no questions, Counsel?"

Charlie feigned reticent acquiescence. "No, sir," he replied as though he was exasperated.

"Okay. Admiral Stone?"

Admiral Stone began the marathon session, with the admirals grilling me unmercifully from shortly after 8:00 all the way until noon, with one short break. At times apologetic, at other times combative, I answered every question they asked respectfully and thoroughly, but I wouldn't concede an inch.

In front of me, I kept a yellow note pad on which I wrote down the admirals' questions before answering. In my left hand, which for the most part I kept concealed in my lap, I held onto a brand-new, freshly stamped *Greeneville* command coin, bearing the ship's logo. The coins were awarded by the commanding officer to crewmembers for outstanding performance of his duties, or simply for a job well done. The night before, Doug Coffman had brought the coin to our home.

To me, the coin represented everything for which I was fighting: my own integrity and that of my shipmates. In a strange way, I felt as though I had a piece of the *Greeneville* with me in the witness stand. Beyond that, as the admirals asked me questions, before answering each one, I turned the coin over in my hand, just as a reminder to slow down and think through the questions before answering.

The admirals went back over all the mounds of material they had accumulated in their questioning of others over the past eleven days. Why were nine sailors out of position at the time of the accident? Why did we not compensate more fully for the broken AVSDU monitor? Why was the ship running late that day? Why did we not spend more time at periscope depth and get a clearer picture of the surface situation? Why did we do the emergency deep in the first place, let alone the emergency blow?

The admirals especially castigated me for ordering young Mike Coen, known to be slow and methodical, to take the ship to periscope depth within five minutes instead of the usual ten minutes—a physical impossibility, the admirals asserted. Impossible or not, we had done it. They especially focused on whether I had rushed the preparations prior to the emergency deep, whether I had taken enough time to perform an adequate periscope search before taking the sub down and bringing it back up in the emergency blow.

The admirals repeatedly attempted to elicit a confession from me that the *Greeneville*'s crew and I had acted irresponsibly, had performed poorly, had not done our jobs, or had done them too rapidly. I refuted the admirals at every point, knowing that they were getting more and more angry with every question. The admirals' voices rose in frustration, and the veins in their heads seemed ready to pop, but I refused to give ground.

I adamantly disputed the notion that I ran an informal, lax ship. "I was not informal," I told the admirals when they picked up on a comment that Admiral Konetzni had made to me a year or so prior to the accident. "I didn't micromanage my crew. I empowered them to do their job."

At times, the inquiry seemed like we were players in a Hollywood movie. At one point, one of the admirals asked an obviously inappropriate question, and Charlie popped up immediately. "Excuse me, Admiral! Objection!" he called.

"Excuse me, Counselor," I said to Charlie. "Can I take this one? I think I can answer this."

Charlie waved his hands in the air and brought them down, slapping his thighs. "Sure, please do," he replied in his best feigned exasperation. "Go right ahead." It took all I could do to keep from laughing as Charlie plopped down in his chair to listen to my answer. He was an incredible showman, not to mention a brilliant lawyer.

Later, I stated to the admirals that I thought that I had done a thorough periscope search, peering intently in the direction of the two known contacts yet seeing none of them. I acknowledged that I truly believed that I had had a good picture of the surface situation before I called for the emergency deep. Apart from that, I held onto the high ground. If I was going down, at least it would be for the right reasons. The truth would be known.

When we broke for lunch, Charlie was ecstatic. On the way up the stairs to Kimberlie's office, he couldn't contain his glee. "You kicked butt! Scott, you were awesome! Really great job! But Scott, you gotta give them something. You're too much in control. You need to let them win once in a while."

When we reassembled for the afternoon sessions, the admirals came back with a vengeance. Apparently they figured, *Now that we have him, let's go after him.* And they did. Again and again they came at me with tough, blistering questions coupled with their acerbic comments.

I got the feeling that much of their ire was sheer posturing. They'd ask a legitimate question couched in a lecture. But I did my best to answer. To follow their line of reasoning, I wrote down their questions on a yellow legal pad as they spoke.

Before I answered, I'd say something such as, "As I understand it, Admiral, you are asking a five-part question. Is that correct?"

I'd go down through my notes ticking off each point as I addressed it, thoroughly answering every part of the run-on question. Before relinquishing the floor, I would turn to the admiral who had asked the question and ask, "Did I answer your question to your satisfaction, sir?"

By that time, the admiral usually couldn't even remember what he had asked me.

Despite everything else, I admitted to the admirals that much of what happened on the *Greeneville* on February 9 fell short of our own high standards of "safety, efficiency, and backup," the three tenets of submarining that I drilled into my men and myself again and again. But on that day, we fell short of our own standards. "The teamwork broke," I told the inquiry, "and no one raised a flag."

I acknowledged that nine of thirteen watch stations were not manned by the designated crewmen who had been assigned for duty in those spots that day. Similarly, one sonar station was manned by a trainee, rather than by a veteran crewmember. Worse yet, I hadn't known that the trainee was working without close supervision for a short period of time, about an hour before the accident occurred.

"That, to me, does not meet this standard of yours," Admiral Stone said snidely.

"It was not effective planning. I don't refute that," I replied. What could I say? The admiral was right. "It's obvious that the plan was not efficient, because the plan didn't work."

We revisited the periscope issue again and again, trying to ascertain why I didn't see the *Ehime Maru* when I did my visual search. As Patrick Seacrest had testified, I had the scope trained on the correct spot, in the direction that we had been tracking contacts earlier in the day. I had ordered the submarine up two feet higher to get a better look, yet I still hadn't seen anything with the periscope at high magnification. There was no explanation for why I didn't see that ship. Finally, I simply said, "I don't know why I didn't see the *Ehime Maru*. I know that I didn't."

When I had answered all of the admirals' and Captain MacDonald's questions, each of the legal teams was permitted to present closing arguments before the close of the inquiry. It was then that I saw Charlie Gittins in his best form. Charlie was magnificent in his closing statement, imploring the admirals to consider the evidence and not to recommend a court-martial. Charlie reminded the court that this accident was the result of a series of "extraordinary circumstances that could not be duplicated."

Charlie spoke long, loudly, and with intense passion. He spoke with incredible conviction, pouring every emotion and every ounce of his energy into protecting me. For a while, I thought that Charlie himself might lose his composure. He came close, but he didn't, pulling himself together to conclude, "Commander Waddle exercised his judgment, and he did his level best. He may have fallen short on that day, but his actions weren't criminal."

The final session of the inquiry concluded at about 4:30 in the afternoon. It had been a long, intense day, but at the end of the inquiry, we felt that we had made our case. Now it would be up to the admirals. They'd take a few weeks for deliberations and make a report to Admiral Fargo. He then would decide my fate.

Our legal team gathered for one last meeting. Charlie slapped me on the back and said, "Great job, buddy. You hit a home run in there today." Kimberlie Young and Jennifer Herrold expressed similar sentiments.

Mark Patton, the man who had risked his career to come to my defense, said, "Good job, classmate. I'm proud of you."

The inquiry was over. The court had called thirty-one witnesses, each one of whom recounted the horrible accident from his own perspective. Ironically, none of the distinguished visitors were called to testify before the inquiry, although they did provide statements to the National Transportation Safety Board. Nor did the court ever call Admiral Macke, the man who had arranged for most of the civilians to be on the *Greeneville* that day in February. In his closing remarks, Charlie raised the specter that perhaps Admiral Macke had a conflict of interests, but by then, I really didn't care. I just wanted it all to end.

For twelve solid days, I had repeatedly relived the accident from every possible position, through the eyes and ears of Captain Onishi, of my crew and officers, my superior officers, the Coast Guard rescue team, and most of all, through my own horrific memories. I felt as though every part of my being had been dragged over hot coals, time and time again.

I walked out into the fresh air. In an interview with *Time* magazine several weeks earlier, I had stated that one of my final acts of command would be to help the victims' families gain some sense of closure concerning the tragic accident. If we'd accomplished nothing else, I felt that we had at least succeeded at that. Now, for all practical purposes, my career as a U.S. naval officer was over. A bevy of reporters bludgeoned me with more questions, but I was through talking for the day. There was nothing more I could say.

CHAPTER 24
THE WAITING GAME

During the days following the court of inquiry, my life was on hold. Nobody knew how long it would take for the admirals to deliberate, review their notes, write a report, and present it to Admiral Fargo for his decision. According to Navy rules, once the court of inquiry filed its report, Admiral Fargo had one month to issue a verdict—either move ahead to court-martial, issue reprimands, or exonerate the persons involved. I assumed the process would take at least a few weeks, so I took some of the leave that I had accumulated and tried to recuperate. Eventually, though, I had to go back to work.

While we awaited the report from the court of inquiry, I was still in the Navy, so I reported for work each morning. My immediate boss was Captain Kai Repsholdt, a fine Christian man whom I got to know not just as my superior officer, but also as a brother in the Lord. On several occasions, we went out for coffee and talked candidly about our faith. We talked a lot about my questions concerning the accident. Kai helped me grapple with the difficult questions, such as, "Why did this happen?" After the exhausting court of inquiry, I better understood how it happened in a practical sense, but what purpose did this horrible accident serve in the larger spiritual sense? That was the mind-boggling issue that I just couldn't grasp. I knew that God loved me; I knew that He loved those nine Japanese victims equally as much. Could He not have prevented this accident from happening? Couldn't God in all His power have somehow drawn my attention to that white spot in the haze that day?

Of course He could have. But for some reason, He chose not to do so. Why?

My most wrenching prayer was not "Why me, Lord?" or "Why this?" But my most troubling prayer was "God, why did those nine people have to die?"

Kai and I talked at length about those issues. We didn't always come up with answers, but just being able to honestly and openly talk about my questions and the deeper spiritual issues they represented was helpful. On more than a few matters, we had to admit that we might never know the answers until we get to heaven. Until then, my attitude was going to be like Job, who said, "Though He slay me, I will hope in Him" (Job 13:15). Kai was a tremendous encourager, and I appreciated his friendship and support.

Kai's boss, and mine, was Captain Robert Brandhuber, the COMSUB-PAC chief of staff. Captain Brandhuber was still angry that the *Greeneville* event had happened and, even more so, that he had been dragged into the controversy since it had happened with him aboard. Like most officers, Chief of Staff Brandhuber probably had dreams of advancing in rank and position in the Navy. The *Greeneville* incident undoubtedly put a damper on those dreams. He testified during the court of inquiry that as the highest-ranking officer on the ship that day, he harbored concerns that we were moving too fast, yet he didn't question or caution me about it.

That begged some rather sticky questions from the admirals to Captain Brandhuber, and the ignorance in his answers was glaring. Even the admirals grew frustrated when Captain Brandhuber repeatedly responded, "I don't know," or "I can't recall." He knew he had to justify his decisions before the admirals, but he was caught between a rock and a hard place. He had been duly impressed with the *Greeneville*'s crew on the day of the accident, so he didn't offer any warnings that we were going too fast or that there was anything out of line about how we were operating. He testified at the court of inquiry that as a skipper I was "a strong presence and strong leader," a captain who "knew how he wanted the ship to run."

But when the admirals questioned him about our performance, Brandhuber said that he had been concerned about the rapid pace of our maneuvers and had even planned to caution me out of earshot of the crew and guests that we were going through our maneuvers too fast, that I was not giving the crew time enough to do their work with precision and skill.

That was a crock. Brandhuber knew it and so did I.

Nevertheless, I still felt awful that the *Greeneville* incident had stalled Brandhuber's career. When asked about the effect the *Greeneville* accident would have on Brandhuber, Admiral Konetzni hinted that it might even end his career. Konetzni acknowledged that when Brandhuber is next reviewed for promotion, "he probably won't get the nod," a devastating rejection for a career Navy man of Brandhuber's rank. "This was an accident," Admiral Konetzni said. "But will it affect your marks? You're darn right it will."

I put in for leave as often as I could, and Captain Kai Repsholdt, my new boss, tried to protect me from Brandhuber. But Brandhuber seemed intent on making my life miserable. He wanted to know where I was and what I was doing every hour of the day.

During the time between the inquiry and the admirals' report, I could do nothing but bide my time. I was mentally and emotionally drained after the inquiry, so the rest was welcome. I stayed at home, read, worked on my computer, and exercised a lot. After a while, though, I started getting bored. I needed to look ahead to the future. Not knowing when the Navy would release me, I tried to figure out what life outside the military might look like. But there was really nothing I could do and nowhere I could go. All I could do was wait . . . and wait . . . and wait.

During this time, we learned a bit of good news. In an interview back on the mainland, Acting Secretary of the Navy Robert Pirie, who had been on Admiral Nathman's flagship, the *Coronado*, in San Diego, said publicly that he didn't feel that the actions taken by the crewmembers of the *Greeneville* warranted taking the captain off the ship. Secretary Pirie was subtly saying, "Look, fellows, think carefully about what you are doing. There's not a valid reason for a court-martial here." I appreciated Admiral Pirie's remarks, but he was a long way from Pearl Harbor.

I scanned e-mails and Web sites for hours to see what people were saying about the *Greeneville–Ehime Maru* incident. Many people were extremely supportive of me. Others were critical, but only a few felt I deserved severe punishment. That was encouraging! On the other hand, some of the more radical responses were downright scary. The most jarring comments came from people who apparently were still fighting World War II in their minds. "We didn't get all of those Japs at Okinawa. Glad you got a few more of them. You should have killed them all! Why'd you let twenty-six get away?" It was hard for me to believe that there were actually people with those attitudes running around loose in society. But I found many of them. Or, I should say, many of them found me.

When Jill would come in and see me on the computer, she'd shake her head and say, "Scott, why are you reading that stuff?"

"I don't know. I guess I just want to know what people think about all this."

On Wednesday, April 18, 2001, the *Greeneville* was scheduled to be taken out of dry dock and back to sea for the first time since the accident. It had cost more than two million dollars to repair the damages to the ship.

The *Greeneville*'s interim captain, Tony Cortese, and I talked the day before the *Greeneville* was to embark. I told Tony that I'd be honored if I could greet the guys and wave good-bye from my front yard as they headed out to sea.

"Sure, I think we can do that," Tony said. "We'll look for you."

Jill had started a tradition that as we went to sea, she'd stand on our front yard and wave good-bye. Now it was my turn. This time, however, as the guys headed out to sea, they'd be going . . . without me.

On Wednesday morning, I dressed in my Navy whites and stood in front of our house, looking at the waters of Pearl Harbor. It was a stomach-wrenching feeling, knowing that my ship, with the guys I had trained, would soon round the bend, but I would not be on it. Nor would I ever be again.

The *Greeneville*'s crew knew that I'd be standing in the yard as they went by, so as many men as possible crowded on the deck of the ship as it passed. Instinctively, as I saw the *Greeneville* approaching, flags flying, I stood at attention and snapped to a salute.

As the *Greeneville* slipped through the narrow channel in front of our house, the guys sounded the whistle, as a special way of saying hello. I'll remember that sound for the rest of my life. On the bridge, Captain Tony Cortese waved to me as the ship passed by. I held the salute until I could no longer see my ship. When the ship rounded the corner and dipped out of sight, I turned away from the water and walked back to the house. "That was the hardest thing I have done in my life," I told some friends who had gathered with me for the special occasion. I went into the house, changed out of my uniform, and collapsed in a chair.

In the early days following the accident, Stone Phillips of NBC recognized that there might be an intriguing story developing. Even before the court of inquiry, *Dateline*, the NBC newsmagazine television program hosted by Jane Pauley and Stone Phillips, sent producers and camera crews to cover the proceedings and to interview me. Not knowing how the inquiry might turn out, I was somewhat reticent about granting any interviews. But because of the amount of time required to gather all the necessary information and to shoot the footage necessary for the piece, I had granted the interviews the weekend after the inquiry concluded on March 20. NBC assured me that they would not air the footage until the final outcome was announced.

By April 10, the admirals delivered their report to Admiral Fargo. Unfortunately, at the same time, the promotions department at NBC mistakenly aired an ad using the prerecorded interview with me.

When I first heard that NBC was running the commercial, I panicked. The network wasn't supposed to air anything until *after* Admiral Fargo's decision, and the admiral had thirty days to review the report and consider his decision! To air the interview before the admiral's decision could easily give the impression that I was trying to influence his assessment.

I wasn't the only one who was concerned. When he heard about the interview, my friend Captain Pete Daly, Admiral Fargo's executive assistant, came over to our home, along with Phil Davidson. "Can we talk?" Pete asked.

"Sure, come on in and sit down."

"Scott, we understand that you've done an interview with *Dateline*. Is that correct?"

"Yes, it is." I could tell Pete was deeply troubled. This was something the Navy couldn't control.

"Can you tell us about it?" he asked.

"No, sir."

"Can you stop it?"

"I probably can."

"What are you going to do?"

"I'm planning to go to New York immediately after Admiral Fargo's decision. I'll be doing some more interviews with NBC."

"Is that what you really want to do?" Pete asked. "Scott, do you think that's wise? We're not here on Admiral Fargo's behalf. We're here as your friends and neighbors, and we want to help you. Do you really think it's in your best interests to do this sort of thing?"

"I don't know, Pete," I replied honestly. In my heart, I didn't really want to go until after everything was settled, but I had already committed to NBC. "I feel strongly that I need to keep my commitment to NBC to go to New York to support their efforts, but I'm not sure just yet what I'm going to do. I'll let you know."

Steve Cheng of NBC called and apologized for the mistake. "Scott, I'm really sorry."

"Steve, this is exactly why I didn't want to do the interview until after everything was settled. But you guys said you needed it in advance, and you assured me that you'd keep it under wraps until after Admiral Fargo's decision. Now you're out there advertising this interview, and you're going to influence the admiral's decision!"

"We'll do our best to make it right," Steve assured me.

The next day, I attended a change of command ceremony at Pearl Harbor for one of my classmates, Dennis Murphy. Afterward, Admiral Konetzni approached me about the interview.

"Scott, what are you going to do?"

"Admiral, I really feel that I have no choice. I have to go to New York. This interview was supposed to be embargoed until after the admiral's decision. It wasn't supposed to be released. Now, if I don't go, they'll air it anyhow."

"Just tell them to pull it," the admiral said. "You can do that. You don't have to go to New York. It's your choice."

I went home and called Steve Cheng. "Steve, do not air the piece," I said. "Please do not air anything about my case until it is resolved."

"We won't," Steve promised.

"Also, I won't come to New York if you guys air this piece on a date that is not agreed to, until after Admiral Fargo's decision."

"Okay, Scott. If that's the way you want it."

"That's the way it has to be."

Maybe I was being too stubborn for my own good; I don't know. But I did what I felt was right, and I believe God honored the intent of my heart. Amazingly, it actually worked out better for everybody.

CHAPTER 25
GUILTY OR NOT?

On April 22, I received the classic "good news–bad news" message. The good news was that I was being called to admiral's mast, a nonjudicial punishment meted out by Admiral Thomas Fargo, commander of the Pacific Fleet. That meant I would not be subject to a court-martial. The bad news was also the fact that I was being called to admiral's mast. Clearly, I had not been exonerated as a result of the court of inquiry, nor was I to be exonerated by Admiral Fargo. The admiral could impose a fine, confine me to quarters, or prescribe a variety of other restrictions. He would also give me a written and verbal reprimand. The one positive point was that it was unlikely that I'd serve any prison time.

On Monday, April 23, 2001, I prayed for wisdom as I prepared to go to admiral's mast. The private mast was to be held at Admiral Fargo's conference room, and only my lawyer and Admiral Konetzni were permitted to attend. The admiral's executive assistant, Captain Pete Daly, and his JAGC officer would record the proceedings, but other than that, there would be no spectators. Not even my wife, Jill, was allowed to attend.

I stopped by the Legal Services building to pick up Kimberlie Young, who was to accompany me as my legal counsel. Charlie Gittins was already working another case, but I had talked by telephone with Charlie prior to going to the admiral's mast. "Be respectful, Scott," Charlie cautioned me. "Be sure to say 'yes, sir; no, sir.' Don't make any promises; be sure to write down any articles the admiral mentions."

Kimberlie and I drove over to Pacific Fleet headquarters at Makalapa Compound to Admiral Fargo's office. As we exited Pearl Harbor, a television reporter and cameraman were standing in the median with Pearl Harbor in the background. As we went by, I couldn't resist. I laid on the horn and purposely interrupted their sound bite. The reporter looked over angrily, and I waved out the window and smiled. When he recognized me, the cameraman nearly dropped his camera trying to get a shot as we drove by, but we were moving too fast for him. It was the only moment of levity we would know on this extremely somber day.

Kimberlie and I walked over to Admiral Konetzni's office. We drove in separate cars across the Pearl Harbor base to Admiral Fargo's office. Admiral Konetzni and I both were dressed in summer Navy whites as we walked in to Admiral Fargo's office conference room.

"Come in," Admiral Fargo greeted us cordially. "Have a seat." He motioned to two chairs across from him. Pete Daly, the admiral's executive assistant, was already there, as was Captain Michael Hinkley, the admiral's JAGC officer.

I took a seat at the large walnut conference table across from Admiral Fargo, with Admiral Konetzni seated on my left. I remained silent and waited for Admiral Fargo to speak. As I did, I glanced around and noted the stately beauty of the conference room. I was surrounded by Navy memorabilia, including sabers in display cases, large oil paintings depicting famous Pacific naval battles, and a large painting of Admiral Nimitz. The admiral's office was almost like a museum of the Pacific Fleet. It was heartbreaking to gaze on those symbols, since they represented a heritage and culture of which I would no longer be a part. This was the end of my naval career.

Admiral Fargo called the mast to order, and he reviewed the charges and elements of the case. He asked Konetzni for his appraisal of my performance as the former commander of the *Greeneville*, and although Admiral Konetzni was extremely kind and complimentary, it didn't matter. Everything had already been said. Admiral Fargo had twelve days' worth of inquiry transcripts, plus the admirals' report. He really didn't need any further information.

The admiral asked me what I had learned through this horrible situation and what I would do differently. "I'd take more time to do a higher periscope search, sir. And a longer search."

The admiral pulled no punches. He was extremely blunt during the mast. "You violated time-honored processes, and you cut corners, you violated your own standard orders, you pushed your crew too fast, and you caused this accident," Admiral Fargo said to me.

I wasn't about to argue with him, and it wouldn't have done any good anyhow. I did, however, challenge the admiral concerning the unfairness of my not being allowed to have Chris Reismeyer represent me. Admiral Fargo's rationale for refusing to grant my request was that it would have set a bad precedent and would have been cost-prohibitive. Although I held my tongue, I thought, *Apparently, you weren't concerned about those issues when it came to the other attorneys involved in the case.*

The admiral spoke somberly, "I find you guilty of two of the three charges, dereliction of duty and improper hazarding of a vessel." I breathed a sigh of relief. The admiral had not found me guilty of negligent homicide. "You will be fined a half-month's pay for two months, and your pay will be suspended for six months."

The admiral went on to give me a searing verbal reprimand, reminding me of the enormous damages done and what a discredit my actions had brought upon the Navy.

Admiral Fargo didn't throw me out of the Navy, but he made clear that my resignation was expected. He said, "Scott, if you choose to stay in the Navy, I'm going to ask you to show cause. Put it in writing. If you want to stay in the Navy, justify why the Navy should keep you, and then a board will review your request."

"Admiral, it is my intent, immediately after this mast, to submit my request for retirement at the earliest possible date."

Fargo nodded. I doubt that he honestly expected me to remain in the Navy, but it was his duty to at least offer me the option, which I appreciated. We talked further, and I once again expressed my desire to go to Japan to personally apologize to the victims' families whom I had not been able to speak to during the inquiry, as well as to the people of Uwajima Fisheries School. "I'd really like to get there," I said, "but I don't have the funds to do so."

Admiral Fargo promised that the Navy would fly Jill and me to Japan so I could make the appropriate apologies.

"Thank you, Admiral," I said.

"You're welcome," the admiral replied. "You're dismissed."

The entire proceeding took about one hour, and I hated every minute of it.

Following the admiral's mast, Admiral Fargo held a press conference announcing to the world what he had just told me—that I had been found guilty of two charges, but not negligent homicide, and I would be allowed to resign from the Navy, to be honorably discharged with my earned pension. He said the collision between the *Greeneville* and the *Ehime Maru* happened because my crew and I didn't conduct adequate sonar and periscope searches of the area before surfacing. The admiral emphasized that he held me responsible.

When asked by the media if the punishment was a mere slap on the wrists, Admiral Fargo came close to defending me as he defended his decision. "Commander Waddle has been stripped of his command," said the admiral, "and his career effectively terminated. For a naval officer who served for twenty years to his country, I would tell you that this is absolutely devastating. He has paid dearly."

Admiral Fargo said that he had not recommended that I be subjected to court-martial because the inquiry produced no evidence of criminal intent or deliberate misconduct. He kindly noted that prior to the accident, my career and service record were excellent.

The admiral was not reluctant, however, to affix blame. "This collision was solely the fault of the USS *Greeneville*," he said. "This tragic accident could and should have been avoided by simply following existing Navy standards and procedures in bringing submarines to the surface." The admiral summed up the incident as "a tragedy in which mistakes were made, for which our people have been held accountable."

I went home, walked in the door, and said nonchalantly, "Well, that's done." Jill knew better. She understood that my almost flippant attitude was a cover-up for the searing pain in my heart. She didn't say much. She just came over and hugged me, and we tried to console one another as best we could. It was the end of an era in our lives.

The outcry in Japan was instantaneous, with many people expressing outrage that I had "gotten off."

Gotten off? I wondered. *Gotten off with what?* Granted, I wouldn't have to endure a court-martial or go to prison. But my life was devastated. My career was a shambles, and my family was forced to leave our home, our friends, our community, everything that we held dear. The only thing we were walking away with was our lives and a meager military pension, hardly enough to live on in the civilian world.

But the Japanese press insisted that I'd have been treated differently had I been tried in a civil court rather than in a military environment. Mitsunori Nomoto, father of Katsuya Nomoto, a seventeen-year-old boy who died in the accident, expressed similar sentiments. "If that is their system, what can we do?" he asked plaintively. "If it were not the military, there would be a harsher punishment."

I was especially disappointed in the reactions of some of the family members of the victims. I had honestly thought that I had gotten through to them and that they truly understood the awful remorse I felt over the accident. But apparently I was wrong. Ryosuke Terata, whose seventeen-year-old son died in the accident, chided, "It's unforgivable that the matter should be settled with this sort of punishment after so many questions were left unanswered by the court of inquiry." Several other family members said that I should have had to face a court-martial. I was saddened by their response but nonetheless determined to get to Japan to formally apologize again.

About the only encouraging word came from a surprising source. In an unrelated television interview, Matt Lauer, host of NBC's *Today* show, asked President George W. Bush about the judgment of the court of inquiry and Admiral Fargo's decision. The president of the United States responded by referring to me as "a fine American patriot." I was surprised the president even knew my name! When asked about my punishment, the president supported the Navy's decision. "I don't want to second-guess the Pentagon," said the president. "Like any good commander, he is taking the heat."

Monday afternoon, I received a phone call from NBC. The *Dateline* interview was definitely going to air the following evening. Could I be in New York for a Wednesday-morning "live" interview with Matt Lauer on the *Today* show? NBC offered to fly Jill, Ashley, and me to New York. I had already planned to take leave following the admiral's mast, so I had the time. "Sure, why not?" I said.

On our flight from Hawaii to New York, we changed planes in Los Angeles. As we walked through first class on our way to our seats, I noticed a familiar face. It was former Chairman of the Joint Chiefs of Staff, General John Shalikashvili. Jill and I took our seats in business class as the remaining passengers boarded. A woman going down the narrow aisle noticed me and began saying to her husband, "That's him! That's him. That's Commander Waddle."

They pushed on back the aisle, but a few minutes later, a flight attendant delivered a note from the woman. "I'm so proud of you for doing the honorable and right thing. It is so refreshing to see someone in a position of responsibility being accountable."

During the flight, I asked a flight attendant if it would be okay for me to go up front to first class to speak to General Shalikashvili.

"Sure, go right ahead."

I walked up to where the general was sitting and said, "Excuse me, General, I'm Commander Scott Waddle."

The general looked back at me coolly and said, "Yes, I know."

"Would you do me a favor, sir?"

"It depends," the general answered.

"Sir, I know that you are close to Secretary Colin Powell. The next time you see him, would you please relay to him my deepest apologies and regrets for the embarrassment this incident has caused the nation and the distraction it has caused him from performing his duties?"

The general remained aloof, but he replied, "I'll deliver the message."

On Tuesday, April 24, NBC aired the *Dateline* piece. Jill and I were in the air most of the day, traveling from Honolulu to New York, so by the time we finally arrived in our hotel room on Tuesday evening, the last thing I wanted to see was another rehashing of the *Greeneville–Ehime Maru* accident. But the *Dateline* piece was riveting. It was not entirely complimentary toward me, but I felt it was a fair presentation of what had happened and my response to it. Stone Phillips later did an interview with Katie Couric on the tenth anniversary of *Dateline*, in which he commented that the *Greeneville* story was one of the most memorable and poignant stories he had covered during his ten years of doing the program. Stone stated that he was most impressed that I had granted an interview with him prior to knowing what Admiral Fargo's decision was going to be.

I was interviewed by Matt Lauer on NBC's *Today* show on Wednesday morning. Everyone we met at NBC was extremely kind to us. Also appearing on the program that morning was actress Uma Thurman, who talked at length with Ashley and Jill. Uma told Ashley that she looked like her when she was her age—that made the trip worthwhile for Ashley!

I met Tom Brokaw, who was also extremely kind and cordial to me, even though we were not scheduled to do an interview. I also met actor John Goodman. Surprisingly, John was genuinely excited about meeting *me!* "I want to meet the commander!" he told one of the assistants in the makeup area. We met in his dressing room, and I wasn't prepared for John's enthusiasm. "I can't believe I'm getting to meet you," he said as he shook my hand vigorously. "How about that? I'm getting to meet the commander. It is such an honor."

"Yeah, and I'm getting to meet Fred Flintstone!" I quipped. We laughed, and John and I talked for a while. I was shocked. This was so different from what I had been experiencing for the past two months. Coming from the base at Pearl Harbor where many people were trying to distance themselves from me, John Goodman went out of his way to spend time with me.

I also did an interview on CNN's *Larry King Live* on Thursday evening, April 26. Larry had once been on board a submarine, the USS *Ohio*, for a distinguished visitors' cruise with Admiral Konetzni, and he had emerged immensely impressed. Better than most, he understood what the Navy was trying to do through the distinguished visitors' program.

Although I was technically on my own time, I was still an officer in the U.S. Navy, so I wore my Navy uniform on the air for all the interviews I did that week. That created quite a stir back at COMSUBPAC, but I didn't care. The uniform had been my identity for more than twenty years. For me to have gone on television wearing a business suit would not have been an accurate portrayal of who I was.

At some point in each of the interviews, I tried to emphasize that I was responsible for the accident. I told Matt Lauer that after twenty years of service to our country, "An eight-minute period of time in my life . . . resulted in the tragic loss of nine lives."

One of the lighter moments on the Larry King show occurred off-camera, when the producers received a call from some guys claiming to be on board the *Greeneville*.

"Yeah, right," the producers said, and hung up on them three times. Later we learned that the *Greeneville* had just returned from the sea trials they had embarked on a few days earlier, and when they saw me on *Larry King Live*, the guys really had called from the ship. It would have been fun to them to have been on the air with me.

During one of the last commercial breaks, Larry asked, "How do you feel about your wife joining you on the set?"

"I don't know, Larry. I'm not sure how comfortable Jill would be doing that."

"Well, she's ready, and we already have her wired with a microphone."

"Okay, bring her on!" I said.

Jill came on the show with us, and she was incredible. Once again, Jill was a natural, and she brought an "everyday family" aspect to our plight.

At the conclusion of the program, Larry told me that he was on his way to Washington, D.C., to interview Vice President Dick Cheney.

"Would you be willing to give him a personal letter from me?" I asked.

"Sure, I'd be glad to," Larry responded.

I wrote a quick letter to the vice president, expressing similar sentiments as I had to Colin Powell. Ten days later, I received a warm letter of response from Vice President Cheney, commending me for the manner in which I stood tall and conducted myself during the *Greeneville* incident proceedings.

Another interesting development spawned by the Larry King interview was my meeting with business magnate and former presidential candidate Ross Perot. About fifteen minutes before the end of Larry's program, during one of the commercial breaks, Larry leaned over and asked me, "Scott, what are you going to do when all this is over?"

"I don't know, Larry. I really don't. I've been in the Navy for twenty-four years. It's been my life. I don't even know where to start in finding a civilian job."

Larry nodded and said, "I'm going to help you find a job, Scott."

I could hardly believe my ears. But the red camera light was back on and we were back on the air, so we left it at that.

On the way back to Honolulu, Jill, Ashley, and I stayed overnight in Los Angeles. While we were there, I got a call from Ross Perot. True to his word, Larry had passed on my name and contact information to the enigmatic Texas multimillionaire.

At first, I thought I was talking to someone imitating Dana Carvey doing one of his famous *Saturday Night Live* routines, but it was really Ross Perot on the line. "Commander Waddle," he said in his shrill, high-pitched voice.

"Yes, sir?"

"Ross Perot."

It was 7:15 in the morning! We talked for forty-five minutes, and Mr. Perot invited me to come visit his company in Texas to interview for a job. He asked, "Where's your wife from?"

"Jill is from the state of Washington," I replied.

"Oh, that's okay," said Perot whimsically, "we can make a Texan out of her."

"Yes, sir, we can."

"Well, how soon can you get here?"

"I don't know, sir."

"How about next week?"

"I'm not sure, sir; I'm still obligated to the Navy. I don't know what my schedule is going to be these next few weeks. I'd be glad to come, though, as soon as I get some leave."

"Good. Get here as soon as you can. I want to talk to you, and we're going to figure out what we can do for you."

When eventually I was able to visit with Mr. Perot, he was incredibly kind and gracious to me. A graduate of the Naval Academy and a staunch supporter of military men and women, Ross Perot was amazingly encouraging in helping me to make the transition from military life to civilian life.

After touring Mr. Perot's complex, he suggested we go out to dinner. We walked downstairs and got into Ross Perot's personal automobile—a beat-up, four-door sedan that looked as though it had about 200,000 miles on it. Ross drove the car himself, talking and gesturing so enthusiastically as he steered that he didn't even notice when he ran over several curbs along the way.

We went to a small, quiet restaurant and enjoyed a private dinner and relaxed conversation. During the meal, Ross Perot said to me, "Here's what you're going to do. I want you to write down all the negative experiences you have encountered over the past several months. Then I want you to wad that paper up and throw it away. Put it behind you, Scott. You can move on."

It was the best advice anyone could have given me.

As we finished our meal, I excused myself as though I were going to the restroom, and I found the maître d'. "Here's my credit card. Charge the meal to me."

"Sir, Mr. Perot is paying for dinner."

"No, tonight, Mr. Waddle is buying Mr. Perot dinner."

"No, sir, we can't do that."

"What's it going to take? Thirty percent tip? Whatever it takes, put it on my card." The maître d' smiled and acquiesced.

When the bill came, Mr. Perot reached for the tab as usual. I lightly put my hand on his arm. "Mr. Perot, tonight I'm paying for dinner. It's a small token of my deep appreciation for your kindness toward me."

Ross Perot looked back at me with a smile of understanding. "Well, you're welcome," he said, relaxing his grip on the bill. He allowed me the privilege of being one of the few people in the world to have ever beaten him to the tab.

I came away from my meeting with Ross Perot with immeasurable respect for a great American patriot and businessman. For a variety of personal reasons, I didn't pursue the employment opportunity with Ross Perot, but I will always be grateful to Larry King and to Ross Perot for the effort they extended in helping me, and more importantly, for believing in me.

CHAPTER 26

TAKING "FLIGHT"

When I arrived back at Pearl Harbor, I had to go back to work for Captain Brandhuber. I was still in the Navy, and I would be until my retirement papers were signed, sealed, and delivered. In the meantime, I was given busywork to do.

For instance, Captain Brandhuber assigned me the task of determining the total cost per day to operate a submarine at sea. It was an interesting but meaningless chore.

It was almost impossible to get an accurate estimate in real dollars and cents. What does it cost to operate a nuclear reactor every day? How much does it cost for food, drinking water, dishwashing detergent, and other basic commodities? What if you practice firing torpedoes or Tomahawk missiles? That's not exactly the same as buying some shotgun shells down at the local hardware store. Nevertheless, I worked diligently trying to ascertain what it actually cost to run a nuclear submarine for a day. I came up with a figure of about six hundred thousand dollars per day to operate a nuclear fast-attack submarine.

I took my results and presented them to Captain Brandhuber, along with some excellent Power Point presentations. Silly me. I thought he actually wanted to know. Brandhuber took one look at the material, and without even reviewing it, he simply said, "That's not good enough. Go back and do it again."

I didn't say a word. I simply turned on my heels and went back and worked for Kai.

Shortly after that, I heard that the Ruehlin job transition seminar was to be conducted at Camp Smith, the Marine base in Kailua, a few miles from Pearl Harbor, so I determined that I wanted to attend. The seminar is run by Admiral Ruehlin, a former naval supply officer who does his best to encourage men and women to stay in the military. But ostensibly, the primary emphasis of the seminar is intended to help career officers make the transition to the business world and civilian life. Basically the seminar is a "dress for success," three-day event, culminating in a mock interview with potential employers following the seminar.

A friend of mine, Colonel Johnson, worked out an extra seat for me. The cost was five hundred dollars per person, but the Marine Corps was paying for the seminar so it wouldn't cost the Navy or me anything but my time . . . and the permission of my superior officer. I asked Captain Kai Repsholdt if I could attend the seminar, and he said, "I think it's a good idea, Scott. Just check in with me in the afternoon and let me know how things are going." I understood what Kai meant. He knew that Captain Brandhuber would be all over him if he couldn't tell him where I was and what I was doing.

I attended the seminar and was getting excited about what I was learning. While there, I received a phone call from John Rodgers, an F-15 pilot known to his men as "Jolly." I had met John Rodgers while I was XO on the *San Francisco*, stationed in Hawaii. One afternoon, John brought his son by and asked for a tour. I took time out of my day to show John and his son around the sub.

After the *Greeneville* accident, John saw the Larry King interview and heard me express my lifelong dream to fly in a jet. John called and offered a special invitation to me. "I'd like you to come to Tyndale Air Force Base, in

Panama City, Florida, to speak to the 325th Fighter Wing about accountability in leadership. It's a group we call the Warrior's Club. I'll get you a hop in an F-15."

I wasn't excited about speaking to anyone. After all, I wasn't exactly known as a motivational speaker yet. But that potential jet ride got my attention. From the time I was a little boy, I'd always wanted to fly in a fighter jet like my dad.

"Sure, Jolly," I said. "What do I have to do?"

"Well, you'll need to get a physical before you come, that's all," Jolly replied.

"Great, let's set it up."

I went to get a flight physical at Hickam. That's where the doctor put a damper on my flight plans. "Scott, you're twenty-five pounds over the flight weight that the ejection seat is rated for, so we'll need to get a waiver if you want to fly."

Oh, no! I thought. *If I apply for a waiver, people are going to make a big deal about me doing this trip, and that's the last thing I need right now.* Life was tense enough around the office.

But I really wanted to fly.

"Okay," I said to the flight surgeon who examined me. "Jolly and I agreed that I'd get this done ahead of time. Let's put in for the waiver. This might be my last chance ever to get in a fighter jet."

"You got it, Scott," the doc said. I left the medical office and didn't think much more about it.

Friday afternoon, while still at the Ruehlin seminar, I received a phone call from Captain Brandhuber. "Get down to my office, now!" he ordered angrily.

"Why, sir? Is something wrong?"

"Why is CINPAC fleet asking me about you flying in a jet?"

I really didn't want to deal with Brandhuber just then, so I said, "I'm not sure, sir."

"Get down here now!"

I left the seminar and drove over to Pearl Harbor, still in my business suit, which was the attire for the transition seminar.

"Why are you in civilian clothes?" Captain Brandhuber railed when he saw that I was not in uniform.

"I've been to the Ruehlin seminar . . ."

"And who gave you permission to go there?"

"Captain Repsholdt did, sir." I nodded toward Kai, who had most graciously accompanied me to see Captain Brandhuber.

"Why didn't you do that on your own time?"

I could tell that Captain Brandhuber was just nitpicking, and that angered me. I looked back at him and said, "Well, *Captain* . . ." Technically, I was not being disrespectful. Brandhuber's rank was that of *captain*, but he was also *chief of staff*, and that's how everyone else in the office referred to him. Everyone except me. "When you hosted the Ruehlin seminar here on the base back in February, while I was preparing for a court of inquiry, do you mean to tell me that all the men who attended that seminar did so on their own time?"

"Well, I don't know about that . . ."

"And how about you, Captain? Did you use your free time to attend that seminar?" I asked. I could see the blood vessels popping up in Captain Brandhuber's forehead. I wasn't being rude or disrespectful, but I didn't have much to lose anymore. What was he going to do? Take my birthday away?

"Well, er . . . ah, no, okay; I see your point." Brandhuber quickly changed the subject. "Let's talk about this hop at Tyndale. If you go, you are going on your own time. You do not represent the Navy. You are not permitted to wear a Navy uniform. You are not Commander Waddle; you are Scott Waddle. You represent yourself. You don't represent the submarine force and you don't represent the Navy."

Although the Air Force requested my presence and cut orders to that effect, Captain Brandhuber refused to allow me to go to Panama City on Navy time. I had to take my personal leave to make the trip. Eventually, I was able to go to Florida to speak for Jolly Rodgers's Warriors, but thanks to the military stonewalling, I was not permitted to actually fly in the F-15. I was disappointed, but Jolly arranged for me to get into an Air Force simulator for three hours. The Air Force simulators, similar to the submarine simulators at Groton, are incredibly realistic. If you didn't know better, you'd think that you really were flying. It's truly the next best thing to being there. I even shot down four MIGs. I was in heaven!

Just as we neared the end of the simulator session, I looked below and saw Jolly "flying" at about three thousand feet below me, five miles ahead, so I shot him down too! "I'm an ace now!" I hooted. I even landed the jet without running off the runway.

When we landed, Jolly said, "Scott, it's too bad you weren't able to get into the Air Force. I've never seen anyone grasp these instruments so quickly. You're a natural."

"Thanks, Jolly. Flying an Air Force jet is something I've always wanted to do."

Standing up in front of Jolly's men and speaking to them about leadership and accountability meant a lot to me. About five hundred pilots, male and female, were in the room that day as I told them about my career and the *Greeneville–Ehime Maru* accident. The Air Force guys treated me with incredible respect and gave me a standing ovation when I finished.

Back in Hawaii, I waited impatiently for my retirement date to come through. Jill and Ashley and I were living in limbo, not knowing when we were moving or where we were going. Nor did I have a job to go to. What was I going to do with the rest of my life? I felt like a kid starting college, wondering what's out there in the big world for me.

Jill and I had a ton of moving details that needed to be attended to. Everyone knows what a chore moving can be. When you are not only moving from your home, but also transitioning in your career, leaving your friends and coworkers, your church family, school, and your lives, the stress level can be excruciating. School would be starting soon, so we decided the best thing we could do would be to relocate to Olympia, Washington, near Jill's family, until my retirement from the Navy came through.

The Navy had scheduled our lovely home on Ford Island to be renovated, so in August we moved out, and Jill and Ashley went to Olympia.

Meanwhile, I moved in temporarily with our good friends, retired submarine captain John Peters and his wife, Joan. The Peterses had gone away for the summer, so I basically had their home to myself.

Admiral Fargo and I had agreed that I would retire sometime around October 1, 2001, but for some inexplicable reason, every time I tried to get my superiors to give me a firm date when I could retire, my official retirement from the Navy kept being put off. It wasn't as though I was a big help around the base. One might think that after the *Greeneville* incident, the Navy would be anxious to say good-bye to me, especially some of the officers with whom I worked each day. I wasn't an office guy. I was a submariner. I was an albatross around the Navy's neck, no longer an asset to the service. Why not just let me go, and we'd all be happier for it?

Quite the contrary, the attitude was "This man has cost us dearly, so let's see how much pain we can exact from Waddle before he gets out of here." Whether that was the case or not, it sure seemed that way to me.

I was growing increasingly frustrated with all the foolishness and delays. Funny, I had spent twenty-four years in a Navy uniform, counting my days at Annapolis, but now that I knew I had no more future in the Navy, I just wanted out—the sooner the better. I had fulfilled my obligation and now I was ready to leave. I wasn't doing the Navy any good by being there, and the Navy was not helping me to get on with my life by stonewalling my retirement.

Finally, I went to Commander McDonald, the Pacific Submarine Force staff judge advocate. I knocked on his door, and asked, "Hey, Commander, do you have a minute to talk?"

"Sure, Scott. Come on in. What can I do for you?"

I sat down and laid out what had been happening in regard to the perpetual delays of my retirement. "This is what has transpired, and you may want to go talk to the chief of staff. If I don't get my terminal leave approved within the next twenty-four hours, I'm going to file Article 113 charges against the chief of staff for harassment." I proceeded to explain to the JAGC officer the rules of retirement and the inconsistencies that were evident in my case. "Now if you don't want me to make a big deal about this,

I suggest that you convince the chief of staff to approve my terminal leave immediately. If you want to play hardball, I will. If I don't get this approval, I'll take it to the press; I'll take it to Congress, and you'll get more attention than you guys ever wanted from me."

Commander McDonald looked at me and gave me the typical Navy response. "I'll get back to you on this, Scott."

"Fine," I said. "I'll be back tomorrow. If you don't have my terminal leave in place, it's going to hit the fan."

When I returned to the JAGC officer the following day, my terminal leave papers were approved and signed by Captain Brandhuber. My formal retirement papers came through on September 25, for a retirement of October 1. I had no retirement ceremony.

I walked out the door on October 1 as though I was simply leaving for the day. Nobody presented me with a gold watch. Nobody was there to say, "Thank you for your service, sir." After twenty-four years in the Navy, it was over, just like that.

I did have a quasiretirement ceremony several months earlier. Before the *Greeneville* had shipped out in August for its six-month deployment, some of the guys and their wives, including Jerry Pfeifer, Mike Coen, Tyler Meador, and others, had gotten together with Jill and me for a farewell dinner at the Aloha Tower at Gordon Biersch restaurant, the military enclave on Waikiki Beach. As a special going-away gift, the guys presented me with a model of the *Greeneville*. It was a priceless gift to me and a special evening that I will always cherish, especially after all we had been through together.

CHAPTER 27

DOING THE
RIGHT THING

Of the thousands of cards and letters I received expressing support and offering prayers from around the globe, I read only two that were sharply critical. I may have received more than that and not been aware, since Jill shielded me from a lot of material in the early days after the accident. One critical letter was from a German physician, a naturalized American living in Miami who thought that my effusive tears and expressions of emotion were not masculine, and were instead an insult and an embarrassment to the men and women in uniform. I received a letter expressing similar sentiments from a former Blackhawk pilot, an American of Asian descent who managed a Japanese restaurant in Oakland.

It took me awhile to track them down, but I called both men by telephone. I said, "I want you to know that I got your letter. I thank you for taking the time and effort to write to me. I've read and acknowledged what you have to say, and although I don't necessarily agree with your sentiments, I respect them and appreciate your insights."

The German physician's answer surprised me. "You must be a strong man if you were willing to pick up the phone and call me," he said. "If you're ever in Miami, I'd like to take you out for dinner." I received a similar response from the man in Oakland.

Although I couldn't respond to every letter I received, I tried to acknowledge as many as possible, especially those from people who had experienced some troubling accident or tragedy in their lives—and believe me, that includes a lot of us.

Many of the letters I received said, "Because of what you did, your example gave me the courage to do the right thing in my situation."

I wrote back, "Weakness is the inability to admit when you've done wrong. Strength is facing your wrong and having the courage to confront it, admit it, and address it. You are strong."

One of the most poignant letters I received was from Ryosuke Terata, a Japanese woman who had lost a loved one aboard the *Ehime Maru*. She wrote me an angry letter and sent it to the *Honolulu Observer* as well. In her letter she said, "I don't know if I will ever be able to forgive you." I met with her and tried to better explain how the accident occurred. And I apologized to her again. When the apology was made, we connected. I told her as I have so many others since then, "Judge me as you would; give me the punishment you feel is warranted. I will shoulder that burden. I must accept full responsibility for my actions."

I promised that I would visit Japan soon to apologize in person to the other family members who were unable to attend the inquiry. Only then will they know the sincerity of my sorrow, and only then will I be able to find an element of closure on that part of the accident. I have no illusions of ever having complete closure.

The accident is the first thing I think about each morning and the last thing that crosses my mind at night. And I still have nightmares.

Even now, the haunting memories of the accident sometimes catch me by surprise. I may be going along with life, keeping busy with my daily activities, when suddenly I'll see a Japanese young person or a white boat or some other reminder, and all the horror of that day comes streaming back. At times, I'll dream about the accident, and in my dreams I am helpless to do anything to assist the kids who are dying. I'll wake up in a cold sweat. In those moments, I must recall what some of my friends have reminded me, "God has big shoulders. Transfer that burden to Him and let Him carry it."

Many people, including Matt Lauer on the *Today* show, have asked me if I think the Navy's distinguished visitors' program should be discontinued.

Absolutely not! The American people deserve to know what a great treasure we have in our submarine force. Moreover, the need for submarines to defend and protect our country is greater now than ever before. Many countries, both those friendly to the U.S. and those hostile to America, still ply the seas in heavily armed submarines. During the court of inquiry, Admiral Konetzni stated under oath that he is aware of at least 270 foreign subs in the water today. Of that number, the admiral warned, 193 are not friendly toward the United States. Many nations have diesel submarines capable of challenging the U.S. nuclear submarine force. Iran, for example, has heavily armed diesel submarines. Vietnam and Yugoslavia also operate midget-class subs.

North Korea has at least twenty-eight midget subs, armed with two or four twenty-one-inch torpedoes or sixteen mines. Their primary mission, it seems, has been the clandestine insertion of agents into "enemy" territory. In September 1996, one of the North Korean subs grounded about one hundred miles east of Seoul and was captured by the South Koreans. The crew promptly committed suicide. These boys are playing for keeps.

The threat of a rogue submarine armed with nuclear weapons disrupting the shipping lanes of Middle Eastern oil tankers is a very real concern to many in COMSUBPAC nowadays. In contrast to the large number of hostile submarines lurking near current political hotspots, at the time I left the Navy, the commander of the Submarine Force, U.S. Pacific Fleet had a mere twenty-six fast-attack submarines and eight Tridents at his disposal. Clearly, the odds are against us, and this is not a time to back down militarily. It's a time to be diligent and wise in our preparations. More importantly, it is a time to make sure our hearts are right before God.

■ ■ ■

People often ask me, "Scott, what have you learned through this experience?"

One of the most important truths I've learned is simple but profound. We all make mistakes, but some mistakes cost much more than others. In eight minutes, my life was totally changed. I failed to maintain the big picture; I genuinely thought that what I was doing at the time was right. My crew did too. My crew trusted me. When I said that there were no visual contacts out in the haze, that there were no ships or other obstacles on the horizon, they believed that there were none. And so did I. Unfortunately, it wasn't so.

All of us have those pivotal moments in life. When you take your eyes off the road for a moment, and suddenly there's a child on a bicycle right in front of you. Or you allow yourself a momentary indiscretion that has lifelong implications. Or you change the figures on your income tax forms to reflect something that you know is not true. Those seemingly insignificant, inconsequential moments in our lives can suddenly take on a proportion we never dreamed possible. We think, *This could never happen to me.*

But it did.

And my mistakes and those of my crew cost the lives of nine people. Your mistakes may not be so costly, but there is always a price tag when we willfully do the wrong thing.

Certainly, the *Greeneville* incident exacted a high cost of the other officers aboard the boat that fateful day. The same day that I went to admiral's mast, Admiral Fargo also formally reproved four other *Greeneville* crewmembers by giving them "letters of admonishment." Although an "admonishment" is not as bad as a formal reprimand, it is still a serious blemish on the officers' permanent naval record.

My executive officer was admonished for his lack of administrative oversight and execution of the enlisted watchbill. Prior to the accident, my XO was clearly on his way to being a standout commander, but he lost his career advancement hopes the moment we collided with the *Ehime Maru*. Eventually, he returned to service aboard the *Greeneville*, but he was later relieved following another incident involving the submarine, when the boat was grounded off the shores of Saipan while attempting to enter the port. The ship's navigator was also fired after that incident, as was the *Greeneville*'s new commander after only four months on the job. Sadly, following the *Ehime Maru* incident, one of the most outstanding boats and crews in the Navy suddenly encountered one problem after another.

The chief of the boat was also admonished following the *Ehime Maru* accident, and the sonar supervisor was disciplined for permitting an unqualified sonar operator on the watch. Captain Robert Brandhuber, Pacific Submarine Force's chief of staff, was admonished by Admiral Konetzni for failing to question my decision to surface quickly and for failing to ensure the chain of command.

Lieutenant Michael Coen, the officer of the deck, was "counseled" by Admiral Fargo about safe navigation of his ship and proper supervision of watch personnel. "Counseling" is one of the least severe forms of nonjudicial, administrative punishment. Petty Officer Patrick Seacrest also received an admonishment from Admiral Konetzni. He returned to work aboard the *Greeneville*. Before we left Hawaii, Jill and I had Patrick Seacrest over for dinner one evening. We wanted him to know that there truly were no hard feelings between us. Patrick was most gracious. He humbly apologized, saying, "I'm sorry, Captain. I let you down."

Ironically, the *Greeneville* was involved in another accident on January 27, 2002, when it collided with the USS *Ogden* during a personnel transfer off the coast of Oman. Although both vessels left the scene under their own power, the accident punctured one of the *Ogden*'s fuel tanks, spilling thousands of gallons of fuel into the ocean. The captain of the *Ogden* was fired, and the captain of the *Greeneville*, who had been in command for less than six months, received an admonition.

Certainly, the cost of the *Greeneville–Ehime Maru* accident in sheer dollars and cents has been astronomical. Within days of the accident, *Scorpion II*, one of two of COMSUBPAC's remotely operated deep submergence recovery vessels, was on board a ship, being transferred from California to Hawaii to begin searching for the *Ehime Maru*. The ship was found and photographed on February 16, 2001, resting in an upright position on the bottom of the ocean floor, 2,003 feet below the surface, about one thousand yards from where I saw it go down.

The U.S. government spent sixty million dollars to recover the *Ehime Maru*, raise it off the ocean floor, and haul it to a location in one hundred feet of water so divers could get into it and retrieve the remains of the victims. Eight of the nine victims were recovered; one student, Takeshi Mizuguchi, was never found.

The Navy spent another two million to repair the damages to the *Greeneville*, originally thought to be minor damage to the sail and propulsion system. After closer examination, it was discovered that large portions of the sub's rubber sound-dampening coating had to be removed and replaced.

In addition, the Japanese requested thirty million dollars in compensation: eleven million to build a new vessel, plus millions more for post-traumatic stress and compensation to the family members who lost loved ones in the accident. All totaled, the *Greeneville–Ehime Maru* incident cost a lot of money that could have been used for good. We could have fed a lot of hungry children for the nearly one hundred million dollars the accident cost.

Eight minutes. Oh, how I wish I had those eight minutes back. Just eight minutes of getting out ahead of my crew and not giving them the chance to catch up to me. Eight minutes, and how eternal are the results.

People often ask me, "Scott, what got you through this ordeal? Other people have crumbled in the face of far less pressure. How have you survived? How have you been so strong?"

My answer is simple: my friends, my family, and my faith in God. From the moment the accident became public knowledge, Jill's and my friends rallied around us. We will never be able to repay the many friends who helped us in tangible ways and the myriad people who prayed for us, called us, e-mailed, and wrote cards and letters to us. When I had so much self-doubt, God showed me His love through strangers, through their expressions of love, their unmerited gifts, cards, and acts of kindness. The United States is an incredible nation, and the American people are truly amazing.

Nor will I ever forget those men who put their careers on the line for me. After the court of inquiry and the admiral's mast were over, Admiral Konetzni and his wife invited Jill and me to dinner at their home. During our dinner conversation, the admiral asked me, "Scott, what can I do?"

"Please recognize Kimberlie Young for her outstanding service," I replied. "And please recognize Mark Patton for what he's done for me." Mark was my Annapolis classmate who willingly became my technical expert during the inquiry, with full knowledge that by doing so, he might jeopardize his own advancement within the Navy. I was asking Admiral Konetzni to protect my friend.

"It's already been done," said the Admiral. "Mark will be awarded a meritorious service medal for his support of you."

"And please make sure his career isn't harmed because of his helping me."

"I assure you he will do fine," the admiral said.

From all indications, the Navy has respected Admiral Konetzni's wishes. Today Mark Patton is regarded as a man of great honor, a man who did the right thing.

Unquestionably, my wife, Jill, has been my greatest advocate throughout our marriage. A catastrophic event such as what happened to the *Greeneville* and *Ehime Maru* and the subsequent impact it made on our lives will do one of two things: It will either destroy a marriage or make it stronger. I'm a fortunate, blessed man. It made our marriage stronger, largely thanks to Jill. She never gave up on me. She never said, "How could you have been so foolish? Why were you not more careful?" She could have left me, but she didn't.

In fact, when the *Greeneville* first came in to the pier at Pearl Harbor the morning after the accident, I walked across the brow of the ship to hold Jill in my arms. After our initial conversation, I suggested to her, "Why don't you and Ashley go to your mom's house for a while? This is going to get ugly."

Jill looked back at me with love in her eyes. "You've got to be kidding, Scott. We're not going anywhere. We're staying right here with you."

Jill faced every grueling trial with me, and she spoke to the media with great dignity, without public affairs or media training. Most of all, she continued to love me unconditionally. On those days when I was upbeat and together, or those days when I was so overcome with grief I could barely function, Jill loved me just the same.

My daughter, Ashley, continues to be the joy of my life. To Ashley, regardless of what I had done, I was still her dad, and she loved me regardless of what some of her insensitive classmates said. She had to put up with a lot of flak, too, especially while we were still living in Hawaii and many of her classmates were military kids.

My father, Dan Waddle; my sister, Michelle; and I have grown much closer through the tragedy we have experienced. My stepdad, John Coe, has been supportive as well.

Sad, isn't it? That sometimes it takes a tragedy to pull our families together. Weddings and funerals are the only times many relatives even see each other nowadays. If I've learned anything through this nightmare, I've learned never again to take the people I love for granted.

Most of all, my faith in God has sustained me. Not that it has been easy. In the weeks following the accident, I felt so lonely and isolated, at times I wondered if it was worth it to carry on. Only my faith in God kept me from ending my life. Ever so slowly, I came to regard every day as His gift to me, and I realized how foolish I would be to throw that gift away.

I used to go through periods of doubt and reaffirmation of my faith. I'd doubt, then God would allow something to happen that would reaffirm my faith. Now I've come to the place where I trust Him completely through my doubts, in spite of my doubts. I still have many unanswered questions. But they don't matter anymore. This accident has strengthened my faith. All I know is that Jesus gave His life for us, and by trusting in Him, we can live . . . even if we die.

■   ■   ■

How has this experience changed me? For one thing, I'm much less cocky these days; I walk much less arrogantly. Oh, I still hold my head up high because I know that I am a child of God and that my heavenly Father has forgiven me, and yes, He approves of me. But He's been teaching me much about humility through this incident.

Certainly, I have a new appreciation for family and friends. Never again do I want to take a day for granted. Never again will I take for granted the touch of my wife's hand or a hug from my daughter. When I go to my daughter's bedroom to kiss her goodnight, I know that there are four Japanese families who can't do that. Their children are gone, their lives snuffed out by a submarine exploding out of the ocean at my command. It pains me severely, because I can't give back what the tragic accident took away. I'll take those consequences of my actions to my grave.

In addition, I've discovered that I've had to deal with my anger. That surprised me. I expected to feel guilt, despair, and other emotions, and I have. But shortly after the accident, I noticed the anger beginning to build inside me, slowly at first, then bubbling and seething like a volcano ready to erupt. I found myself being angry at God for allowing the accident to happen, angry with myself for the mistakes I made, angry with certain friends who chose to distance themselves from me following the accident. The anger kept growing and spreading like a forest fire during a drought.

Eventually I went to the Navy clinic and talked with a clinical psychologist, who was able to help me realize that my anger was unhealthy. Anger, blame, resentment, and other emotions that we often make excuses for may be natural, but that does not necessarily mean they are productive. I began to see my anger for what it was, a counterproductive emotion in my life.

God has also given me great compassion for others whose lives have been torn apart due to some unexpected nightmare, whether because of a national tragedy, such as the 9-11 attacks, or a personal tragedy, such as the death of a loved one, divorce, bankruptcy, getting fired, laid off, downsized, or replaced. When it's your world that crumbles, it doesn't matter how big the calamity was that caused it.

Regardless of what you are facing, you can make it through. The Bible says, "No temptation has overtaken you but such as is common to man; and God is faithful, who will not allow you to be tempted beyond what you are able, but with the temptation will provide the way of escape also, that you may be able to endure it" (1 Corinthians 10:13). That doesn't mean that tough times won't come your way. It simply means that no trial can shake you. There's no test you cannot pass with God's help. God will give you the strength. You can hold your head up high. You can do the right thing.

The most important thing we have is our integrity before God, our family, friends, and before the world. Colin Powell said, "Integrity is something that you cannot afford to compromise." Your superiors will see it. Your peers will notice. When it's compromised, you can't get it back. Only God can restore to you what the enemy has stolen. I remind myself of that each new morning.

Of course, I'm still human, and I miss the guys on the boat terribly. The U.S. Navy has been such a major part of my life. I love my country; I love people, and I love seeing them work together for a common goal, to help others. My crew on the *Greeneville* was my extended family, and I will never forget them.

Lately, though, I've become convinced that God isn't finished with me yet, that He has more for me to do than driving a submarine. Realistically, because of the *Greeneville* incident, many doors of opportunity have closed to me. But on the other hand, as the saying goes, when God closes one door, He opens another. My task now is to see which door of opportunity God is opening for me. The question of whether I will go through it has already been settled.

I still have a desire to serve—to serve God, my country, my family and friends, and my fellow man. It's easy to talk about serving, but God sees through all our smoke and mirrors. He knows our hearts. In God's service, there are no strings attached, no chains binding me, only chains of love. I know that I can go spiritually AWOL (absent without leave) at any time. But I don't want to. I've committed my life to God. I'm learning to trust Him more each day, not only with my own life, but also with my family, my career, and my future.

I enjoyed my career in the Navy, and I regret the way it ended. But my life is no longer defined by or dependent upon my success in the Navy. I serve a much higher Authority. I serve the King of kings and Lord of lords! While I am no longer the captain of the *Greeneville*, I serve the Captain of my soul, and I am available to Him for whatever He wants me to do, wherever He wants me to go.

My prayer these days is rather simple: "Here I am, Lord. I'm reporting for duty; I'm ready for new orders. I'm committed to You. Help me to take the next step in faith and obedience. And help me to do . . . the right thing."

PROMISES BROKEN; PROMISES KEPT

On Friday, December 13, 2002, Scott's long-anticipated trip to Japan to offer his personal apologies to the family members of the victims of the *Ehime Maru–Greeneville* accident became a reality.

Ironically, despite the Navy's earlier commitment, the emotionally charged trip was funded and facilitated not by the U.S. Navy or the United States goverment, but by Commander Waddle. To the Japanese public, Scott's apology was not an admission of guilt, but a gesture of integrity, humility, and honor. They recognized the importance of having Commander Scott Waddle stand before the family members and bring as much closure as possible to the incident that took the lives of their loved ones and sparked a firestorm of international controversy.

Truly, God has brought good from what the enemy intended for evil. "Let us pursue the things which make for peace and the building up of one another" (Romans 14:19).